A Place of Care, Love, and Hope

A Place of Care, Love, and Hope

A History of Arkansas Children's Hospital

Steven G. Hanley

August House Publishers, Inc.
LITTLE ROCK

Published by August House, Inc.,
P.O. Box 3223, Little Rock, Arkansas, 72203,
501-372-5450.

Printed in the United States of America

10 9 8 7 6 5 4 3 2 1

LIBRARY OF CONGRESS CATALOGING-IN-PUBLICATION DATA

A Place of Care, Love, and Hope:
A History of Arkansas Children's Hospital

Steven G. Hanley — 1st ed.
p. cm.
Summary:
ISBN 0-87483-368-X (pb: alk. paper): $15.00
1. Arkansas Children's Hospital—History 2. Children—Hospitals—Arkansas—
Little Rock—History I Title. [DNLM: 1. Arkansas Children's Hospital.
2. Hospitals, Pediatric—history—Arkansas. WS 28 AA8 A7h 1994].
RJ28.L58A754 1994 94-33432
362.1'9892'000976773—dc20 CIP

First Edition, 1994

Executive in charge: Ted Parkhurst
Project director: Amy Oliver
Design director: Jan Diemer

Unless otherwise stated, all photos are courtesy of Arkansas Children's Hospital
Public Relations Department

This book is printed on archival-quality paper that meets the
guidelines for performance and durability of the Committee on
Production Guidelines for Book Longevity of the
Council on Library Resources.

AUGUST HOUSE, INC. PUBLISHERS LITTLE ROCK

Acknowledgments

SO MANY PEOPLE HAVE HELPED ME in researching and writing the history of Arkansas Children's Hospital that naming them all would make a book in itself. I want to express my thanks to former Chief Executive Officer Dr. Randall O'Donnell for authorizing this book. His successor, Dr. Jonathan Bates has been a source of encouragement.

Blanche Moore, Director of Institutional Relations, located records without which the manuscript could not have been completed. Jane Miller, manager of the Playaway Gift Shop answered countless questions and provided many leads in my quest for information.

Long-time ACH supporter Stella Boyle Smith invited me into her home and shared her colorful memories. Virginia Bellue recalled her experiences as a patient the first year the hospital opened. Jim Young of Lafayette, California reminisced about growing up in the orphanage, and Don Moore of Springdale sent me a wonderful letter, part of which is quoted in chapter four.

Jewell Mainard and Pat Wright of the ACH nursing staff offered valuable insight. Medical Director Dr. Betty Lowe and Dr. Robert Fiser were never too busy to return my phone calls. They have given me a greater appreciation of their professions.

For creative editing and patience beyond measure I am grateful to my long-time friend David Davies, assistant professor of journalism at the University of Mississippi. Amy Oliver, ACH Director of Public Relations, also read the manuscript and offered many helpful suggestions. To all who helped in telling the story of Arkansas Children's Hospital, I can only say thank you. While many people have helped, interpretation of the material reflects my own judgment and the responsibility for any factual errors rests solely with me.

Steven G. Hanley

August, 1994

Orphanage residents break ground for children's hospital
October 1923

Orphanage residents, ca. 1926

One

FOR THE AMERICAN PEOPLE, the early years of the twentieth century were a time of optimism and confidence. The wonders of modern science and technology seemed to promise almost unlimited progress and prosperity. Between 1860 and 1900, the United States had jumped from fourth to first place among the industrialized nations of the world. New techniques of mass production gave the growing middle class an abundance and variety of inexpensive consumer goods, items which could be purchased at any hardware, dry-goods or clothing store.

Their rising standard of living did not blind all Americans to the problems caused by the nation's rapid industrialization. Reform-minded people organized to combat the social ills which had accompanied recent changes. Around them they saw slums, crime, poor sanitation and sickness. Children, the most helpless victims of these conditions, were a major focus of the reform movement. Much of this heightened interest in the well-being of the nation's young stemmed from recent advances in the biological and social sciences, especially psychology. For the first time, children were seen as subjects worthy of legitimate scientific inquiry, and people began to realize that an understanding of childhood behavior could unlock the secrets of adult behavior.

In 1909, President Theodore Roosevelt convened the first White House Conference on Children. "Surely nothing ought to interest our people more," admonished Roosevelt, "than the care of those children who are destitute and neglected but not delinquent." With this new focus on the needs of society's youngest members, reformers confidently predicted that this would be the "Century of the Child." At long last children were going to be rescued from the ignorance, neglect and abuse of the past.

Across the land many dedicated men and women were working toward that goal. One such individual was Horace G. Pugh, a Little Rock, Arkansas, real estate dealer. He dreamed of founding a home for children who had been orphaned, neglected or abused.

Horace G. Pugh

His own youth had been difficult. Horace Gaines Pugh was born on a farm near Blue Grass, Illinois, on January 13, 1874, the first of three sons born to William Matthew and Martha Elizabeth Jones Pugh. William Pugh was a veteran of the Civil War, having served in the Thirty-third Indiana Volunteer Infantry. After the war he married and settled in Vermillion County, Illinois. William Pugh died in the fall of 1876, leaving a widow and three small children.

During his boyhood Horace Pugh attended the public schools of West Lebanon, Indiana. In his early teens, Horace left school and worked to support his mother and younger brothers. Due to this hardship he received no college training.

In 1896, after completing an apprenticeship in printing and engraving with a firm in Indianapolis, Indiana, Pugh moved to Little Rock. For a time he was employed by the *Arkansas Baptist*, a publication of the Southern Baptist denomination. Later, while selling real estate, he dreamed of founding his own printing firm.

Pugh was married on April 28, 1904, in Malvern, Arkansas, to Jamie DeAnna Ward. Five years younger than her new husband, she was a graduate of Ouachita Baptist College in nearby Arkadelphia. Horace Pugh would later serve on that educational institution's board of trustees.

The young businessman was active in church and civic work. He was a member of the First Baptist Church in Little Rock, where he served as a deacon and Sunday School secretary. Over the years he would serve as president of the Young Men's Christian Association of Little Rock and as president of the United Charities Association of Pulaski County, and would play an active role in many other worthy causes in the community.

Most of all, Horace Pugh wanted to help those who were too young to help themselves. In 1910 he established a home in Little Rock for orphaned, neglected and abused children. After less than a year of operation, however, the home was forced to close its doors due to a lack of financial support. Horace Pugh was discouraged but not defeated.

In November 1911, the same year that the orphanage failed, the firm of H.G. Pugh & Company was incorporated. The new printing house, located at 417 Main Street in the capital city, was advertised as "The Business Man's Department Store." Within a few years one observer of the firm's work wrote that "all kinds of printing are contracted for; the work done is of excellent quality, the reputation of the house being of the best; but a specialty is made of bank work and of copper plate and steel die work."

In the aftermath of the failure of the children's home, the self-made business executive wrote to the National Children's Home Society requesting that it consider the establishment of a branch in Arkansas. The Society, headquartered in Washington, D. C., was dedicated to the care of orphaned and neglected youngsters.

The Society agreed to help, and in February 1912, the Reverend Edward B. Dillard, an experienced Children's Home Society worker, came to Little Rock from Kansas. Details of the Reverend Dillard's background have been lost, but his actions reveal a person gifted with an ability to persuade others to take up his cause.

"Reverend Dillard came to Arkansas for the definite purpose of organizing a state society," Horace Pugh later wrote, "and at once enlisted General B. W. Green and General Jonathan Kellogg, who had been interested in a society doing similar work a number of years before. He also secured the cooperation of Governor (George) Donaghey and of other Little Rock citizens in the work."

Reverend Edward B. Dillard

General Benjamin W. Green and General Jonathan Kellogg were veterans of the Civil War, having served as privates in the Confederate Army. General Green was a successful local real estate agent. Governor Donaghey had named him Adjutant General of the State Militia in 1909. General Kellogg owned and operated a bookstore on Markham Street in the capital city. Both men were active in the United Confederate Veterans organization, in which Kellogg held the rank of Brigadier General.

According to the minutes kept by Horace Pugh, "The initial meeting for the purpose of organizing the Arkansas Children's Home Society, auxiliary to the National Children's Home Society, was held in General B. W. Green's office, State Bank Building, Little Rock, February 24, 1912, at 8:00 P.M." This organizational meeting was attended by Horace Pugh, Reverend Dillard, General Green, General Kellogg, William H. Garanflo, Ulysses S. Bratton and Charles D. Cone. Garanflo was president of the State National Bank, in whose building the meeting was held, and Bratton was postmaster of Little Rock. Nothing is known of Cone's background.

On motion of General Green, William Garanflo was elected temporary chair, and Horace Pugh was elected temporary secretary. Reverend Dillard read the proposed constitution, which was referred to a committee consisting of Kellogg, Dillard, Bratton and Pugh. This committee was to report in one week with recommendations for possible changes or revisions in the proposed governing document.

The formation of a board of directors was the main topic at this first meeting. It was decided that the Society's Board of Directors should be composed of no fewer than fifteen nor more than twenty-one members. It was also unanimously agreed that Governor George Donaghey be named president of the Board. William H. Garanflo was elected vice president and Reverend Edward B. Dillard was elected state superintendent. Horace Pugh was elected secretary and Judge William M. Kavanaugh was elected treasurer. Kavanaugh, a former county and probate judge, was president of Little Rock's Southern Trust Company and of the Little Rock Railway & Electric Company. Charles D. Cone would be named assistant superintendent of the Children's Home at a later date.

Three other members named to the Board at this first meeting were Dr. J.H. Estes, a Little Rock physician; Dr. Thomas Mason of Siloam Springs, a Methodist minister who had served as the first president of Philander Smith College; and James M. Oathout, a Booneville businessman. None was present at the first meeting, but each had expressed a willingness to serve when approached by Reverend Dillard. Eleven other members would be named later, bringing the total to twenty-one. Also at this first meeting the articles of incorporation of the Arkansas Children's Home Society were read and signed. The meeting was adjourned, with the next meeting scheduled for the following Saturday evening.

At the second meeting, Secretary Horace Pugh read the report of the committee concerning the proposed constitution. After some amendments, the constitution was adopted by the Board. The document's preamble was a statement of purpose for the Arkansas Children's Home Society which reflected the sociological thinking of that era. It read:

"Whereas there are thousands of orphaned, homeless and dependent children who by birth, poverty, desertion and criminality and vicious environment, do not and cannot have the proper influence and training to fit them for the requirements of life, or enable them to have the advantages which they are justly entitled by nature and

"Whereas a large percent of our paupers, criminals and undesirable citizens come from this class and

"Whereas there are thousands of good religious homes where every need of said child can be met and every good influence brought to bear so as to correct, train and prepare them for the duties of good citizenship and

"Whereas the experience in more than thirty states has shown that these homes are not only willing but in many cases anxious to adopt or indenture said children and raise them as their own and

"Whereas this system has not only demonstrated by years of experience its success in thus protecting, saving and training said children, but also is the fact that it is beneficial to society and the homes of the country as well as the children under whose protecting care they are fostered. This system has been found to be expedient, practical and inexpensive, and the National Executive Committee of the National Children's Home Society has authorized the organization of the ... Arkansas Children's Home Society."

The main body of the document consisted of seventeen amendments outlining the bylaws under which the organization was to operate. Amendment Four declared that the Arkansas Children's Home Society "shall be absolutely non-sectarian and without political bias, but distinctly religious and inter-denominational."

A committee was appointed to officially notify Governor Donaghey of his election as president of the Society. "There is no estimating the future results of this work," said the fifty-six-year-old chief executive. "Think of 250 children housed, reared and educated so as to make good citizens. I am proud to be president of such an institution."

At the Board's third meeting, a committee was appointed to seek suitable housing for the children's home. The search proved difficult, primarily due to financial limitations. This difficulty was resolved in May 1913, when Emma Hannaford of Morrilton, Arkansas, offered to deed some property to the Society for use as a children's home if the Society would locate in the Conway County community. The Board voted to accept her generous offer.

The Sayle-Hannaford Memorial Home, ca. 1915

The property, thirty acres of land located on the first ridge south of Morrilton, was known as Sayle Hill. The house, a stately old Victorian, had been built by Hannaford's first husband, the late Dr. W.A.C. Sayle, who had practiced medicine in Conway County for more than thirty years.

In its first year of operation, 157 children entered the new Sayle-Hannaford Memorial Home, and 125 others were placed in foster care. By February 1914, Superintendent Dillard had made vast improvements on the property, which now housed 200 children. He was commended by the Board for his work.

"Homeless children have found an asylum here," wrote Reverend Dillard in his 1914 annual report. "While the work is imperfectly done and not yet complete, these buildings mean a home for the homeless and protection for the weak. The widow may bring her fatherless children here and not be required to die to save her boys."

As superintendent of the Arkansas Children's Home Society, Reverend Dillard took an active role in every aspect of the institution's work. "On last Thursday, that terrible rainy day," he noted in one of his reports, "the deputy sheriff and I saddled our horses and rode in the woods until we found the old dilapidated tent, the half crazy mother and the child. The child did not have a whole rag of clothes on her body. This girl is now well clothed and in a good home."

Feeling that he had done all that he could, Reverend Edward B. Dillard resigned as state superintendent in the summer of 1915. "The work of the Society made some progress under Dillard's administration," Horace Pugh later wrote, "as he was a man of ability and an untiring worker." From June 1915—the date of Dillard's resignation—until November 1916 the Society made very little progress. Several men were elected to the superintendent's position during this time, but served only short periods, and with little success.

Governor George W. Donaghey

Without strong leadership, public interest and support of the children's home declined and the Society fell into debt. "It was during this time of depression of the Society," wrote Horace Pugh, "that the Board of Directors decided that the receiving home at Morrilton could not be made a success." Plans were made to sell the property, pay off the debt and seek a new location in Little Rock.

This plan was dropped, however, when Emma Hannaford made it known to the Board that she wanted the Society to use the property as a receiving home or for other charitable purposes, not sold for debt. Otherwise, she proposed that the property be deeded back to her. After some discussion, the Board decided to return the property to Hannaford. It also extended a resolution of thanks for her interest in the work of the Arkansas Children's Home Society.

In December 1916, former Governor George Donaghey resigned from the presidency of the Board of Directors. The building contractor turned politician had failed in his bid for a third term in the state's highest office and wanted to devote more time to his wide-ranging business activities. Little Rock businessman Max Heiman, who was a partner in the Blass Department Store, was elected to the post. Governor Donaghey would return to a seat on the Board in 1924, serving until his death in 1937 at the age of eighty-one.

Dr. Orlando P. Christian

"Without a permanent superintendent, property given up at Morrilton, the receipts very small and uncertain and at the same time with ten or twelve children to take care of, the outlook for the Society was indeed gloomy," wrote Horace Pugh. "In the fall of 1916, we learned of the work of a California superintendent, who made good in the West in the work of the Children's Home Society. In the course of a few weeks' time an arrangement had been consummated with Reverend O.P. Christian, and on Thanksgiving Day, 1916, Dr. Christian arrived in Little Rock and was ready for work."

The new superintendent's interest in orphaned and neglected children was deeply rooted in his own harsh childhood. Orlando Philander Christian had been born in Ingham County, Michigan, on March 9, 1855, the second of ten children. His father, Philander Christian, was a mechanic, working in gristmills and sawmills. It was a struggle for him to feed and clothe his large brood.

When Orlando was six years old his father was stricken with rheumatism, which left him an invalid for several years. Two years later, Orlando was "bound out" to a Michigan farmer. His childhood became a dreary round of chores. Even school was denied him, his entire early education consisting of one year's schooling. While still a boy, he determined to gain an education.

At seventeen his desire for knowledge was far too compelling for him to go on working as a farmhand. Deep in his heart was a longing to prepare himself so that he could help other waifs like himself. As a first step, he secured a place in a marble shop and soon mastered the stonecutter's art. Twelve hours was the average workday, but the ambitious youth was no stranger to hard work. The nights belonged to him, and he took advantage of them to study. From time to time he would appear before teachers for rigorous examinations. With the encouragement of his pastor, he began to prepare himself for ministry in the Methodist Church.

At the age of twenty-nine, he entered the ministry, and over the course of the next seventeen years he was appointed to six different pastorates. But it was not until 1901, when he was forty-six years old, that he realized his dream of working with underprivileged children. He began work on the staff of the Wisconsin Children's Home, and transferred first to Idaho, then to California, before coming to Arkansas in 1916.

"Dr. Christian," observed Horace Pugh, "was master of the situation from the first day." Many years later, Reverend Christian recalled the early days of his administration. "Misfortune ... had reduced the number of children in the Arkansas Home to only seven, and a bad debt had so impaired their credit that it looked as though failure would engulf the struggling institution." The new superintendent began the task of rebuilding the Arkansas Children's Home Society in a rented house, with an improvised table made from a stable door, a few blankets on the floor for a bed and soap boxes for chairs.

"Under Dr. Christian's careful management," said Horace Pugh, "the Society began to take on new life." The children were brought from Morrilton to Little Rock. Their new home, located at 2428 Louisiana Street, was donated to the Society by Mrs. David Terry, the wife of Arkansas' future congressman. During 1917, the first year of Reverend Christian's administration, the Society received 116 children and placed 101 of them in foster homes.

When Board President Max Heiman died in November 1917, Governor Charles H. Brough was named to succeed him. In accepting the post, the former college professor said, "I accept with pleasure the honor conferred on me today by election to the office of President of the Society. Personally, I regard this Society as being one of the greatest constructive humanitarian works in the state of Arkansas."

With an energy and enthusiasm which amazed his co-workers, the new superintendent led the Society's fund-raising efforts. He spoke to church, school and civic organizations about the function of the children's home. "We receive children into the Society, and train the mind for transplanting into a new home," he explained. "During this time we become acquainted with their needs, disposition, and tendencies, and establish a fixedness of purpose, and create a wholesome desire for the best.

"When the child is ready, we seek out the home most suited for that particular child, and when a suitable home is found, we try to establish a perfect adjustment between the foster parent and the child before adoption takes place.

"We have found that if a child is really loved it is never neglected, never over-worked; that it is given the privilege of church, Sunday School and will be kept in public school for the full school year. We must be sure of all this before we will consent to adoption."

In talking with groups of school children, Dr. Christian urged them "to help us in finding homes for the many children who have no homes, no kind father and mother to care for them ... Will you ask your teacher to appoint a day when you can bring something to send to the Children's Home Society for these needy children? It will help so much!" Thanks to these efforts, the Society was soon able to pay off its debt.

On January 3, 1918, Captain E.S. Hilliard, a cotton planter from Grand Lake, Arkansas, donated $5,000 to the Society to establish a fund to buy property suitable for a receiving home. A few weeks later, a building at 3210 West Twelfth Street was selected for the E.S. Hilliard Receiving Home. The purchase price was $6,500—$5,000 cash, $1,000 in sixty days, and $500 in four months.

On March 22, 1918, as plans were being made to move the children to the new location, Dr. Christian shared with the Board his vision of the future. "We next need a free child's hospital. There are many of the children that need a minor attention, it is but little to be sure, but that little means much to them.

The E.S. Hilliard Receiving Home
housed the Arkansas Children's Home Society from 1918 to 1920

"The equipment of the hospital will be furnished by the different counties in the state, whose children will be sent here for treatment," explained Dr. Christian. "In my long years of experience, I know of nothing that is so much needed and so greatly appreciated by the people as a place where the child of the poorest parent can have the same advantages as the child of the well-to-do.

"To allow these children to go without this attention means that a large percent of them will become a liability upon the state, while to give them this needed attention they may become an asset.... It is a shame and a crime," he declared, "to allow children to go through life maimed, when they might be fully restored; to remain a sufferer, when pain can be removed; to be blind, when sight may be restored; and deaf, when the surgeon may unstop the ears." No action was taken on Dr. Christian's proposal at this time.

On June 27, 1918, Dr. Christian was given a salary of $150 a month by the Board. Also on this date, W.G. Prichard, a friend of Governor Brough, made the first contribution toward the building of a children's hospital. His gift was a check for $1,000. Other contributions followed, and on April 15, 1919, Dr. Christian further outlined his plan:

"It should be large enough to accommodate the full needs of the Society in the way of a school room, hospital, isolation hospital, dormitories, nursery, baths, laundry, root cellar, etc. The hospital ward need not have over five beds, this with a well provised operating room, bath, etc. will be ample to care for all those children that come to us for treatment. The larger building will soon become a necessity if we carry out our county co-operation theme." Dr. Christian estimated that "about twenty percent of the children taken by the Society are not physically fit for placement until they have been under the care of a physician, and in many instances under the surgeon's knife."

On May 14, 1919, the Executive Committee of the Arkansas Children's Home Society kicked off a campaign to raise at least $100,000 for the construction of a children's hospital. Dr. Christian addressed the gathering. "We are living in a day of great things," he declared. "Men think great things, and are willing to undertake great things.... We are here tonight to discuss subjects that shall change the whole physical, mental, moral and spiritual conditions of future generations, and will affect hundreds, yes thousands of future men and women. Our actions tonight will 'Heal the sick, cause the lame to walk, the deaf to hear, the blind to see,' and change the menace and liability to an asset and a blessing. The question," he concluded, "is no longer what should we do, but how and when shall we begin our task?"

During the following year the Society's fund-raising effort made steady progress. So encouraging was the effort that on September 23, 1920, the Board of Directors approved Dr. Christian's plan to build a children's home and hospital at a total cost of $200,000. It was a goal worthy of the "Roaring '20s."

The Boys' Home, ca. 1925

The Girls' Home, ca. 1925

Two

THE DRIVE TO BUILD A CHILDREN'S HOSPITAL was launched during an economic upswing for Arkansas, its first in many years. As had been the case for nearly a century, the state's economy remained overwhelmingly tied to agriculture. Despite farmers' efforts to diversify, cotton was still the principal crop. World War I had brought a measure of prosperity to Arkansas. Many commodities produced in the state—such as lead, zinc, coal, bauxite and especially cotton—were in great demand during the conflict and for a few years afterward.

For the first time in memory, a touch of real prosperity reached the rural South. Money—not much, but more than they were used to—found its way into the pockets of those who lived on the land. Thousands of Arkansans joined the nation's consumer revolution, buying such modern luxuries as radios, cookstoves, refrigerators and even Model-T Fords.

The increasing number of automobiles on the state's roads led to the establishment of the Arkansas State Highway Commission. License fees and a gasoline tax were enacted to help pay for much needed road improvements. Service stations, garages, restaurants and "tourist courts" began to appear along the roads in the more populated sections of the state.

For the South as a region, and for Arkansas in particular, the touch of prosperity was short-lived. As demand dropped, the prices of cotton and other commodities fell even faster than they had risen during the war. The response of many farmers was to grow more cotton to make up for the lower price per pound. Such increased production merely flooded the market, further depressing prices. By 1924, cotton prices had fallen so low that crops were left to rot in the fields because the owners could not afford to pay field hands to pick them. For Arkansans—who were dependent on cotton for all or part of their livelihood—the Great Depression would come early.

But this grim reality was not apparent for some time. Thus the first two years of the Arkansas Children's Home Society's fund-raising efforts were a rousing success. The largest single contribution to the campaign came from the estate of Captain E.S. Hilliard. Captain Hilliard died in December 1920, bequesting $50,000 to the Society. C. Matthew Cashion of Eudora, Arkansas, executor of the Hilliard estate, promised an added $25,000. Also at this time, Mr. R.G. Bruce, a former Board member who had moved to Memphis, contributed $5,000 to the hospital fund.

In June 1922 the Board of Directors voted to purchase a ten-room house and six lots located on Ninth and Wolfe and Battery Streets for $20,000. The seller, Mrs. C.A. Forney-Smith, valued the property at $40,000. She considered the sale to be a $20,000 contribution to the Society given in memory of her two sons who had been killed in World War I. Three additional lots on the northeastern corner of the block were purchased from Charles Phillips Waters, a local real estate broker, for $6,000. This gave the Society ownership of three-quarters of the block, or nine lots in all. These last three lots were purchased for the purpose of erecting a children's hospital.

Mrs. C.A. Forney-Smith

The new C.A. Forney-Smith Receiving Home was occupied by the Society on September 10, 1922. The old E.S. Hilliard Receiving Home at 3210 West Twelfth Street was sold in November to a Little Rock physician, Dr. Robert L. Saxon, for $11,000. (This was a profit of $4,000, the original purchase price having been $6,500, with an additional $500 spent on improvements.) Dr. Saxon also made a $5,000 donation to the Society at this time.

Shortly after the move, former Governor Charles H. Brough resigned as president of the Board. Fellow Board member William A. Hicks was elected to succeed him. Hicks was a vice president and cashier of the American Bank of Commerce & Trust Company. Governor Brough retained a seat on the Board and was named honorary president. He would resign his seat four years later due to poor health.

In his annual report to the Society's Board of Directors on May 16, 1923, Superintendent Orlando P. Christian observed, "We have been making steady progress in the accumulation of property, the number of children received and cared for, and the amount of subscriptions received for current expenses and for our new hospital.... Since the incorporation of the Society, March 5, 1912, we have received 1,027 children. During the present administration, we have received 527 of these children. These have been provided for either by placement in selected family homes, returned to their parents or sent to other institutions. This leaves fifty children on hand, April 30, 1923.... The publicity given throughout the state in procuring funds for the hospital has brought the work of the Society before the public in such a way that we are receiving an increasing number of applications for admission into the Home."

Children on swings / Boys' Home, ca. 1925

The new receiving home served as the girls' dormitory. A boys' dormitory was the institution's most pressing need. "To meet the present urgent need for a boys' dormitory," explained Dr. Christian, "we remodeled the attic and we have passed the winter quite comfortably. Yet, as demands for entrance increase from month to month, it will soon be impossible for us to make room for them. At the present time we have nineteen boys and only ten beds."

While living at the home, all of the children took the last name of Christian and were dressed alike. The children came under the care of the Society for various reasons. Some had been orphaned through illness, accident or abandonment. Others came because of poverty, abuse or neglect.

Not surprisingly, many of these unfortunate youngsters often had serious behavioral problems. In his annual report, Dr. Christian spoke of these troubled young people with honesty and a touch of gentle humor. "They are untrained, disobedient and rebellious. A large percentage of them are either covered with vermin or some skin disease, and sometimes both. They hate a bath and refuse to co-operate with the Matron in keeping themselves clean. They have never had any good examples set before them, they lie when the truth would serve them better, steal when they could have for the asking. Added to all this care the Matron must watch each new and untrained child lest he turn on the water and flood the ceilings; meddle with electric connections and short circuit the lights; or turn on the gas and cause an explosion. Strenuous, most strenuous and exacting is the work!"

Such behavioral difficulties were among the reasons cited by the superintendent in support of his plan for the establishment of a school within the institution. "When you take into consideration that our children come to us largely untrained, some of them with bad habits and associated ideas that it takes a long time to eliminate ... you will understand more readily why we need our own school.

"Then again people sometimes come long distances to see the children and you can readily see how impracticable it would be to go to our public schools and ask of the teachers the privilege of calling our children out for interviews. And that might occur two or three times a day. Our children are shown better when seen together. The prospective parents insist on seeing the children—all the children—to help them in their decision. Oftentimes, prospective parents come with the preconceived idea of taking a child of a certain age, but when they see the children together, they change their minds and take either an older child or a younger child than they had anticipated.

"Our Society should maintain an ungraded school. The child of ten or twelve years who has never been to school a week in his life, may be received into a class adapted to his need without any embarrassment. The child being treated for defective hearing or impaired eyesight, may go into school to see and hear as much as possible while having treatment at the hands of specialists. The anemic child may be excused at recess to go for the much needed glass of milk or fruit, if necessary, and be under the supervision of the Society all the time. There is every advantage in having a school of our own, and we should provide for this as soon as possible."

Dr. Christian also urged that a building committee be named to select an architect and enter into a contract for construction of a children's hospital, declaring, "The public has been held long in suspense. There are those who are waiting to make a subscription when they see we are doing something, and we have the assurance that a good and substantial sum will be added when they see the hospital is really being built."

A building committee was named, and on June 23, 1923, John P. Almand, a Little Rock architect who specialized in church and hospital architecture, was awarded the contract for construction of a children's hospital. The contract price was $133,370. In September, upon completion of the blueprints, Mr. Almand and Dr. Christian went to New York City to confer with a noted expert on hospital construction.

In January 1924 the Society received a bequest of $25,000 from the estate of Joseph P. Kendrick, a Little Rock businessman. The will also gave the Society ownership of a house and three lots located at 801 Battery Street. In accepting this gift, the Board assumed responsibility for a $15,000 mortgage on the property. After some remodeling, this house became the girls' dormitory, and the C.A. Forney-Smith Receiving Home became the boys' dormitory.

By this time the drop in the price of cotton was taking its toll. The farmers and those who depended on them—small-town merchants, bankers, farming equipment suppliers and hardware dealers—were feeling the pinch. Donations to the hospital fund drive slowed. As of September 25, 1924, the four principal contractors for the hospital building—Herman and McCain Construction Company, Shaw's Gas and Plumbing, Arkansas Electric Company and John P. Almand, the architect—had been paid a total of $89,864.95. This left a balance due of $43,505.05. With the building nearing completion, and with contributions lagging behind, the Board voted to borrow $50,000 from the Bankers' Trust Company of Little Rock in order to pay off the contractors and purchase necessary equipment for the hospital.

The hospital building was completed on November 6, 1924. In February of the following year, after conferring with the Pulaski County Medical Society, the hospital's first medical staff was named. This first all-volunteer medical staff consisted of twenty-three local physicians, two X-ray technicians and one laboratory worker. Because of the state's faltering economy, it would be more than a year before the new medical facility would be able to open its doors to the children of Arkansas.

Due to a lack of funds, most of the state's seventy-five counties were unable to assist in furnishing the hospital. Thus, when the hospital finally opened on March 9, 1926, it had a fully equipped operating room, but only two beds. John N. Heiskell, editor of the *Arkansas Gazette*, donated $150,

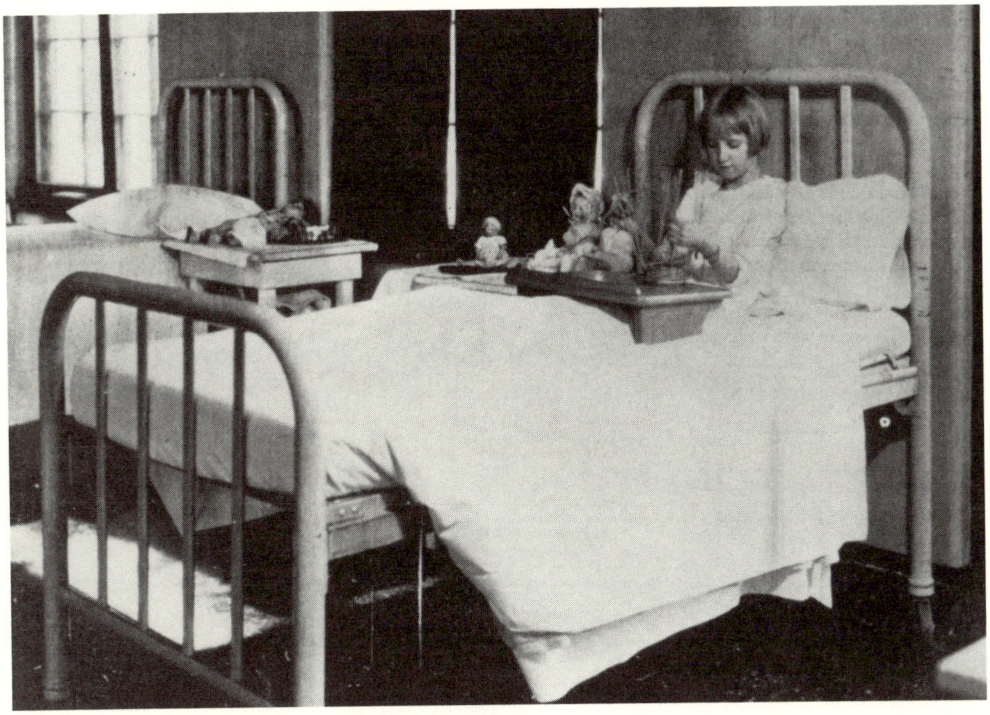

Patient/Girls' Ward, ca. 1929

three-month's salary for a nurse. He also gave $75 to the Society's general fund. Three other individuals contributed a total of $1,500 on this long-awaited day. This date also marked Superintendent Christian's birthday.

"Dr. Christian," reported the *Gazette*, "will celebrate his seventy-first birthday by bringing to the Children's Home for needed surgical treatment two children of families living in different parts of the state, one two years [old] and the other two months old, who were born with the distressing but remediable deformity of harelip. One child has no palate and the other, a cleft palate. Parents of these children appealed in the most moving way to Dr. Christian. They could not themselves meet the expense of the needed treatment, but they realized as only parents can what failure to have the operation would mean to their unfortunate little children."

These first two surgical procedures were performed by Dr. Joseph F. Shuffield. A native of Arkansas and a 1923 graduate of the Tulane University School of Medicine, Dr. Shuffield would serve on the staff of Arkansas Children's Hospital for over thirty years.

As Dr. Christian had predicted, the opening of the hospital generated an outpouring of public interest in the work of the Arkansas Children's Home and Hospital, as it was now officially known. In May, two months after the hospital opened, a group of local women formed a ladies' auxiliary to aid

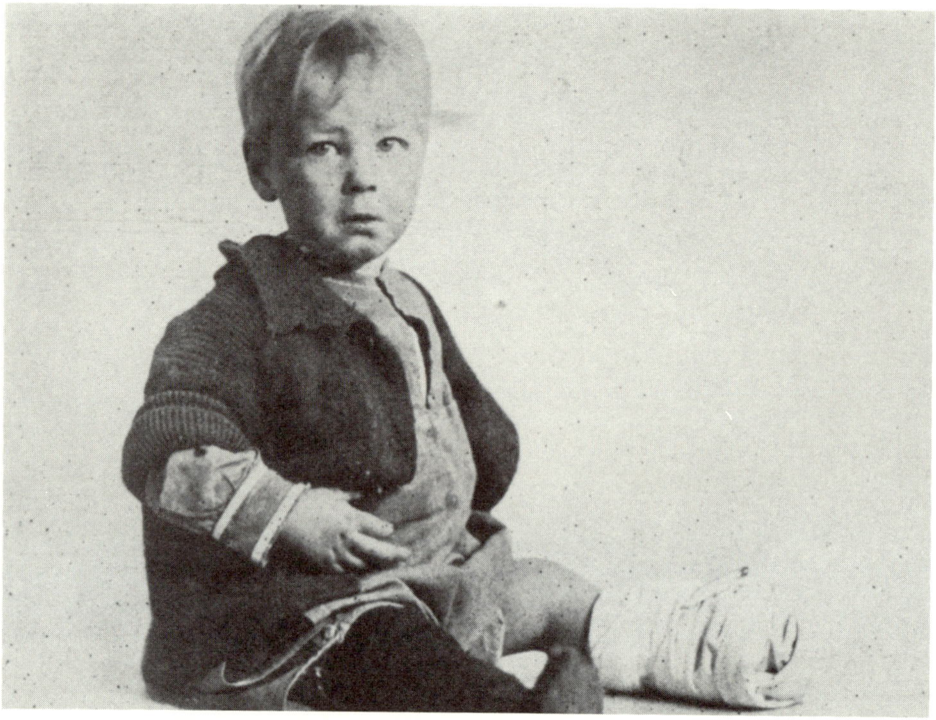

Before Ortho Surgery, late 1920s

After Ortho Surgery, late 1920s

the struggling institution. By September, the auxiliary had nearly eight-hundred members and had raised over $800. Of this sum, $180 was used to pay nurses' salaries.

In late 1926, President William A. Hicks resigned his seat on the Board of Directors for health reasons. Hicks had worked tirelessly to realize the dream of a children's hospital. He was succeeded in the top post by Robert E. Wiley, a well-known Little Rock lawyer. The new president had his hands full as the state's continuing economic woes were pushing the charitable organization toward the brink of financial disaster.

At a special meeting of the Board on March 24, 1927, Superintendent Christian reported that while county governments across the state had appropriated almost $31,000 to aid the work of the Society, less than a third of this sum had actually been received due to a sharp decline in tax revenues. The Home and Hospital had a combined debt of $13,452.13. Of this sum, $5,140 was owed to a local bank, which was demanding immediate payment of at least part of the obligation.

The bank received full payment, but other pressing debts went unpaid. By June, the situation was desperate. With the hospital on the verge of closing, and with food, clothing and other necessities for the children being purchased on credit, the Board reluctantly voted to mortgage all of the Society's property to the Bankers' Trust Company of Little Rock for $70,000. They also secured a $20,000 loan. The smaller sum was used to pay all of the Society's outstanding bills. It was hoped that the funds obtained through the mortgage would be enough to keep the home and hospital open until the state's economy improved and full county funding could be restored.

Throughout this time of crisis, the hospital continued to accept new patients. As additional beds were donated, the number of patients increased. Among the patients admitted during this period was twelve-year-old Virginia Preddy. Virginia's parents were sharecroppers. The family lived on a farm near the Pulaski County community of Scott. The active youngster had been thrown from a horse in August 1926. "I was horseback riding and a boy kicked my horse and made him throw me," she reminisced more than sixty years later. "I got up and walked home, but three weeks later I was flat on my back with a high fever."

When the girl's condition grew worse, the doctor told her parents, "If you're going to do anything for her, you had better get her to the hospital." Arrangements were made through Dr. Christian for her to be admitted to the new Children's Hospital. "The doctor took me to Children's Hospital in the back seat of his car, put me in a bed and left me there." The youngster was suffering from severe osteomyelitis, a bone infection, and was not expected to live.

The following weeks were a blur of pain. "I had a high fever for nearly a month. The skin peeled off my palms and feet, and all of my hair came out. Then they decided to do a tonsillectomy. Now that was an experience!" After the tonsillectomy Virginia's condition slowly began to improve, but her ordeal was not yet over.

In December the doctors decided to operate on her left leg, which was still badly infected. Shortly before Easter 1927 she underwent surgery on her left shoulder. "My Mother and Dad were there. They planned to come back to the hospital the following Saturday and bring Easter eggs to all the kids on the ward. Well, that was the year of the flood. The levee on the Arkansas River broke and I didn't know for a month what had happened to my folks. I didn't know if I had any folks left or not."

At the Children's Hospital the little girl waited and wondered. As soon as the flood waters had receded, Virginia's parents made their way to Little Rock by the first available means of transportation—a horse-drawn wagon. "When they walked into the ward," she recalled with a smile of remembrance, "I just couldn't believe that they were really there, that it was really them. I was sure a happy little girl that day."

As she improved, life in the hospital became more pleasant. "They would put us out on the porch in the sunshine in the afternoon," she recalled. "A lot of the children couldn't get around. Well, I could hop around without my crutches, so I would go out and pick up persimmons and take them to the children who couldn't get any.... A friend of my Aunt Lilly would visit and give me ten or fifteen cents. That was my spending money. A little boy who could walk would go to a store just down from the hospital on Seventh Street and buy some pickles and wieners. We would sit out on the porch and eat them.

"I remember one girl named Gladys. I don't remember where she was from. They asked her if she'd had her tonsils out. She said 'yeah' the doctor back home had taken out six and she didn't know how many she had left!"

In February 1928, after almost a year and a half in the hospital, Virginia Preddy went home. Eventually, she resumed horseback riding. The sharecropper's daughter, who was destined to become a schoolteacher, had been among the first of the thousands of children whose lives would be touched by the work of Arkansas Children's Hospital.

The flood of 1927 had dealt a crushing blow to the state's already depressed economy. At the height of the disaster, nearly half of Arkansas was reported to be under water, and over 143,000 people were being sheltered in refugee camps established by the American Red Cross and other relief organizations. Cotton, the backbone of the state's economy, could not provide sufficient income to quickly make good the vast losses. Recovery would be slow and painful.

There was now little hope that full county funding would soon be restored, but press coverage of the benevolent institution's dire plight brought forth some gracious offers of assistance. In January 1928 a group of Little Rock laundry men offered to provide laundry service to the Children's Home and Hospital at no charge. The different laundry firms planned to rotate the duty every two months. Upon the recommendation of Superintendent Christian, this offer was cheerfully accepted.

On April 11, 1928, the management of the Capitol Theater offered to donate the receipts from a new Sunday afternoon matinee to the Children's Hospital. The minutes of the Board meeting at which this offer was discussed do not provide details of the discussion which preceded the Board's vote to accept the gift, but it must have been a lively debate. Showing movies on Sunday was illegal under state law, and the prominent businessmen who sat on the Board were well aware of these so-called "blue laws." In voting to accept this controversial donation, they were helping to provoke a court test of the state law.

The movie shown on the following Sunday afternoon as a benefit for the Arkansas Children's Hospital was a comedy entitled *Tillie's Punctured Romance* starring W.C. Fields. The movie played to a full house. Receipts from the entertainment totaled $413.15. (The film was apparently shown several times.) At the conclusion of the movie, theater manager Ed Bowley was arrested by officers of the Little Rock Police Department. He was booked and released on $100 bond. The arrest was front-page news in both of Arkansas' statewide daily newspapers.

The laws restricting business and recreational activities on Sunday had been the subject of lively debate throughout the 1920s. As automobiles became more common, the debate had intensified. In an era when a six-day work week was typical, many people wanted to attend movies, baseball games and other leisure activities on Sunday afternoon. On the other side of the emotional debate, many thoughtful and sincere religious people felt that the modern world increasingly tempted people to use the Sabbath as a day for pleasure rather than worship. Now the issue was before the court.

On the following Wednesday morning the theater manager was brought before Municipal Judge Harper Harb. Among the charges preferred against him by Deputy Prosecuting Attorney E.G. Shoffner, were showing a motion picture on Sunday, laboring on Sunday and compelling eight employees to labor on Sunday. "It looks like persecution to me," Ed Bowley told the *Arkansas Democrat.* "I did not ask a single employee of mine to labor on Sunday, but all volunteered and were glad to perform their services in the interest of hundreds of deserving crippled children over the state.

"While I am being prosecuted on ten different charges growing out of the operation of a business on Sunday ... for a charitable purpose," he pointed out to Judge Harb, "there are no efforts being made by the constituted authorities to close many filling stations, drug stores selling other than necessary drugs, cold drink parlors and other businesses being operated for private gain and in violation of the letter of the law."

The prosecution countered that the Arkansas Supreme Court had ruled that the operation of a motion picture theater on Sunday was in violation of state law and that no exceptions were made in the case of charity. Ben Brickhouse, attorney for the defendant, in turn countered that the state Supreme Court had never been called upon to decide a case similar to the one in question, since in the previous instance the question of charity had not been involved. "Moreover," proclaimed the defense, "the operation of a place of amusement for charitable purposes, is not a business, according to court decisions as to the nature of business enterprises." On these grounds, he contended that the charges against his client were without foundation.

Briefs of the arguments were submitted by the lawyers. A few days later, Judge Harb ruled that since no profit had been made by the theater, the showing of the movie on Sunday had not been a violation of the state law. In view of the fact that the eight theater employees had volunteered to work on Sunday without pay, their employer was found not guilty of compelling them to labor on Sunday. The other charges were dismissed.

While the ruling had not overturned the ban on Sunday movies, it had established that showing movies on Sunday for charitable purposes was legal, thus creating a loophole in the law. The debate over Sunday recreation would continue to rage, and there would be other court tests of the law. By 1931 the state legislature would legalize both Sunday movies and baseball games. Thus even though the Arkansas Children's Home and Hospital had been a neutral party in the court case, it had played a key role in bringing Sunday recreation to Arkansas.

The Capitol Theater held several more Sunday afternoon matinees to benefit the children's hospital. In May 1928 the theater management presented the Society with a check for $2,000. The money was desperately needed. With the fall in county funding, the Society was struggling to keep its doors open.

Loyd W. Judd, a real estate and insurance agent, succeeded Robert E. Wiley as president of the Board of Directors in June 1928. In addition to his work with the Arkansas Children's Home and Hospital, Judd was active in the Young Businessman's Association and served on the Little Rock City Planning Commission. Under his innovative leadership the institution turned to the Arkansas General Assembly for financial assistance.

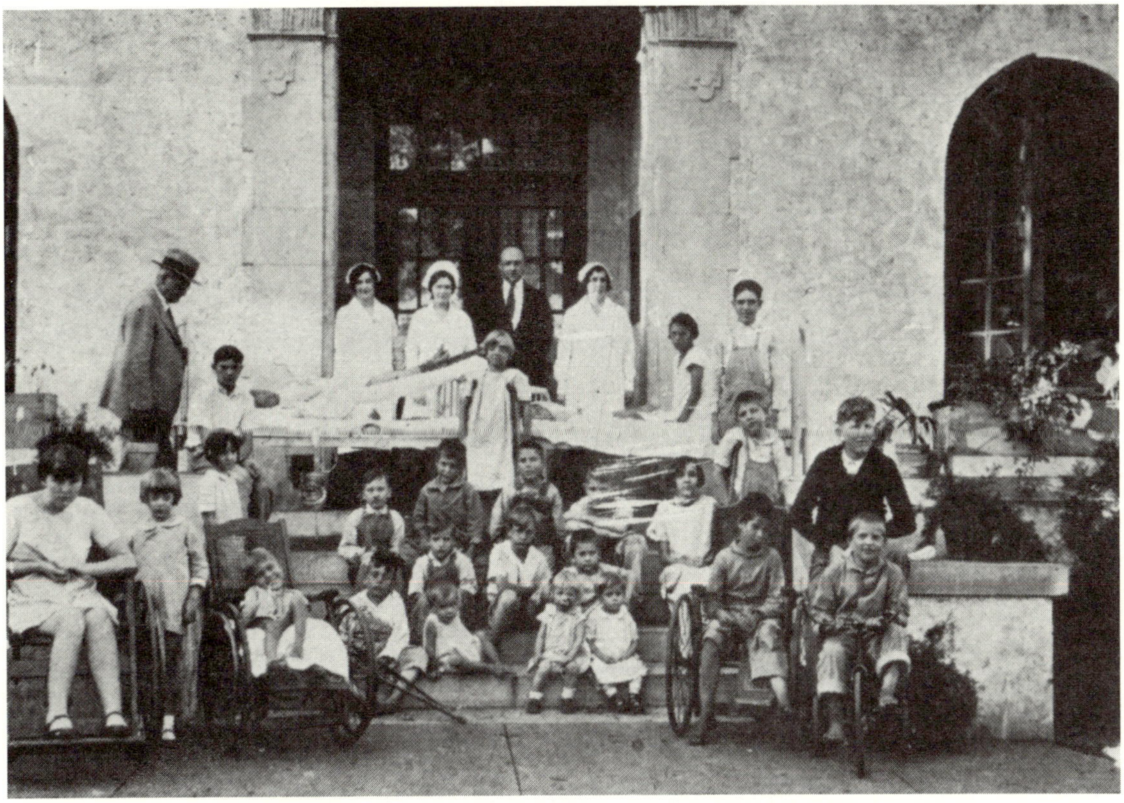

Hospital patients and Dr. Christian (standing in back row)
ca. 1926

In April 1929 two bills were passed by the legislative body to aid the Society. The first was an "act to create and adopt the Arkansas Children's Home and Hospital as a state agency for the care of dependent and neglected and crippled children." The second was an "act appropriating money for the partial support and maintenance of the Arkansas Children's Home and Hospital and of the dependent, neglected and crippled children therein." This bill guaranteed the institution a maximum of $625 per month in income from the state. Both bills were signed into law by Governor Harvey Parnell.

Also in April, Dr. Christian and his wife were presented with a house and three lots by Mrs. C.A. Forney-Smith. The property was located on the corner of Maryland Avenue and Battery Street, just south of the Home and Hospital. In his thirteenth year as superintendent of the Arkansas Children's Home Society, the seventy-three-year old Dr. Christian was in failing health. Still, he continued to labor in behalf of the children.

On the opening page of his 1929 annual report, the superintendent sought to assuage concern regarding the state of his health. "For four years I have suffered from a complaint which threatened my life," he declared, "but I am glad to say to you that I am enjoying a degree of health that is astonishing for one of my age. I am better than for twenty years."

His annual report was far more candid in discussing the Society's financial health. He pointed out that the slump in its income over the past year was due to a combination of circumstances, some of which dated back to 1927. Arkansas was still struggling to recover from the millions of dollars in devastation wrought by the floods and windstorms that had swept the state in that year. In addition, a recent ruling by the state Supreme Court had brought a penalty against county judges who appropriated funds above the ability of the counties to pay.

According to the report, the Children's Hospital now had fifty-five beds. In July 1929, there were fifty-two patients in the hospital. The average daily census was twenty-eight. The average length of a hospitalization was thirty-one days. The average cost per patient per day was $1.27. Local physicians continued to provide their services free of charge.

A total of 243 children had been cared for by the Children's Home during the fiscal year just ending. Of these children, sixty-six were currently living at the Home while awaiting placement, thirty-eight had been sent to live with relatives and eight had been transferred to other institutions. The remainder had been returned to their families or placed in foster homes.

The superintendent expressed the hope that the prolonged financial crisis was almost over. It proved to be a false hope. By October the monthly expenses incurred by the Home and Hospital were totaling $6,000 per month, while income was approximately half of that sum.

On October 29, 1929, the stock market crashed. It would be several months before the full impact of the crash became apparent, but as the supply of investment money dwindled, factories and businesses were forced to close or lay off workers. The jobless could not purchase products, causing still more shutdowns and cutbacks. As unemployment grew, millions of people across the nation suddenly found themselves living in poverty. Thousands could not meet payments on homes and property. The Great Depression had begun.

Board President Loyd W. Judd resigned his post in the aftermath of the stock market crash in order to devote more time to his struggling business enterprises. Fellow Board member Aurthur L. Wooten was elected president of the panel. Wooten was manager of the real estate department at Twin City Bank.

In February 1930 the Board voted to request an extension of the two mortgage notes which were now past due with the Bankers' Trust Company. The following month Dr. Christian informed the Board that he had been offered the position of State Superintendent with the Missouri Children's Home Society. In order to retain his leadership, the board raised Dr. Christian's salary to $200 per month. Under the terms of the contract, this salary was to continue throughout his lifetime regardless of his work with the Society.

Less than two weeks after the resolution of the leadership crisis, the Bankers' Trust Company demanded payment of the $20,000 mortgage loan. The Board voted to try to raise $5,000 plus the interest due on the note. Their efforts failed. In September, with foreclosure proceedings looming, Dr. Christian spoke to the members of the Board. He expressed the frustration which they all felt.

"The conditions over which no one has any control have brought us a double burden: the securing of funds to pay the current monthly expenses, and caring for children already in our care, to say nothing of trying to appease the several counties in the state who have made appropriations and paid them, and who demand that we shall take their children who are in need of hospital treatment, or in need of a home and mother.

"Our financial distress is not owing to any lack of management on the part of those who have had the responsibility of the care of the children either in Home or Hospital. If we alone suffered, we could find a remedy. The same conditions prevail everywhere. Our city is facing a deficit. Pulaski County is running behind, and even the great state of Arkansas is complaining of the shortage of funds. This same condition seems to prevail throughout the United States in every line of business.

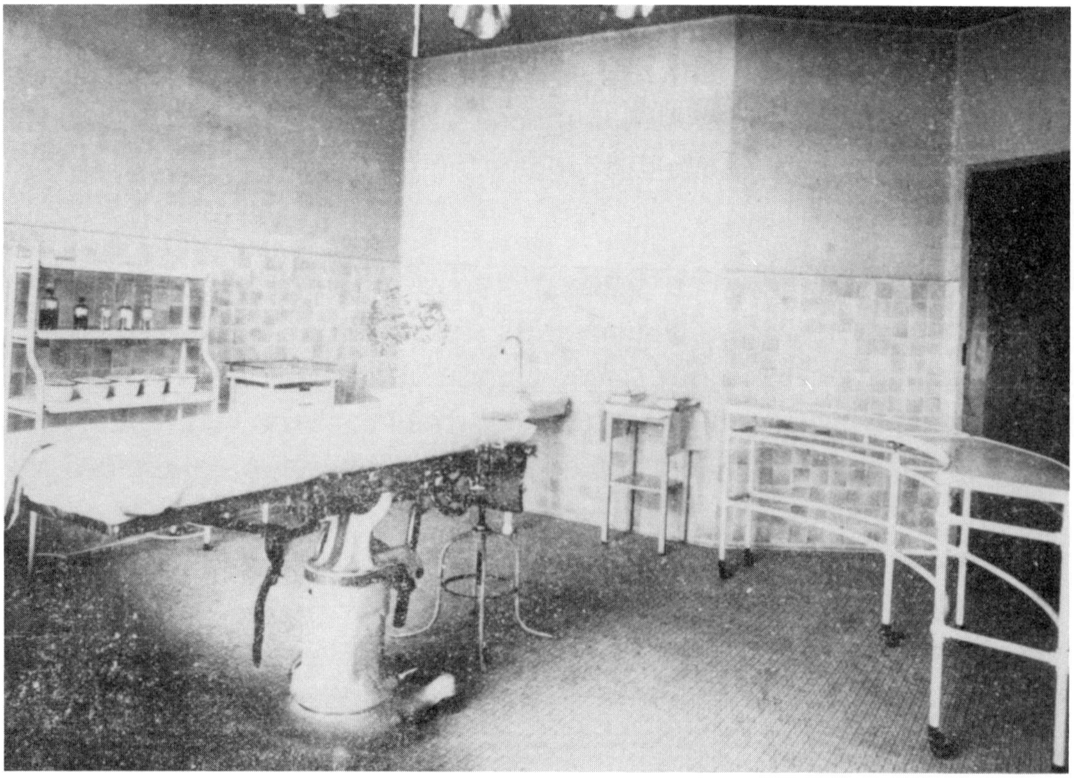

Operating Room, ca. 1929

Laboratory, ca. 1929

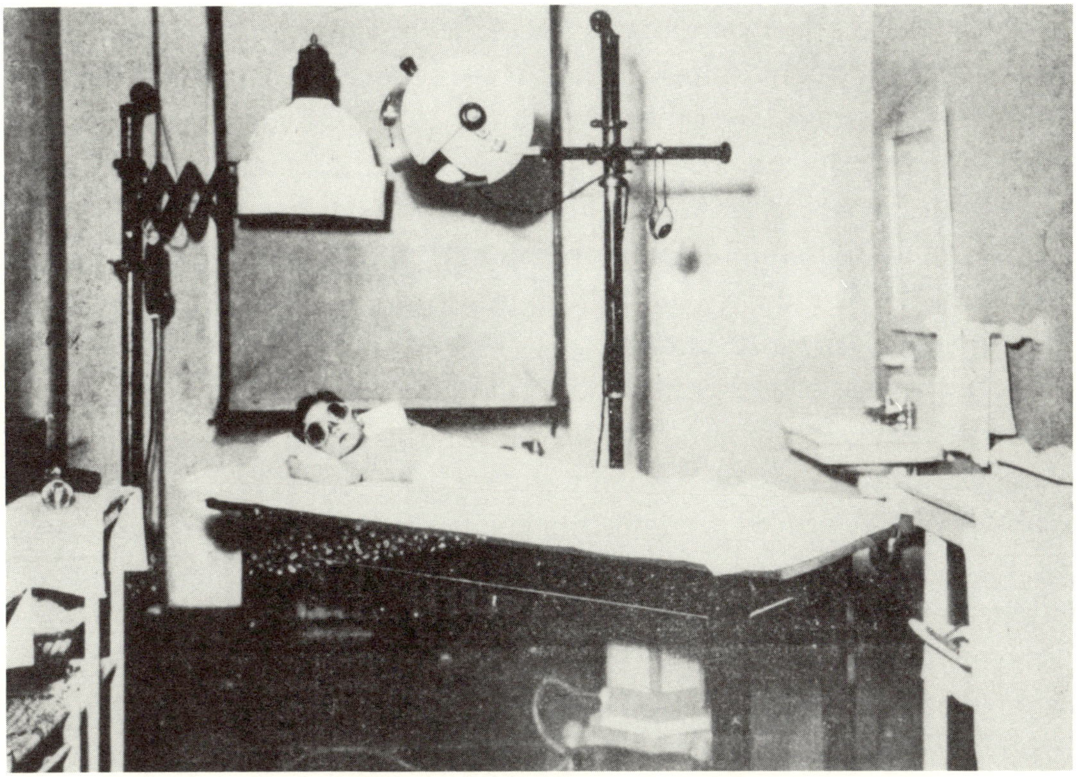

Physical Therapy Department, ca. 1929

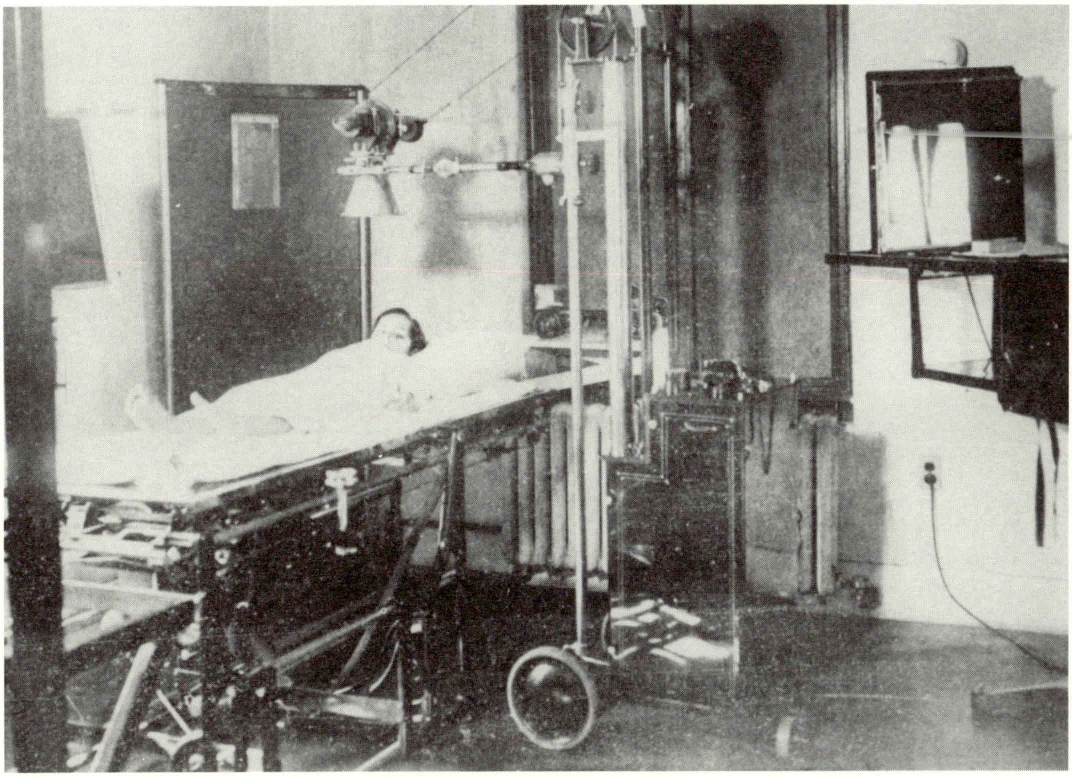

Radiology Department, ca. 1929

"Our creditors are demanding payments on the grounds that they too have obligations which compel them to insist upon the payment of our bills. If we could only collect the amount due us from the several counties, which amounts to over $3,000, and [if] the Community Fund [was] more prompt in its payments, and if conditions over the state were normal so that we could obtain subscriptions from individuals who heretofore have co-operated with us, we would have sufficient funds to pay our bills and keep up the good name of the institution."

Foreclosure was averted when the Bankers' Trust Company agreed to grant a one-year extension on both the first and second mortgage notes in exchange for the immediate payment of the $2,085 in interest due on the two notes. While engaged in these critical negotiations with the bank, the Board received word that the Children's Hospital had been given a Grade-A rating by the American Medical Association.

The institution's second decade had been difficult. Even so, it had been a time of great fulfillment. The Children's Hospital had been built, and its doors had remained open despite great hardship. The 1930s would prove to be an even greater challenge.

Arkansas Children's Hospital, ca. 1929

Three

IN 1930 THE AVERAGE ARKANSAN was far more concerned about the weather than about the recent Wall Street crash. Arkansas was locked in the grip of a drought which was to last nearly a year. As weeks passed without rain, cotton and other crops shriveled in the fields. Half of the state's crops were lost to the heat, as cotton prices continued to fall. With their incomes down, planters and merchants could not provide credit to the sharecroppers. Thus the old sharecropping system upon which thousands of Arkansans depended for the basic necessities of life collapsed. No credit meant no food. Long accustomed to grueling poverty, the sharecroppers now faced the prospect of starvation.

The stock market's tumble took the state's small but thriving business community by surprise. In 1930 alone, more than 100 Arkansas banks failed. Thousands of depositors and shareholders lost their savings and investments. Even as President Herbert Hoover assured the nation that "Prosperity is just around the corner," the situation grew steadily worse. By 1933, more than one-fourth of the nation's labor force was unemployed, and more than half of the industries in Arkansas had closed their doors. Across the land unemployed men and boys drifted from place to place seeking work. Millions of hungry people stood for hours in soup and bread lines. Millions more went to bed hungry.

When private organizations such as the American Red Cross ran out of money, local and state governments did what they could to help. As revenues fell, Arkansas was forced to default on its highway bond payments. President Hoover's major program to combat the Depression, the Reconstruction Finance Corporation (RFC), offered emergency loans to banks, railroads, insurance companies and other businesses. The agency also provided some money to create jobs for the unemployed. Arkansas Governor Harvey Parnell authorized public works projects in each of the state's seventy-five counties. Arkansas spent its entire RFC allotment in only eight months, with little improvement to its dying economy.

Like the rest of the nation, the Arkansas Children's Home and Hospital was caught up in this economic catastrophe. In 1930 alone, more than 10,000 letters appealing for donations were mailed out. Field representatives of the Children's Home Society crisscrossed the state speaking to church, school and civic groups stressing the urgency of the organization's need.

Stella Boyle Smith of Little Rock was a member of the Society's small but dedicated band of volunteer fieldworkers. Smith and her husband had moved to Little Rock from the Hot Spring County community of Malvern in the early 1920s. "When we moved to Little Rock," she reminisced at the age of ninety-seven, "the Children's Home was asking for volunteers to help investigate the homes of people who wanted to adopt children from the orphanage. Well, I had always been interested in orphans, and I had free train transportation around the state [her husband was chief accountant for the Missouri Pacific Railroad], so I volunteered, and when the Home's Board of Directors decided to add a hospital in 1923, I was there when they turned the first shovelful of dirt."

Most of all, she remembered the children. "The seventh patient ever treated at Children's Hospital was a little girl named Minnie Fay from Arkadelphia, who was born with spinal and bone deformities. Everybody called her 'Sunshine,'" said Smith, "and I used to call her 'Froggy' because she was in a body cast.

Adoption Poster, ca. 1933

Poster/Milk Donations, ca. 1933

"I remember one time we had five youngsters brought to the orphanage because their parents were in the penitentiary for bootlegging. We couldn't get the baby to drink milk—and then we discovered that the parents had been giving him moonshine instead! I had to go down to the courthouse and get some of the 'evidence' to mix with the milk until we could get that baby weaned from moonshine."

Then there was the seven-year-old who was so dirty and full of lice that the nurses would not touch him. "I had to use coal oil and scrubbed that child so hard I was afraid his skin was coming off!"

During the hard times of the Great Depression, Stella Boyle Smith took an active role in the Home and Hospital's fund-raising efforts. "Dr. Christian would call me and say, 'We need more money,' so I'd hop on the train and go all around the state collecting donations. I would keep track of everybody who gave me even a quarter. Sometimes, if they didn't have money to give, they'd give me sheets or pillowcases or something else that the home or hospital could use."

In one small Arkansas community, she approached two local businessmen, a banker and a store owner, both of whom were notoriously reluctant to donate to charitable causes. She persuaded each man to donate $25 if the other would agree to do the same. "I'll tell you, I sure didn't let any grass grow under my feet in going back to each of them to collect!"

Despite such determined efforts, the Society's budget deficit continued to mount. In March 1930, William P. Hamilton succeeded Aurthur L. Wooten as president of the Board of Directors. Hamilton was vice-president of the O.K. Houck Piano Company of Little Rock. By the middle of the year, the Arkansas Children's Home and Hospital was on the verge of closing its doors, a victim of the times. There was but one final avenue of appeal, one last hope of saving the institution.

"It would be an easy matter," Superintendent Orlando P. Christian told the members of the Board on September 18, 1930, "for us to say 'Let us close our doors.' This would mean sounding a death bell of the Arkansas Children's Home and Hospital. We could not go before the quorum courts and ask for an appropriation for an organization that was not functioning. There would be no hope of receiving an appropriation from the state of Arkansas with our doors closed. There are hundreds of other reasons, if we would stop to think of them and name them, why we must continue our work. The greatest of all is, the children themselves demand it of us.

"About a week ago, a mother, poorly clad and with a saddened face, called upon us to arrange for the boarding of her three children. She gave their ages as two, four and six. She said, 'I do not want to give my babies away, but I want to board them and will pay all I can so I can keep them.' It was not possible for us to take them under those conditions, and I sent her to the charity organizations for help. Yesterday, I was asked by the County Probation Office to take these children as the mother had found no work, and must give them up for adoption. Could any story be more sad than this? If this was our only case, we could easily remedy it, but multiply this by hundreds, and you have a problem that challenges the united efforts of all the people of Arkansas."

Poster thanking Arkansans for help, ca. 1934

Poster for donations, ca. 1933

Dr. Christian implored each member of the Board of Directors to personally take up the challenge by pledging to secure at least three solicitations from their friends of $25 or more. He urged that these pledges be made by the first day of October, and that they be paid in full on or before the first day of December 1930.

"This organization," declared Dr. Christian, "can be saved and must be saved through the combined cooperation of every member of the board of directors. We each have our friends. We each can tell the story in our own way. This will broaden our field by placing upon our books many names of persons who will be an annual contributor to the Society, ... and with a proper appeal to individuals we believe that we may be able to secure sums equal to 1929. What we need and must have is immediate help ... to extricate the Society from its financial embarrassment."

The Board members rose to the challenge, themselves giving far beyond the amount that Dr. Christian had suggested. They appealed for donations from friends in every corner of the state. As a result, the budget report for January 1931 showed a deficit of only $194.98, and the institution's debt had been reduced to $8,805.24. The response of the hard-pressed Arkansas business community had been truly remarkable. Superintendent Christian expressed the hope that the worst was over and that better days lay ahead.

This was not to be the case, however. As the Depression deepened, and as more and more Arkansans lost their jobs, hunger in the state increased. Thus many of the children admitted to the Arkansas Children's Home and Hospital during these dark days were suffering from malnutrition. Stella Boyle Smith recalled one of these malnourished youngsters, "an eleven-year-old boy with pellegra (a deficiency of protein), who weighed only thirty-two pounds. He was cured with whole milk and overripe bananas that I'd collect from the grocery stores every Saturday," she said. "When he went home I bought him a bicycle."

By June 1931 the financial condition of the institution was once again desperate. Dr. Christian was urged to limit admissions to the Home and Hospital until the outlook improved, but he could not bring himself to turn away a needy child. This difficult dilemma gave rise to an innovative program. A group of the hospital's physicians began traveling throughout the state conducting clinics at local schools. Hundreds of children were examined, badly needed medicines were distributed and operations such as tonsillectomies were performed. This program helped keep hospital admissions down and brought health care to countless young people who otherwise would not have had access to it.

Despite such innovative measures, the financial condition of the Society continued to worsen. In July, financial secretary Lillian McDarmott reported that the Hospital's nursing staff had been paid one month's salary. The office help and the Society's one remaining paid fieldworker had received a half month's salary. All other workers had received one full month's salary.

All food and supplies were being purchased with cash. A small payment had been made on the electric bill and the telephone bills had been paid in full. This left the organization with less than $500 cash on hand. The combined debt of the Children's Home and Hospital had risen to almost $17,000.

"Everything possible will be done to economize," Superintendent Christian assured the Board of Directors. All employees of the Children's Home were dismissed with the exception of the cook and the laundress. The children living at the Home were cared for by a small group of volunteers. This was done so that the hospital could remain open. Both the Home and Hospital began accepting only emergency cases. It was the institution's darkest hour.

A committee was formed to seek a solution to the crisis. The committee's report called for a statewide fund-raising effort. Newspapers throughout Arkansas were asked to help in soliciting these emergency funds. The "Goodwill Dollar Unit Campaign" was launched on September 2, 1931. Newspapers across the state featured stories about the fund drive. Most of these stories focused on the Children's Hospital. Many of them included letters of thanks and praise which had been sent to Dr. Christian by grateful parents.

A typical story, which ran in the October 10, 1931, issue of *The Benton Courier*, featured a letter from a Saline County mother whose son had recently undergone treatment at the Children's Hospital. "Charlie has been home three weeks," she had written Dr. Christian. "The wound is entirely healed and he is enjoying himself as I have never seen him do before. I feel I owe it to you and the Children's Hospital at Little Rock that he is alive today.

"Two years ago, before I knew about your hospital, I had taken him to two other hospitals, and both of them sent him home as incurable, but now he is well. It is just like a miracle to me.

"I am a poor widow but I am going to save all I can and send it to your hospital, as I know there must be many mothers who have children who must come to your hospital, for like me, they have no money to pay hospital expenses. My prayer is that the good people will help you to keep the hospital open."

The woman had added a postscript. "P.S. Charlie is going to try to get you five bushels of white potatoes."

Similar donations of food poured in from around the state. In November, as the Goodwill Dollar Unit Campaign was drawing to a close, Superintendent Christian told the Board of Directors that while the drive had been very disappointing in terms of the amount of money collected, it had been a great success in another respect.

"While the people have almost no money," declared Dr. Christian, "they have said what Peter said to the lame man who was lying before the gate of the temple, 'Silver and gold have I none, but such as I have, give I unto thee.' Friends, this is the picture that has been presented to us all over Arkansas. People have said to us with faces full of sympathy and hearts pulsating with ours, 'Gold and silver we have none, but such as we have we give unto you.'

"Some of you have visited our basement and seen the hundreds and hundreds of cans of fruit and cases of vegetables piled [one] on top of the other. In our vegetable room, we have all kinds of vegetables such as farmers raise. A supply sufficient to last us until fresh fruits come again. Such as they had, they gave us. We have been offered corn, hay, wheat and rice. Some of these commodities we have taken, others we may give our consent to take, providing we can find a market for it.

"I think that I can say to you truthfully that the Arkansas Children's Home and Hospital is thoroughly embedded in the hearts of the people throughout the whole state of Arkansas.... I am confident," concluded Dr. Christian, "that when these communities who have furnished us fruits and vegetables so freely have an opportunity to turn their commodities into money, they will give us money just as freely as they have given us fruits and vegetables."

Home residents making party decorations, ca. 1938

Whatever the future might hold, for the present there was little money. In December there was no money for Christmas gifts for the children. Once again, Dr. Christian sought the assistance of the press. The front page of the December 20, 1931, *Arkansas Democrat* featured a story urging childless couples to take a child from the Arkansas Children's Home into their home for the holidays. "There are a lot of tots," proclaimed the *Democrat*, "who would like a 'vacation' over Christmas in some nice home, whether they are to get permanent homes or not, and the opportunity is extended to Little Rock and Arkansas folks to invite a real cheer to their homes for the holiday period."

Many compassionate Arkansans responded to this heart-tugging appeal. Of the forty-seven youngsters living at the Home, all but two were taken for holiday outings, and Dr. Christian and his wife celebrated Christmas with the two remaining children. In addition, each patient in the Children's Hospital received a small Christmas gift. "It was," said Dr. Christian, "a most remarkable and joyous holiday season."

The new year brought little relief to the Depression-ravaged institution. In January 1932, Judge Thomas H. Humphreys succeeded William P. Hamilton as president of the Board of Directors. Judge Humphreys was an associate justice of the Arkansas Supreme Court. Throughout 1932 the seemingly endless financial crisis was the major topic of discussion at all Board meetings. The hospital's medical staff did their part to keep the doors open. In 1932 alone, more than $50,000 worth of time and services were donated to the medical facility by local physicians, surgeons and dentists.

"Among other efforts to reduce expenses," reported Dr. Christian in May of that year, "we have mailed letters to fifty-one different dairymen who bring milk to Little Rock, asking them to give us their surplus milk. This has resulted in the Arkansas Children's Home and Hospital receiving sufficient milk to supply the children's needs. In addition, the bakers of the city have joined together and are furnishing us with bread."

Five months later, in October 1932, the hard-pressed superintendent sent out yet another appeal to long-time supporters. "A short time ago," he reminded them, "we wrote you telling you something of the demand for the services of the Home and Hospital and asking if you could help us with a November contribution.... Depression, a spectre grim and gaunt, looms over many an Arkansas community this winter ready to snatch the bread from the mouths of the children, the shoes from their feet. Barefoot weather is passing fast. The gardens will soon be barren. If you can help us in November, will you let us know within the next week using the enclosed card?"

Such appeals kept the doors open. "That the Arkansas Children's Home and Hospital has been able to keep its doors open," wrote Superintendent

Christian, "speaks volumes for the ... splendid patience and generosity of the good people of Little Rock and the state of Arkansas. Had its creditors compelled us to meet our bills from month to month, the Arkansas Children's Home and Hospital would have been compelled to close its doors more than a year ago." Demand for the hospital's services had never been greater. According to the 1932 annual report 694 patients were admitted to the pediatric medical facility and 458 operations were performed by its volunteer physicians.

In November of that year, Arkansas voters helped to elect Franklin Delano Roosevelt President of the United States. In his inaugural address on March 4, 1933, the new president offered reassurance. "The only thing we have to fear," he asserted, "is fear itself." Under FDR's vigorous leadership the Congress embarked on the most remarkable legislative program in American history. Much of this historic legislation would have a lasting impact on the Arkansas Children's Home and Hospital.

In a letter dated December 30, 1933, Dr. Orlando P. Christian announced his decision to retire after seventeen years as superintendent of the Arkansas Children's Home Society. "I believe," he wrote, "that I have arrived at the time in my life where I must ask for retirement from active service in the Children's Home and Hospital as your superintendent. I find that my strength is gradually failing, and the condition of my wife's health requiring me to give her closer attention, seem to compel me to take this step which I regret more than I can tell. There are four lines of an old hymn that we used to sing when I was a boy which run like this:

My latest sun is setting fast
My race is nearly run
My greatest trials now are past
My journey's just begun.

"However," he added, "I wish to be connected with the Society as long as I live." He had definite plans in that regard. He reminded the members of the board that under the terms of his contract, "when I retire from active service I immediately become Superintendent Emeritus, and am to hold myself in readiness for counsel when needed and also to spare as much of my time as I am able in soliciting funds for the endowment of the Society."

In closing, he offered to remain at his post until a replacement could be hired, and he expressed his gratitude to the Board. "I love every member of the Board of Directors and I feel under very great obligation to them for what they have done for the Society; the way in which they have helped. Without which assistance we could not have succeeded, and so far as I know I have the respect and confidence of every member of the Board."

Dr. Christian was not present when the announcement of his retirement was made. Board president Thomas Humphreys read the letter to the institution's governing body. The resignation was accepted, as was the offer to remain on the job until a replacement had been chosen. The members of the Board may well have pondered whether a new superintendent was even needed. The institution's buildings had fallen into disrepair, and it was again being threatened with foreclosure by its creditors. Who would want the job under such seemingly impossible circumstances?

In January 1934 a young woman named Ruth Beall (pronounced "Bell") brought a little boy from Benton County in northwest Arkansas to the Children's Hospital for treatment. The youngster was suffering from spinal tuberculosis. Beall was county secretary (director) for the National Tuberculosis Association. There was little that the doctors could do for the child. Ruth Beall remained in Little Rock to be near him; within a few days the child died.

Before leaving the capital city Ruth Beall—"Miss Beall" as she was always referred to by her friends and co-workers—paid an unannounced visit to Judge Thomas Humphreys. She expressed her dismay at the run-down condition of the hospital building and told him that the staff was too small to care for such a large number of patients. "The children," she declared, "deserve better." The president of the institution's Board of Directors reminded the earnest young social worker that times were hard. They were, he assured her, doing the best they could do given the limited resources available. The Board was seeking a new superintendent. Would she be interested in the position?

"In any other mood," Beall later told an interviewer, "I would have had better sense than to accept the job, but I had just been through a divorce—the first in the history of my family—and I wanted to bury myself in hard work far away from home."

The new superintendent of the Arkansas Children's Home and Hospital had an abiding interest in the welfare of the less fortunate. Ruth Olive Beall had been born in St. Louis, Missouri, in 1896, the daughter of Charles Carlton and Florance Walcott Beall. Her father, a well-to-do traveling salesman, moved the family to the small community of Rogers, Arkansas, when she was a teenager. Ruth, who dreamed of serving as a medical missionary, remained in Missouri, attending boarding school at Arcadia and later Washington University in St. Louis.

Upon returning home to Rogers, she became the adviser to the local chapter of the Junior Red Cross during World War I. After the war, she briefly served as owner and editor of the local newspaper, *The Rogers Daily Post*, and later moved to Little Rock, where she worked in the state office of the National Tuberculosis Association. An emergency in the Benton County TB office took her back to Rogers in 1926, where she served as county secretary for the next eight years.

During her tenure as county secretary, Beall traveled the back roads of Benton County visiting families who were coping with tuberculosis. She was shocked at the poverty of the rural South. She was particularly distressed by the obvious lack of basic dental hygiene among the school-age children she met.

At her own expense, she purchased a supply of toothpaste and toothbrushes. Then, with the cooperation of the county schools, she spoke to students about the importance of good dental hygiene. After she had demonstrated the proper way to use them, each student was given a tube of toothpaste and a toothbrush. Many of these young people had never used "store-bought" toothpaste, and for some it was their first encounter with a toothbrush.

At one school, Beall was puzzled by the fact that every girl's dress and every boy's shirt bore the same blue-flower pattern. After concluding her presentation she asked the teacher about this. The children's clothes, it turned out, were made of flour sack cloth. The store in their small community stocked only one brand of flour—one that, unlike most others, offered only one pattern on its sacks. Before heading home to Rogers, Beall visited the store and obtained the address of the flour company. She wrote the company and persuaded it to add four or five new patterns, so that the youngsters would no longer be forced to dress alike. This was the woman who became superintendent of the Arkansas Children's Home and Hospital on February 1, 1934.

Ruth Beall brought a nest egg of $80 with her from Rogers. Within six weeks of her arrival in Little Rock she had spent all but twenty-five cents of this sum for urgently needed hospital supplies. One gloomy night as she sat munching on a dry cheese sandwich in the hospital's basement kitchen, Beall had an

Actor Dick Powell, ca. 1939

unexpected visitor, an old friend from Benton County who was interested in applying for the job of cook. As they were discussing the demands of the job, a drugstore delivery boy entered with a seventy-five cent C.O.D. prescription. Beall persuaded her friend to lend her fifty cents, put it with her last quarter, and paid for the medicine. Her friend got the job.

With no money for basic necessities, and with foreclosure looming, fund raising was the new superintendent's first priority. Thirty thousand dollars was needed to postpone disaster for one year. She persuaded Cooper Jacoway, a well-known Little Rock attorney, to head the fund drive. Jacoway made direct appeals to prominent members of the Arkansas business community.

He sent El Dorado oilman Roy W. Spence to Memphis to put the bite on Harvey Couch, founder of the Arkansas Power and Light Company. Couch promised to give $1,000 if Spence could get four Arkansans to donate $500 each. Spence found three $500 contributors, but could not find a fourth. Finally, in desperation, he put $350 worth of small checks together, obtained $150 from another donor, then persuaded the donor to take all of the small checks and give him a draft for $500. Confronted with the four $500 checks, Couch paid the $1,000 that he had promised.

After the deed was done, the oilman's conscience bothered him so badly that he went back to his victim and confessed the deception. "I knew that all the time," said Couch with a laugh. "Nobody in his right mind would give $500 to that bankrupt hospital, and there are only three rich idiots in Arkansas." Couch would continue to support the work of the Arkansas Children's Home and Hospital. Today, the Arkansas Power and Light Company carries on this tradition as a major contributor to the state's only pediatric medical center.

Jacoway's efforts raised $16,000. Somehow the remainder of the money needed to pay the interest on the mortgage was found; no one knows exactly how, although the Masonic Lodges of Arkansas are generally credited with this philanthropy. With $20,000 in delinquent interest outstanding, the bank had first claim on any money raised, but Beall was not about to part with all of the hard-raised cash. She rented a safe deposit box and put the first $7,000 raised into it. Beall used this secret fund to pay most of the day-to-day C.O.D. expenses of the Home and Hospital for the next two years.

Her next move was to persuade Azro L. Barber, a Little Rock corporation lawyer, to become president of the Board of Directors. He would serve for eight years—longer than any of his predecessors. With his legal background he was able to work closely with the institution's creditors. By the time he stepped down from the position in early 1943, the Arkansas Children's Home and Hospital would be almost free of its long-standing debt, and would be financially stable for the first time in its history.

The new superintendent economized in every possible way. She dismissed all of the department heads and personally assumed their responsibilities, and conceived a plan to trim the institution's food budget. As county secretary for the Tuberculosis Association, she had worked with the Benton County Home Demonstration Club. Arkansas had 1,626 such clubs with over 39,000 members. These clubs, a function of the county agent's office, taught health, diet and homemaking skills to rural Arkansans. Here was a vast reservoir of farm women who had little cash, but much good will. She appealed to them for help. Soon, jars of home-canned fruits, vegetables, jams and jellies were pouring in from across the state. Many of these women also applied their sewing skills, turning out pajamas, layettes, bedding and other items for the children.

Other changes not only saved money, but also resulted in a much less institutionalized lifestyle for the children. Beall closed down the home's school and enrolled every school-age resident of the orphanage in the public schools. The youngsters were encouraged to participate in school and community activities. In June 1934 she reported to the Board that "the boys are members of the Boys' Club and have all the privileges of the clubhouse and go swimming at least three times a week, each child taking his own penny with him for his towel."

A library was established at the home in the hope that it would help the children make better grades in school. In March 1935 Beall noted that "the children are all doing better in school now. Regular study hours have been established. The library ... has about one-third of the volumes necessary. The bookcases were built, the lumber furnished and finished by the Kiwanis

Patients and staff ride in parade honoring
President and Mrs. Roosevelt, June 10, 1936

Eleanor Roosevelt and Ruth Beall (on left), March 21, 1937

Club and this has been a wonderful addition to the Boys' Home. The library is to be catalogued and opened at regular hours during the day for the children."

In an echo of the flour sack incident, Beall discarded the last of the uniforms that the children had been wearing and appealed for donations of more appropriate clothing. The response was very disappointing. "There is just absolutely no clothing for children past the age of five years being sent in, with the exception of a few summer dresses and some summer suits for boys of the same age," she reported in June 1935. "Therefore it becomes necessary that we buy shoes, stockings and unbleached muslin."

This report also disclosed that most of the residents of the Girls' Home had joined the Girl Scouts, and that those residents of the Boys' Home who worked in the laundry, went to the market or helped maintain the institution's grounds were being paid ten cents a week as a reward for their labor.

To renovate the institution's run-down buildings, Beall balanced one Depression relief program against another. The materials needed for the work were available to institutions through the Public Works Administration (PWA), but not the labor. Beall obtained $33,000 worth of brick, steel, cement, plaster and other building materials, which she stacked and stored all around the hospital. Then, she went to the Works Projects Administration (WPA), which could provide labor, and thus succeeded in getting the job done.

Beall's next coup was political. She lobbied the Arkansas General Assembly, urging a renewal of county support for the institution. Legislation legalizing such appropriations was passed. She saw federal aid to dependent children coming even before the passage of the Social Security Act, and persuaded Arkansas Attorney General Carl Bailey, father of six children, to issue an official opinion stating that the Arkansas Children's Home and Hospital would be eligible for federal aid. Thus, when federal aid finally came, she was fully prepared to receive it.

In November 1936 Carl Bailey was elected Governor of Arkansas. He promised an activist administration, declaring in his inaugural address, "The people who pay taxes are buying services, not surpluses." He may well have been thinking of the Arkansas Children's Home and Hospital when he questioned the value of political freedoms without economic security. "What good," he asked, "is the right peaceably to assemble to a child so crippled that he cannot look forward to a normal life? What good is freedom of the press to the harassed, careworn mother of hungry, tattered, fatherless chil-

Residents of Girls' Home
Easter Sunday 1938

Residents of Boys' Home
Easter Sunday 1938

dren?" In any case, he quickly moved to nail down the struggling institution's tenuous position by recognizing it as an agency eligible for assistance from the newly restructured and enlarged Arkansas Department of Public Welfare.

Another example of Beall's remarkable foresight was the establishment of the Arkansas chapter of the National Foundation for Infantile Paralysis. (Today this organization is known as the March of Dimes.) The foundation was the brain-child of President Franklin Roosevelt. Roosevelt, a polio victim who could not stand without braces or walk without crutches, was a leader in the fight against the crippling disease. His birthday became an annual fund-raising event in cities across the nation.

Little Rock's first "President's Birthday Ball" was held on the evening of January 30, 1936. The event was a rousing success, thanks primarily to Beall, who flooded the newspapers with heart-tugging photos of young polio victims. This wave of publicity led to the establishment of the Arkansas chapter of the foundation, which by 1950 would be the hospital's largest single source of income.

As the institution's financial situation stabilized, Beall began planning for the future. With the passage of the Social Security Act, she envisioned less need for the home and a greater emphasis on the hospital. "Anybody can break up a home," she declared in her superintendent's report for May 1936, "but it takes a genius to hold families together and that's what Franklin D. Roosevelt had in mind when the clause 'dependent children' was incorporated in the Social Security Act." She favored allowing the Child Welfare Division under the Social Security Act tend to the needs of any child who was orphaned or neglected. Beall expressed the hope that the Home could eventually be closed down and the hospital expanded, on the theory that such a move would provide the greatest good for the greatest number.

President and Mrs. Roosevelt visited Arkansas on June 10, 1936. Their one-day visit was the high point of the state's centennial celebration. More than twenty patients and staff members from the Children's Hospital took part in a parade through the streets of downtown Little Rock in honor of the President and First Lady. On March 21 of the following year, Eleanor Roosevelt returned to the capital city to speak at Little Rock Senior High School. That afternoon, accompanied by Governor Carl Bailey's wife, she visited Arkansas Children's Hospital. She chatted with many of the young patients in the wards and also visited the baby unit.

The hospital that Eleanor Roosevelt visited, like the nation that her husband governed, was slowly emerging from the depths of the Great Depression. As income rose and debt fell, many long-overdue improvements were made. On October 14, 1936, following the installation of new equipment in its operating room, the pediatric medical facility was fully accredited by the American College of Surgeons. Also in that same year, the outpatient clinic was expanded. The medical facility's reputation was growing. According to the 1936 annual hospital service report, 556 patients were admitted to the hospital and 338 operations were performed.

Former superintendent Dr. Orlando P. Christian died on November 14, 1937, at the age of eighty-two, following Mrs. Christian's death in July. The hardships of his early years had instilled in Dr. Christian a burning desire to help less fortunate children. His vision had given birth to the Children's Hospital. "In my long years of experience, I know of nothing that is so much needed and so greatly appreciated by the people," he had declared in 1918, "as a place where the child of the poorest parent can have the same advantages as the child of the well to do." He was buried at Roselawn Memorial Park in Little Rock.

Total income for the Arkansas Children's Home and Hospital in 1938 was $72,274.25, the highest in its history. Further improvements were made in the hospital building, and new equipment was purchased for the laboratory and X-ray departments. "As we approach 1939," observed Superintendent Beall, "I think we can look with a good deal of pride upon our achievements as an agency for the past twenty-seven years....The hospital has many improvements that mean much in the scientific care of its patients. The home standard of living, I personally feel is as nearly like an individual home as it can be made in view of the number of children in each building. There is a security, loyalty and pride among the children relative to their home that is a source of satisfaction to them.

"Our mortgage debt has been cut down, and will continue to be cut down. Our buildings are in a good state of repair and I feel that we have the respect of many of the finest citizens of Arkansas. And so, as we take stock in approaching the new year, we have much for which to be thankful."

It would prove to be a very busy year. According to the 1939 annual hospital service report, a record 765 patients were admitted to the Arkansas Children's Hospital in that year, and a record 550 operations were performed.

Beall summed up the situation matter-of-factly. "Well, we have out-grown our hospital building, haven't we?"

The Arkansas Children's Home and Hospital had weathered the storm known as the Great Depression. Strong leadership and the steadfast support of the people of Arkansas had made the difference. Now, at the dawn of its fourth decade, the institution was considering its first major expansion.

Four

IN 1940 THE UNITED STATES was enjoying a rebirth of prosperity. Economists predicted that the nation's gross national product, the total value of all the goods and services produced, would exceed $125 billion by the beginning of 1941. This was more than twice the GNP recorded in the depths of the Great Depression. For the first time in more than a decade, many Americans were buying such luxuries as new cars, jewelry, clothes, furniture and household appliances. In keeping with this spirit of renewed optimism, "The World of Tomorrow" was the theme of the 1939 New York World's Fair, which foresaw television, the interstate highway system, mass air travel, organ transplants, atomic power and many other future wonders of science and technology.

There were problems, of course. For instance, unemployment was still high. But, for the first time in years the unemployed had reason to hope. The war in Europe, however, cast a dark shadow over this rekindled optimism. The fighting had broken out in September of the previous year, and it seemed all but inevitable that the United States would eventually be drawn into the conflict on the side of England, France and Russia, against Germany and Italy. In Asia, the armed forces of Japan were also on the march, bent on establishing the vast empire that her warlords deemed appropriate for a modern industrial giant. But most Americans did not view Japan as a serious threat. To most Americans Adolf Hitler was the threat—Adolf Hitler was the enemy.

With the possibility of American involvement looming, President Franklin Delano Roosevelt ran for an unprecedented third term. On election day a solid majority of the voters decided that FDR's leadership was needed for another four years. Arkansas voters, however, did not express the same confidence in Governor Carl Bailey. He was defeated in his bid for a third term by Homer Adkins, a Little Rock pharmacist and businessman. For most Arkansans, as for most Americans, 1940 was a year of renewed hope tempered by growing apprehension.

It was a very busy year for the Arkansas Children's Home and Hospital. According to the 1940 annual hospital service report, a record 1,122 patients were admitted to the medical facility, and a record 839 operations were performed by its staff of volunteer physicians. An outbreak of polio that summer was largely responsible for this dramatic increase in admissions. An infectious viral disease which attacks only humans and monkeys, polio was the most frequent cause of crippling among American children during the first half of the twentieth century. Outbreaks of the dreaded disease usually occurred during the summer months, alarming parents and closing public swimming pools.

The number of children in the home was dropping, although not as rapidly as Superintendent Ruth Beall had hoped. In her report to the Board of Directors for the second quarter of 1940, she noted that there were twenty-nine youngsters living at the home. She reported that it had been an eventful summer for them. "The children had a camping trip which was enjoyed by all of them. Some went on one excursion and some on another. Some went individually, but all had a camping experience.

"All the children in the Home Division," she concluded with obvious satisfaction, "are in school now, including the three young children who are going to the Nursery School at the High School. This is being paid for by outside people. All of the children have been to the dentist and their teeth are in perfect condition which is a great compliment to Dr. (Fred) Woods and the staff of doctors he chooses to help him."

The unexpected jump in demand for the hospital's services put such a strain on the institution's budget that income for the year was only $3,755.43 above expenses. In an effort to avoid deficit spending, the Board decided to delay the proposed expansion of the medical facility until the remainder of the institution's long-standing mortgage debt was paid off. Unforeseen events would delay the project far longer than the members of the Board anticipated.

In March 1941 the Superintendent reported that the hospital's average daily census since the first of the year had been sixty-seven. As one measure of the impact of this continued heavy demand on the institution's resources, she noted that 1,670 empty fruit jars had been sent to home demonstration clubs across the state to be refilled and returned in the fall. Donations of food, clothing and other items were arriving daily as Arkansans once again came to the aid of the Arkansas Children's Home and Hospital.

Admissions fell sharply in April and May when the institution was placed under quarantine due to an outbreak of mumps and measles. For several weeks, only those children who had already had both of these childhood diseases could be admitted. With the lifting of the quarantine, admissions to the hospital resumed at a brisk pace.

World events were also moving swiftly. If the American people had doubts about becoming involved in the war in Europe, their president did not. In September of the previous year, at the urging of Roosevelt, Congress had authorized the first peacetime draft in the nation's history. If war came, FDR was determined to be prepared. In his annual message to Congress on January 6, 1941, he had called for all-out aid to those democracies besieged by dictatorships, declaring that the United States must become the "arsenal of democracy."

Soon defense plants throughout the country were working around the clock, seven days a week, turning out armament and other desperately needed supplies for the Allies. Despite their reluctance to become involved in the European conflict, most Americans welcomed the jobs that this defense build-up created.

As the nation's economic recovery accelerated, consumer prices rose. "The increased cost of every item used in operating the Arkansas Children's Home and Hospital has caused a great deal of concern," wrote Superintendent Beall in October 1941. "Good help," she added, "is increasingly hard to get. We lost four nurses in one month to the army."

In contrast to Beall, most Americans simply shrugged off this mild dose of inflation as the price of better times. While the expansion of the armed forces caused some hardship such as the loss of the four nurses, it was *defense,* not *war*, and by and large the American people were enjoying it—or at least the results of it. After ten years of depression, the newspapers were filled with "Help Wanted" ads.

The Japanese attack on the American naval base at Pearl Harbor, Hawaii, on Sunday, December 7, 1941, shattered the illusion of peace and prosperity and plunged the United States into the conflict. The war would have a great impact on Arkansas. Over ten percent of the state's population—more than 200,000 Arkansans—would serve in the armed forces. Camp Robinson in North Little Rock and Fort Chaffee at Fort Smith would become important military installations.

Throughout the early months of 1942, as the nation struggled to convert to a full-scale war economy, there was little visible change in the day-to-day routine of life at the Arkansas Children's Home and Hospital. In January the Board voted to establish a convalescent ward for polio patients on the second floor of the hospital. The refusal of some general hospitals to accept polio patients, many of whom required extensive long-term care, was increasing the demand on the Children's Hospital. The convalescent ward was an effort to meet this critical need.

The institution, however, did not escape the impact of the nation's call to arms. The convalescent ward had utilized already available space, but any further expansion of the hospital would have to be delayed for the duration of the conflict. In April Beall reported that one of the boys from the home had joined the navy. Five members of the hospital's regular medical staff also had gone into the service.

The attack on Pearl Harbor shattered America's belief in the safety of its shores by demonstrating that planes launched from aircraft carriers could strike devastating blows thousands of miles from their home base. Fear of an enemy attack on the American mainland prompted a wave of civil-defense activity. Millions of citizens volunteered to serve as air raid wardens, firefighters, plane spotters and industrial security guards. At a special meeting of the Board on April 14, 1942, Beall disclosed that all of the hospital's window screens had been placed on the inside of the windows as protection against flying glass during air raids. Blackout curtains had also been hung.

"All of this involves a lot of work and detail," she explained. "It is necessary to plan what you would do, if say the operating room was damaged in an air raid, and to have in mind some other place that could be set up in such an emergency. We have planned to move the patients into the halls on the first and second floors of the hospital and to place them under their beds to keep the debris off of them. We already have our sand and water connections ready in case of fire in all of the buildings and plan to have our first drill Monday."

Because both the Boys' and Girls' Homes were wood frame structures, no adequate safety precautions could be devised for them. Even though there was little possibility of an enemy air raid as far inland as Arkansas, the fear of one was real, and their participation in civil defense work gave many Arkansans on the home front a sense of common purpose.

In May 1942 with nearly half of the hospital's regular medical staff now serving in the armed forces, Beall pondered the uncertainty of the times. "How," she wondered, "are we going to continue to serve our children in the future as we have in the past? We have such inadequate medical service

Children's Home residents on swings, ca. 1948

Children's Home residents play baseball, ca. 1948

here tonight for dependent, sick and crippled children. What will our present medical staff be like by August 1? Can we continue to receive as many types of cases for care? Who can say? These things must be faced.... Air raid plans, evacuations and continued diligence for more service with fewer doctors, surgeons and nurses—these facts we must face. The same spirit that has brought us thus far—that spirit of devotion to our cause—will take us through this next year."

The summer months brought a sharp increase in the number of polio cases admitted to the hospital. In the early 1940s, medical science was relatively helpless in treating this crippling disease. More than thirty years earlier, however, a young nurse working alone in the remote outback of Australia had devised a method of treatment using a combination of heat therapy, exercise and massage to alleviate the painful muscle-damaging spasms common to the disease.

This remarkable woman was Sister Elizabeth Kenny. (In Australia, as in Britain, chief nurses are given the title "sister.") For years the "Kenny Method" was viewed with skepticism by many in the medical community. Then, in 1940, when Sister Kenny visited the United States, the National Foundation for Infantile Paralysis and the University of Minnesota gave her an opportunity to explain and demonstrate her method. Doctors were convinced that something new had been found, or at least rediscovered—movement and heat treatment are as old as medicine itself. The American Medical Association approved her method, and in 1942 the Sister Kenny Institute was established in Minneapolis to train nurses and therapists.

Beall was quick to recognize the potential of this new treatment. In July of that year, six technicians who had trained under the watchful eye of the Australian nurse came to the hospital to administer the treatment to patients and to train members of the staff. Sister Kenny herself visited the hospital in August 1942 and noted with approval the loving care with which its young patients were treated. Many polio victims would retain a greater degree of mobility, thanks to the advanced treatment offered at Arkansas Children's Hospital.

"I think you would be interested to know," observed Beall in her superintendent's report for November of 1942, "that of fifty boys examined for the Marine Corps on the day that one of our boys was examined, only nine passed. The others were refused because of bad teeth, bad eyes and bad ears. This home boy was deeply impressed and he realized that the cod liver oil and good care that he had received here had made it possible for him to get in." A total of twenty-one "home boys" would serve in World War II, and one would be killed in the conflict.

In December 1942 as the war entered its second year, the government announced mandatory gasoline rationing. Every driver was issued a windshield sticker designating the type of ration coupons to which he or she was entitled. As a medical facility, the Arkansas Children's Home and Hospital was eligible for the more generous "C" coupons which were awarded to vehicles used in that line of work. With so many children to provide for, the rationing of other consumer goods, such as shoes, had a far greater impact on the institution.

Rationing became necessary not only to make sure that there were adequate supplies for military use and that the remainder were distributed fairly, but also as a hedge against inflation. The United States went from bust to boom practically overnight. By mid-1943 the nation had full employment, and economists were warning that inflation posed almost as great a danger as the enemy. Forced to compete with industry for many of the technical skills it required, Arkansas Children's Home and Hospital was hard pressed to match the high wages offered by the booming war-related industries. "We are having increased problems trying to maintain an adequate staff," observed Beall in her superintendent's report for the third quarter of 1943. "Salaries are too low to attract or keep competent people."

Like millions of others on the home front, the residents of the Children's Home took part in local scrap drives to remedy the shortages of such critical materials as iron, tin and rubber. In the spring of 1943 the youngsters planted their first "victory garden" in a vacant lot near the Boys' Home. They were not alone in tilling the soil to aid the war effort. Americans planted more than 20 million such gardens, which produced more than a third of all the vegetables grown in the United States that year.

For the most part, however, there was little noticeable change in the day-to-day lives of these young people. They continued to take an active role in school and community activities. Going to the movies remained by far the most popular form of recreation. Some local movie theaters offered free admission to residents of the orphanage, requiring them to pay only the tax on the ticket. Most of the youngsters were members of either the Boy or Girl Scouts and continued to spend part of the summer months at camp.

Beall treated these children as if they were her own, and when it came to discipline, she believed that the punishment ought to fit the crime. This was certainly the case when several of the older boys ran away from the home. After learning from some of the other boys that the runaways had talked of "riding the rails as hobos," she notified the authorities to be on the lookout for them. The Pulaski County sheriff soon returned the would-be hobos to the institution. Beall decided to give them a taste of hobo life. After a few days of sleeping on the ground behind the Boys' Home and of cooking their meals over a wood fire—much to the delight of the other children—the boys were convinced that life on the road was not the dashing adventure of which they had dreamed.

The governing body of the Arkansas Children's Home and Hospital had been called the Board of Directors since its formation in 1912, but in early 1943 its name was officially changed to the Board of Trustees. The new title was considered a more up-to-date designation. Also at this time, Little Rock insurance executive George L. Alexander was chosen to succeed Azro L. Barber as president of the panel.

Horace Pugh was now the only surviving member of the original Board. For over thirty years, he had worked tirelessly on behalf of the institution. Although seventy years old and in failing health, he continued to take an active role in its affairs. He was among those present on March 14, 1944, when Board president Alexander announced that the final payment had been made on the mortgage debt which had plagued the home and hospital for so long.

The first group of medical students from the University of Arkansas School of Medicine to be assigned to Children's Hospital as a part of their education came in May of 1943. With more than half of the hospital's regular medical staff in the military, the services of these physicians-in-training were desperately needed. There were six young men in this first group, and they spent six weeks at the hospital. One of them, twenty-two-year-old medical student Roger Bost, would retain vivid memories of the experience. "We were given a room on the third floor of the hospital, and we had our meals with the rest of the staff. Miss Beall? ... She could be very demanding, and she was used to being obeyed, but she had another side, too. She was very caring and compassionate. She knew each of the children by name, knew where they were from, what their medical condition was and what their individual needs were."

The young medical students were kept busy. "We did a lot of orthopedic surgery," recalled Dr. Bost, "and we had to change the dressings on many of the burn patients every day or two. This was very difficult for us and very painful for the patients. There were so few doctors available because of the war that we just did whatever needed to be done. There were a great number of polio patients and so little that we could do for many of them. Our resources were so limited. Our knowledge was so limited. Times have changed so much that it's hard for people today to realize how it was back then. The mortality rate among the polio patients was very high."

The doctors marveled at the new wonder drug called penicillin. Because of the laborious process then used to create laboratory mold, only small quantities of the infection-fighting drug were available. "We couldn't administer very large doses of penicillin," remembered Dr. Bost. "It was too scarce and too expensive. Still, it was marvelous what it could do even in those small doses."

After graduating from medical school, Dr. Bost, a native of Clarksville, served in the navy. Upon discharge from the service, he was accepted by Duke University Medical School. "I've always suspected that I was accepted because I was the first UAMS graduate to apply to their graduate program," he reflected in a 1992 interview. "My experience at Arkansas Children's Hospital certainly contributed to my interest in becoming a pediatrician." Dr. Bost was destined to play a major role in the growth of the institution in the years ahead.

In November 1944, at the request of Beall, John P. Almand, the original architect of the hospital building, and Joe Fry, the original contractor, inspected the structure and recommended that a new foundation be laid, as the old one was cracking. This recommendation was accepted by the board, and Fry was authorized to do the work.

According to the 1945 annual hospital service report, 728 patients were admitted to the Children's Hospital, and 359 operations were performed that year. This was a remarkable accomplishment at a time when the medical facility was coping with the continued shortage of doctors and nurses due to the demand for these professionals in the armed forces.

The year 1945 was in many ways one of the most significant of the century. In April, President Roosevelt died suddenly of a cerebral hemorrhage and was succeeded by Vice President Harry S. Truman. In May, the Allies accepted the unconditional surrender of Germany, and V-E Day—Victory In Europe—was at last a reality. In August, President Truman's decision to use the atomic bomb against Japan brought a sudden and unexpected end to the conflict and ushered in the nuclear age.

While the Arkansas Children's Home and Hospital awaited the return of many of its regular medical staff from military service, it was business as usual. In October 1945, for reasons not clearly documented, the Ladies Auxiliary which had served the hospital since 1926, was disbanded. The passage by Congress in early 1946 of the Hill-Burton Act under which non-profit hospitals could obtain one-third of the cost of new hospital construction sparked a revival of pre-war expansion plans.

This first year of peace was a time of crisis for the Children's Hospital. The Arkansas Department of Health reported a record 408 new cases of polio in 1946. The epidemic underscored the need for more beds and additional staff. "We haven't had a vacant bed for days," observed Beall in her report for the month of September. She also disclosed that the National Foundation for Infantile Paralysis was sending a nurse and two physical therapists to assist in caring for these patients, and that the state chapter of the foundation was planning to purchase $5,000 worth of new equipment for the hospital's Physical Therapy Department.

"During the 1940s and '50s, I remember so vividly the Children's Hospital as just being an extension of my own home," wrote Don Moore, who grew up in a house near the medical facility. "I remember those terrible days of the polio epidemics, and the faces of those unfortunate youngsters who were victims of that dreaded disease. I spent many hours talking to the kids when they were allowed to come out on the hospital porch. They would come out during those hot summer days in their wheelchairs and on their gurneys. My folks were always afraid that I would somehow contract polio as a result of being over there so much."

The youngster had so many friends at the orphanage that he became known as one of "Ruth Beall's kids" and was always invited to special events, such as birthday or Christmas parties. On Saturday afternoons he often went to the movies with his friends. "Miss Beall tried so hard to provide a normal life for those youngsters. She saw to it that they had all kinds of sports equipment available to them, and on summer evenings the neighborhood kids would play softball on the front lawn of the hospital. Sometimes Miss Beall would sit on the porch and watch us play. I remember one evening when we convinced her to come down and play with us. I can still see her standing there at home plate swinging at that softball. There she was

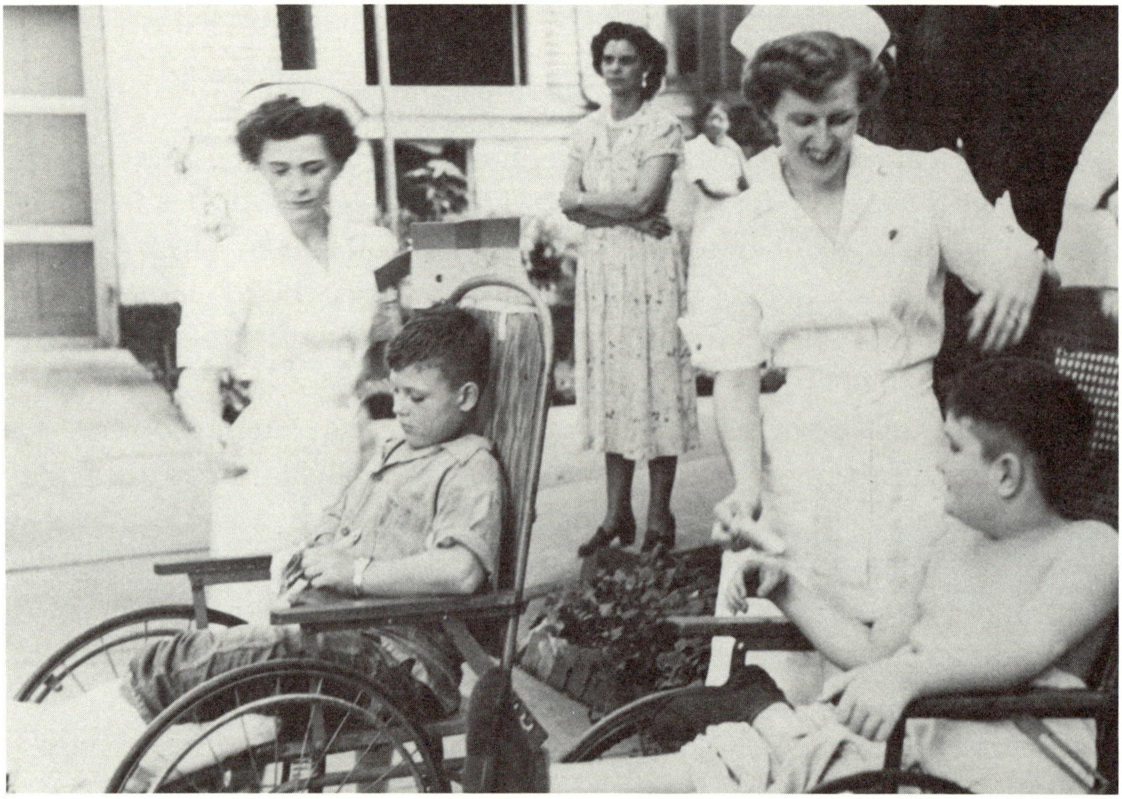

Polio patients on back porch, ca. 1948

in her straight-laced manner, black dress and all, swinging at that softball. What a sight! What a grand old lady!

"... As kids we were both afraid of and in love with Miss Beall.... You always knew exactly what she expected of you. She was at the same time, both strict and loving....Looking back, I realize the hardships she faced. She spent long hours keeping the money coming in any way she could. She did not have a personal life as such. Her whole life was centered around assuring that the hospital would be available to any child regardless of their family's inability to pay.

"... I remember one long ago afternoon when she invited me into her apartment for a Coke. I didn't really want to go," wrote Don Moore in April 1990, "but you just didn't say no to Miss Beall. Well, it turned out to be a wonderful visit. She was interested in what my plans for the future were. She encouraged me to always do the best I could with whatever life gave me to deal with, and she pointed out how fortunate I was to have good health and to have parents who were able to take care of me. The visit lasted about an hour, and I came away not fully understanding what she had meant. It was only as I grew older that I came to understand. I look back on that long ago

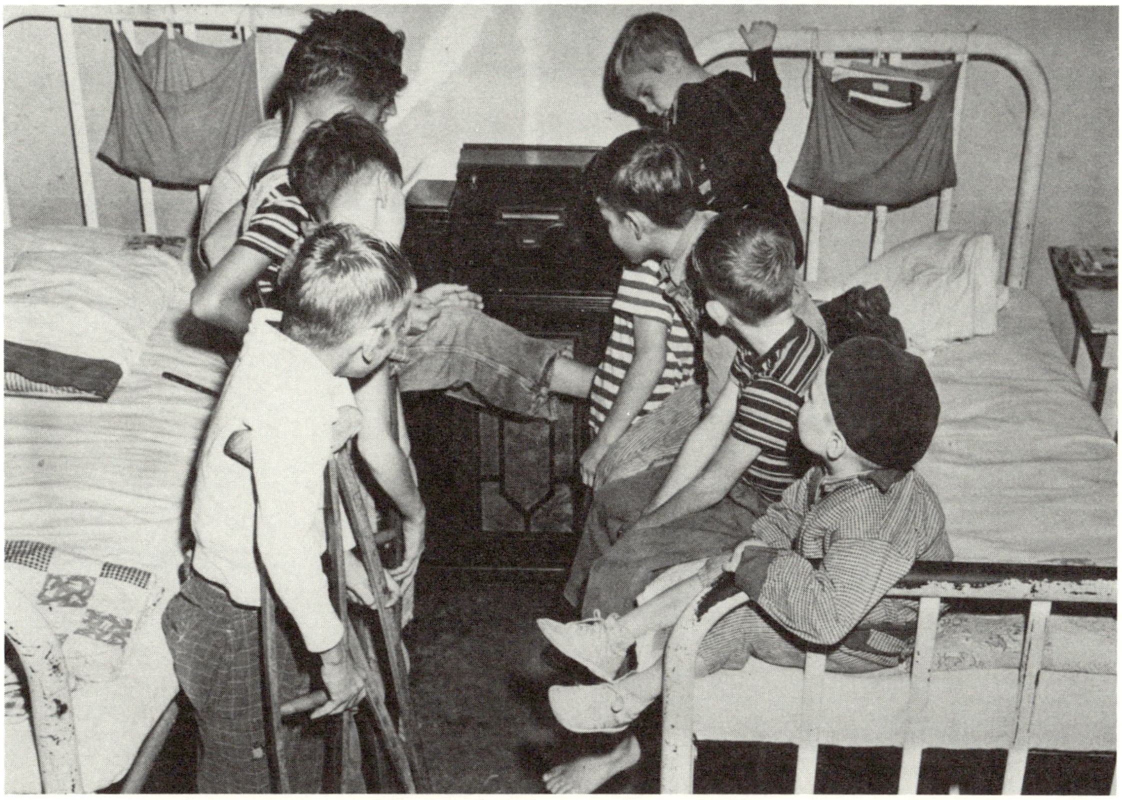
Hospital patients at radio, ca. 1948

Party in girls' ward, ca. 1948

afternoon with gratitude. Her words of wisdom about overcoming adversity and making the most of life have stuck with me all these years."

"Many of the polio patients are being dismissed for Christmas," wrote Beall in late November 1946. "Of course those children with fractures and pneumonia and the critically ill children will not be able to leave the hospital. Many organizations and individuals are providing Christmas for those children, and I think it will be nice as always."

Nor was Christmas the only holiday celebrated by the children. In March 1947 the superintendent reported, "the (home) children are all getting ready for Easter. The Optimist Club is going to have them as their guests over at MacArthur Park on Saturday afternoon, April 5, and of course we will have Easter egg hunts here at the hospital in the wards for those patients who can participate." Once a month the youngsters were also treated to a birthday party complete with cake and ice cream for everyone, and gifts for those having a birthday during the month.

Many of these children came from remote rural areas and had never seen mechanical devices which were commonplace to most people. In one such incident, after being prepared for surgery a five-year-old boy was placed on the elevator to be taken to the operating room. "What's this thing I'm being moved onto?" he asked the attendant. "It's an elevator," was the reply. "Alligator!," yelled the startled child. "This is the first time I've ever ridden an alligator!"

Another boy, aged nine, called Beall to his bed in the boys' ward one day and demanded to know "what kind of an animal is that out there in the hall, running around in a cage?" Startled, Beall rushed into the hall, expecting to find a stray dog or perhaps a squirrel. The *animal* turned out to be an electric fan, the first the youngster had ever seen.

Gratitude for the hospital's services sometimes took unusual forms. A north Arkansas farmer whose sixteen-year-old son underwent successful neurosurgery after being kicked in the head by a mule, left a bill of sale and papers for a registered Jersey bull along with a note saying that he would deliver the bull the following Saturday. At Beall's suggestion, a beef steer was substituted for the bull, and roast beef was soon on the menu.

The young patients often displayed their own special brand of wit. Once when the hospital was overcrowded, a five-year-old south Arkansas boy was placed in a room with several small babies. After a few days he asked a nurse,

"Do I have to take one of these babies home with me when I go? Mama and the neighbor woman always bring one back from the hospital."

Rejoicing over the return of many members of the hospital's regular medical staff and the end of wartime rationing and shortages was soon dampened by the inflation which rocked the nation's post-war economy. "After the war, it was hoped that things would get back to a more so-called normal level," wrote Ruth Beall, "but with the spiraling prices of almost everything, that has just been wishful thinking." Fortunately, most of this jump in operating cost was offset by an increase in donations from individuals as well as from organizations such as the Infantile Paralysis Foundation.

In August 1947 Cooper Jacoway, who had played a major role in the struggle to save the institution from foreclosure and pay off the mortgage debt, succeeded George L. Alexander as president of the Board of Trustees. In accepting the top post, Jacoway expressed his determination to carry forward with plans for the expansion of the hospital.

At the invitation of the Board, Dr. Francis F. Schwentker, a noted consultant from Johns Hopkins University Hospital in Baltimore, visited the Arkansas Children's Hospital in February 1948 to study the facility and make recommendations with regard to its expansion. "I am very impressed," he declared, "with the wonderful job being done with such inadequate resources."

In his report, Dr. Schwentker recommended that the orphanage be closed, and that a new 200-bed hospital be constructed. He also recommended that the new facility be attached to the University of Arkansas Medical Center. "The Children's Hospital should be instrumental in training the young pediatricians of Arkansas," he declared, "and certainly a trained personnel would be very hard to get for a 200-bed hospital if it were not connected with the University." Dr. Schwentker estimated that the total cost of the new hospital would be $2 million.

The following month, Chief of Staff Dr. Ellery Gay, Sr., requested that a specially equipped room be set up for burn patients. "We have from forty to fifty burn cases per season," he noted, "and the hospitalization period is usually from two months to two years.... We are not adequately prepared to handle these cases. What is needed is a room with temperature control and a large immersion tub in the center. This tub should be built some distance from the floor to enable the nurse to handle the patient with more ease."

Dr. Gay had been a physician in the army in Europe during World War II. While helping treat sailors who had been burned when the Germans sank an oil tanker, he noted that those sailors who had been picked up immediately afterward and taken to hospitals all died, while thirty sailors who had not been rescued from the ocean until several days after the ship went down had all survived. He concluded that the sea water had somehow prevented infection and promoted healing. He had returned home determined to test his theory. The board voted to authorize this project "if and when" the necessary funding could be secured.

"People have been unusually nice to the children this year and everything needed to make their Christmas a merry one has been received," noted Ruth Beall in her superintendent's report for the fourth quarter of 1948. She also reported that officials of the district Kiwanis Clubs had pledged to take as their special project for 1949 the piping of oxygen to the different wards in the hospital.

The Arkansas Department of Health reported 992 new cases of polio in 1949, the highest number ever recorded in the state. "We are really in the thick of the care of convalescent polio cases," wrote Beall at the height of the epidemic in June. "We have under care today thirty cases of 1949 polio, and twenty-nine other 1949 cases have been discharged. This is really a big job. It has been a task to get staff. We have polio patients all over the house." With the residents of the orphanage away for the summer, both of the homes were used for convalescent polio patients.

When a distressed father telephoned from the Ozark Mountains saying that his nine-year-old son was suffering from a double hernia, and asking if he could bring him to the hospital, Beall told him, "I don't have a bed right now, but when I get one I'll let you know." Five days later the father and son arrived at the hospital in a borrowed pickup truck. The father unloaded a hand-made bed which he had built after studying a picture in a hospital supply catalogue. "Since you don't have a bed," he explained, "I made you one." Beall set up the bed in a corridor for lack of room space and admitted the youngster. "You don't turn down people who try that hard to help themselves," she commented.

Once again an outbreak of polio had underscored the need for more beds and additional staff. With the institution free of debt and with income rising, the time was right for the long-delayed expansion of the medical facility. In 1950, as the Arkansas Children's Home and Hospital stood on the threshold of its fifth decade of service to the children of the state, the future beckoned bright with promise.

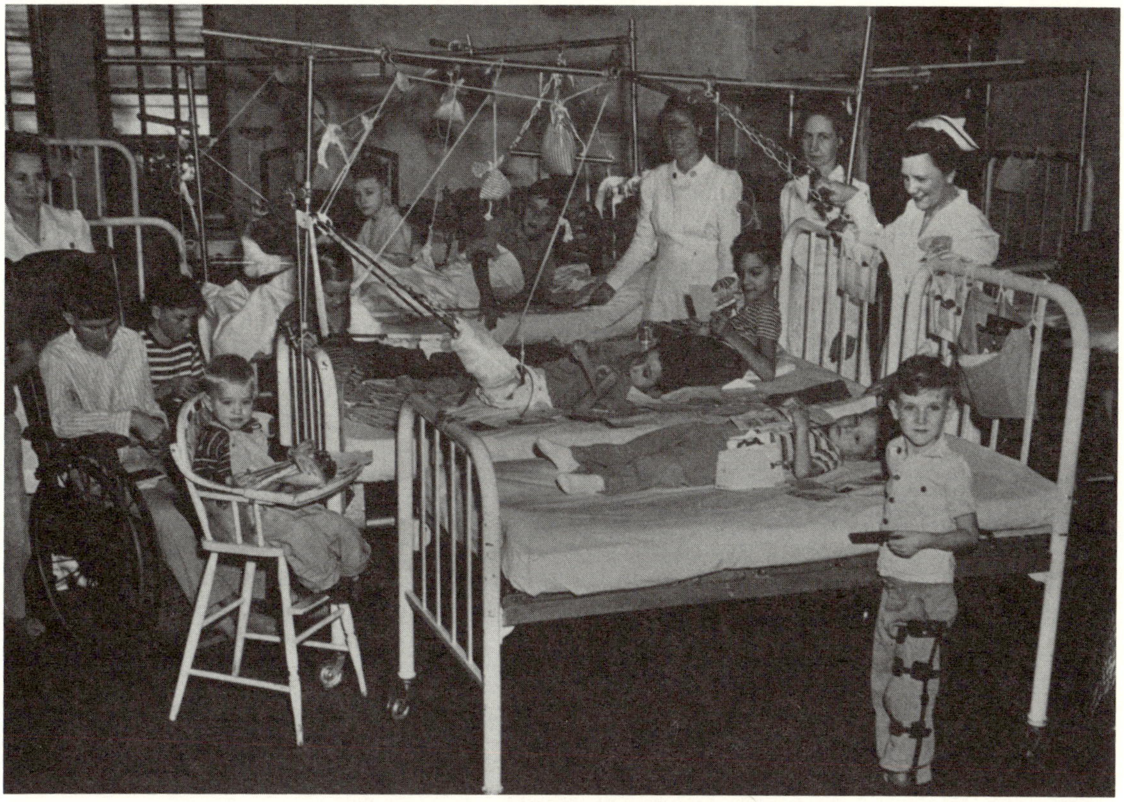

In the 1940s and 50s, seventy-five percent
of the hospital's admissions were orthopedic,
and the wards were filled with patients in traction,
ca. 1950.

Five

DURING THE WAR YEARS MORE than $300 million worth of defense plants and installations had been located in Arkansas. At the end of the war, many of these plants were purchased by private companies and converted to peacetime production, providing continued employment and an industrial base for the state. The postwar era brought profound social and political changes. Indeed, in many respects the Arkansas of today is the product of those years.

For millions who had endured the Great Depression, the war had been a time of opportunity. By one estimate, as many as 20 million Americans—

Members of the Broadview Home Demonstration Club
of Carlisle deliver home-canned food to the hospital, ca. 1955.

about fifteen percent of the population—had left their homes to seek employment. Thousands of Arkansans had migrated to the industrial cities of the North and Midwest. Many never returned. To a lesser extent this trend continued after the war. When the Korean War broke out in 1950, another large migration began, as high-paying jobs were once again available in Texas, California and other states. Between 1940 and 1960, Arkansas lost about eleven percent of its population.

The war had accelerated the mechanization of Arkansas agriculture. Higher prices for farm products had made it possible for farmers to buy tractors and other machinery. With labor scarce, farmers had learned to get along with fewer workers. Agricultural workers had accounted for fifty-two percent of the state's work force in 1940, but by 1955 the figure dropped to thirty-five percent. In 1940, four out of five Arkansans had lived on farms. By 1960, nearly half of the state's population would live in towns and cities.

The war years had also raised the expectations of black Americans by lowering social and economic barriers to their advancement. Millions had abandoned the land and moved to the cities in search of better jobs. For the first time, many had found themselves earning decent wages and coming into contact with other cultures. The civil rights movement of the 1950s and '60s would grow out of a determination to keep and expand on these wartime gains.

In 1950, the impact of most of these social and political changes on Arkansas society was yet to be felt. In that year eighty-five percent of the patients admitted to Arkansas Children's Hospital still came from low-income rural homes, and Superintendent Ruth Beall was primarily concerned with matters relating to the upkeep of the institution. That spring she persuaded the Little Rock Painter's Union to stage a mass demonstration of how fast they could paint the exterior trim of the hospital building; 100 of them were able to do the job in one hour, and of course they charged no fee for their services.

A major expansion of the outpatient clinic enabled the hospital to increase its orthopedic services by nearly 200 percent over the previous year, treating a total of 1,245 outpatients. Part of this increase reflected the fact that for the first time the outpatient clinic was opened to all children regardless of race. Beall had spoken out about the needs of black Arkansans as early as 1936, but the economic and social conditions of the times had prevented any real change. Now, with society's attitude changing, and with a blueprint

Painters from the Little Rock Painter's Union
Spring of 1950

in development for an addition to the hospital, the medical facility began planning to admit children of any color.

The 1950 annual hospital service report disclosed that a record 1,167 patients were admitted to the Children's Hospital, and 780 operations were performed that year. Convalescent polio cases had accounted for 450 of these admissions. In addition, the hospital had treated at least one accident victim from each of the state's seventy-five counties: youngsters who had swallowed the contents of lye cans, been kicked by mules, shot in hunting accidents or burned in fires. It had also treated twenty-four premature babies, one of whom weighed only thirty ounces. Doctors had used their skills to convert rib bones into chins, put living corneas in the eyes of blind children, lengthen legs and correct the effects of spinal tuberculosis.

According to Chief of Staff Dr. Ellery Gay, Sr., seventy-five percent of this caseload was orthopedic, the average case being under treatment a total of four and a half years, of which forty-two days were spent in the hospital. Dr. Gay estimated that sixty local surgeons, orthopedists, pediatricians and dentists, all of them private practitioners, donated $1,100,000 worth of services to Arkansas Children's Hospital in 1950.

In January 1950, J. Harry Stacy succeeded Cooper Jacoway as president of the Board of Trustees. Stacy was the owner of Stacy's Fine Foods, a grocery store located at 1900 West Seventh Street, a short distance from the Arkansas Children's Home and Hospital. He had served on the Board for five years, and was active in the Lions Club and the YMCA.

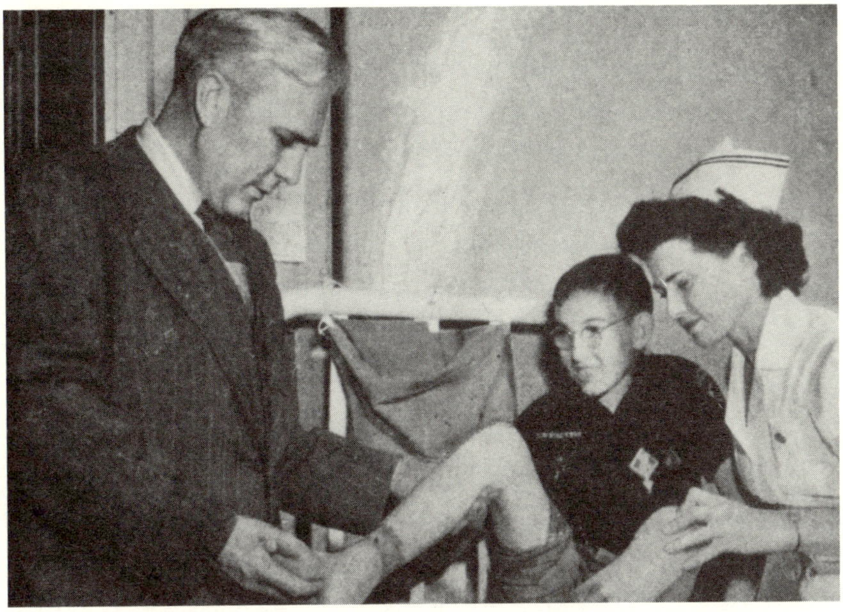

Dr. Ellery Gay, Sr., Cephia Spencer, & John Murray, ca. 1951
Courtesy of The Saturday Evening Post

In the summer of 1950 a young occupational therapist named Betty Sorensen approached Beall about the possibility of employment. A graduate of Texas State College for Women in Denton, Sorensen felt that there was a need within the hospital's rehabilitation section for the type of therapeutic activities which she could provide. Beall replied, "There's no money for occupational therapy, but we've got to have it. We'll just have to work it out somehow. When can you start?" Giving her two rooms on the second floor of the hospital, Beall told her, "I know nothing about this occupational therapy business. It's all yours. Go to it."

And go to it she did. With two rooms, no money and a dream, Sorensen set about contacting anyone whom she thought might be willing to help. The Pulaski County Polio Foundation provided looms and jigsaws, the Junior Red Cross provided a kiln, and numerous other church and civic organizations helped to furnish necessary supplies. Slowly the new occupational therapy department began to take shape.

One afternoon, without informing Superintendent Beall of her intentions, Sorensen paid an unannounced call on Woodlief A. Thomas, Grand Secretary of the Masonic Lodges of Arkansas. Introducing herself, she explained the purpose of her visit. The recently organized occupational therapy program at Children's Hospital was in need of a more appropriate space for its work. Would the Masons consider undertaking the renovation of an area within the hospital for this purpose? Thomas replied that the Masons had recently completed construction of a building at the Booneville Tuberculosis Sanitarium and were looking for a new project. "We wouldn't be interested in renovation work," he declared, "but we would be willing to build you a building." The young therapist could hardly believe her ears.

The Board met with representatives of the Masonic Lodges of Arkansas in September 1950 concerning their interest in financing construction of an occupational therapy wing. These long-time supporters of the Children's Home and Hospital were willing to invest as much as $25,000 in the project. Bids were solicited, and at a November meeting with Beall and Dr. Gay, the Masons agreed to finance the occupational therapy wing even though the lowest bid—that of Little Rock General Contractor Herman Carty—was $10,327 more than they had originally planned to spend. Construction was scheduled to get underway in January of the following year.

In July 1951, the possibility of closing the orphanage was discussed. Beall reported that $1,000 per month could be saved or applied to the hospital if the homes were closed. The Board asked that a brief case history of each child being cared for at the home be sent to each member of the panel. A final decision in the matter was deferred until later.

The occupational therapy wing was completed in August 1951, and like the outpatient clinic, it was open to all children regardless of race. Beall and the members of the Board were pleased with the new department. "Occupational therapy has long been an unmet need of our state," asserted Board president Stacy in a letter to Masonic Grand Secretary Thomas. "This additional treatment will help the children to become more useful citizens. Please extend our thanks to everyone who helped make this gift possible, and tell them to feel free to visit our institution and see the work being done for crippled and indigent children from all over the state."

Although unable to attend the September 14, 1951, meeting of the Board's Executive Committee, Cooper Jacoway sent word that he thought the Board should consider changing the name of the institution to Arkansas Children's Hospital. Jacoway felt that the name change was necessary in order to avoid confusion among the public when the homes were closed. A special committee was appointed to study the matter.

Patients on front lawn, ca. 1951
Courtesy of The Saturday Evening Post

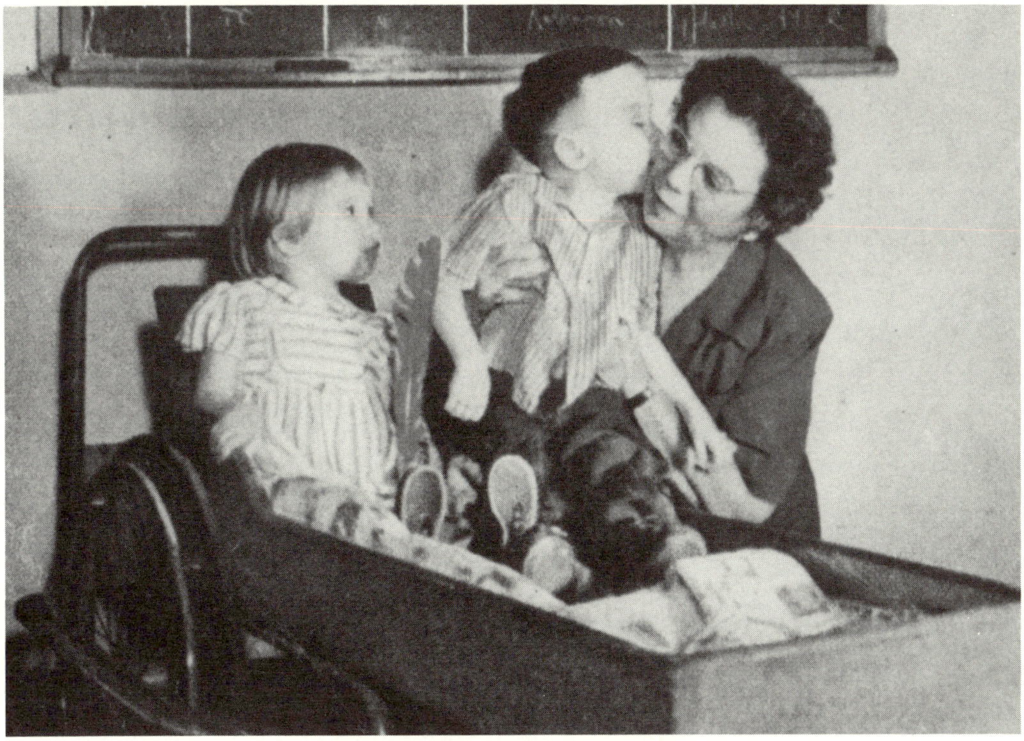

Ruth Beall with patients, ca. 1951
Courtesty of The Saturday Evening Post

The committee's report issued on November 14, 1951, recommended that the name of the institution be changed to Arkansas Children's Hospital. While acknowledging that the services provided by the homes were very useful, the report concluded that the services provided by the hospital were of even greater usefulness. Thus the report recommended that the homes be closed as soon as feasible in order that all available resources might be devoted to the expansion of the hospital.

The recommendation concerning the change of name was approved, but the Trustees were sharply divided on the question of closing the homes. Finally, in June 1952, after nearly a year of sometimes stormy debate, a compromise was agreed upon. Under this plan the Girls' and Boys' Homes would be combined into one. The children—four girls and three boys—would be housed in one of the homes and the other would be converted into an administrative office building. Since the care of dependent children would continue, the Board decided not to change the name of the institution at that time.

Horace G. Pugh, founder of the Arkansas Children's Home Society, died on August 19, 1952, at the age of seventy-eight. As with Dr. Orlando Christian, the hardships of his early years had instilled in him a burning desire to help the less fortunate. He had served on the institution's governing body for over forty years. "From the time of his arrival in Arkansas as a young man of twenty-two, until the day of his death," proclaimed the resolution passed by his fellow Trustees, "Mr. Pugh was active in a great variety of unselfish endeavors to alleviate human misery and to improve the life of all persons about him." He was buried at Oakland Fraternal Cemetery in Little Rock.

Without formal ceremony, the long-awaited burn treatment center—the first such facility in the state—was opened on February 24, 1953. On that day, a twelve-year-old girl with third-degree burns over half her body was wheeled into the shiny new room, and a team of doctors and nurses headed by Dr. Gay went to work. Her body was washed in the specially built tub and then bandaged in soft muslin cloths. The entire procedure took only twenty minutes. Without this special equipment and the remodeled room—both gifts of the Arkansas Masonic Grand Lodge—the procedure would have taken about two hours.

The new method of treatment would soon prove itself by cutting the average hospitalization time for the young burn patients in half. This and

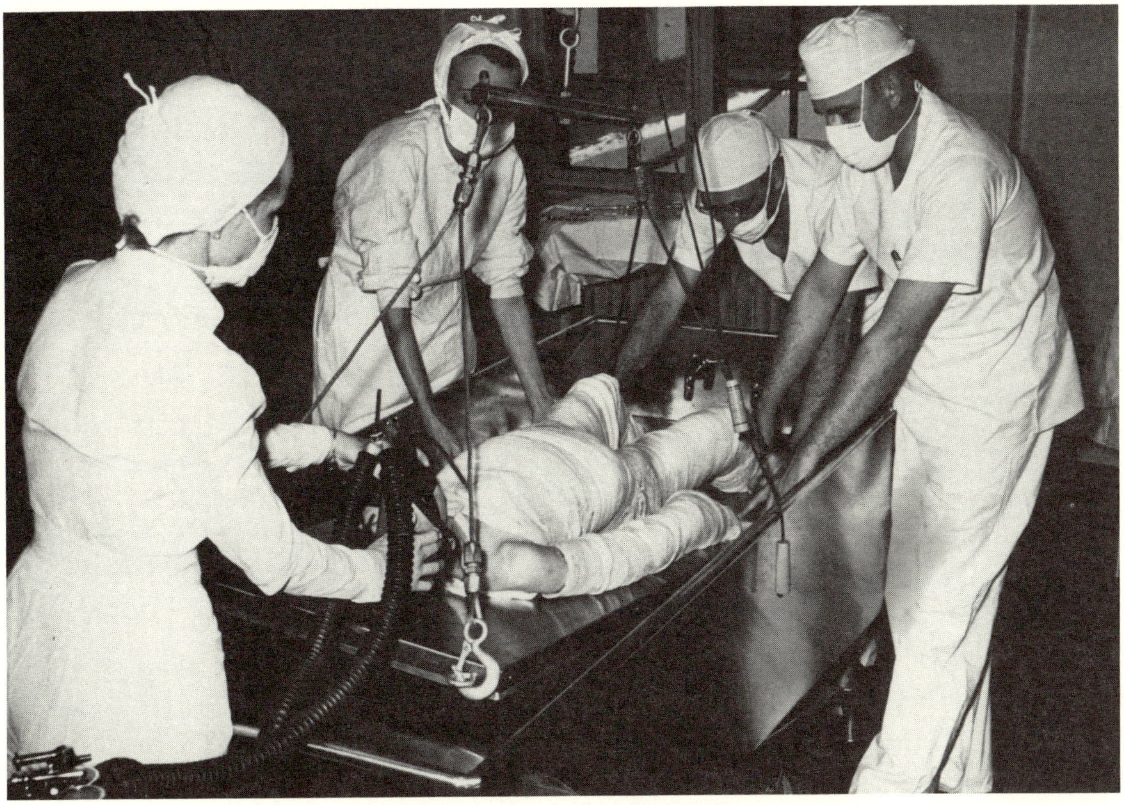

First patient treated in special burn unit
February 24, 1953

other innovations pioneered by Dr. Gay would help to make the burn center at Arkansas Children's Hospital one of the finest in the nation.

In October 1953 the Board of Trustees voted to retain James A. Hamilton and Associates Hospital Consultants of Minneapolis to make a study of the institution. The cost of this study was $3,500. The following month, Louis Rosen succeeded J. Harry Stacy as president of the Board. Rosen, who had served on the panel for five years, was a partner in the Williams and Rosen Insurance agency.

In July 1954 Hamilton and Associates issued their report. It was the opinion of the consultants that the volume of hospital services had leveled off to a reasonably normal figure for the size of the facility, but the number of dependent children receiving care in the home had dropped so drastically that this service should be discontinued.

Pointing out that construction of new facilities was underway at both the University of Arkansas Medical Center and St. Vincent Infirmary, the report concluded that these expansions would provide acute pediatric care, but that certain phases of specialized pediatric care would still be lacking. In view of this fact, the principal recommendations of the study with regard to the future of the hospital were:

- ❖ That by the year 1957, or earlier if feasible, the hospital modify its present program to provide primarily children's orthopedic care, supplemented by such other care as plastic surgery, treatment of burn cases, and the like for which there is a demand in a specialized facility.
- ❖ That in this modified program the hospital's capacity be sixty beds. Also that a sixty-bed convalescent unit be constructed.
- ❖ That some private cases be admitted, the number to be dependent upon the demand for charity services, but that charity patients always be given full preference as both in and outpatients.
- ❖ That the hospital provide fully adequate dental service to both in and outpatients, and that some private patients be accepted, the number to be dependent upon the demand for charity services.
- ❖ That consideration be given to establishing a child guidance clinic as part of the outpatient services.

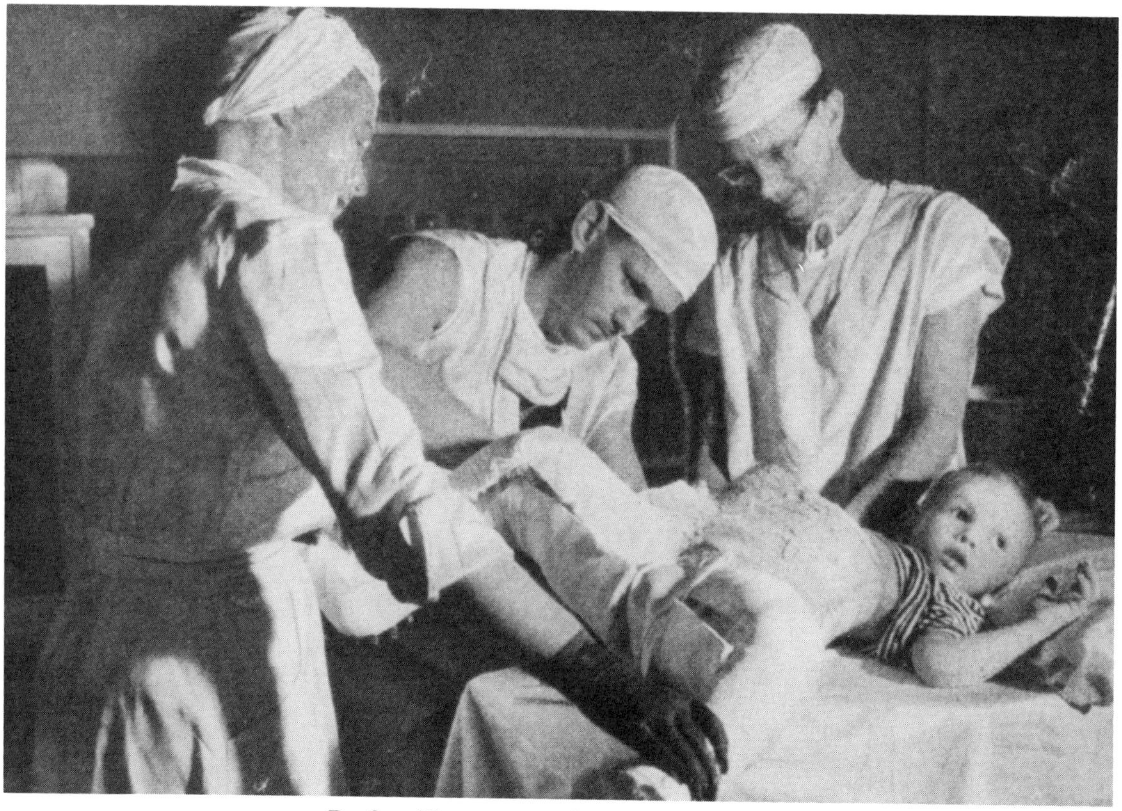

Dr. Sam Thompson and Dr. John Christian
and an unidentified nurse remove the cast of Raymond Thomas, ca. 1951
Courtesy of The Saturday Evening Post

The conclusions of the Hamilton and Associates study differed greatly from those of Dr. Francis F. Schwentker's 1948 study. Clearly there was no longer a need for the 200-bed children's medical facility outlined in the earlier study. On July 27, 1954, after reviewing the recommendations of the report, the Board voted unanimously to close the home and change the name of the institution to Arkansas Children's Hospital.

"The whole social picture has changed since Arkansas qualified for federal-state child welfare aid in 1937," Ruth Beall told the *Arkansas Democrat* in the aftermath of this vote. "The policy of keeping orphaned or abandoned children in the care of either remaining parent, or a suitable relative or in an approved foster home, has been adopted and followed. Emphasis is placed, in this program, on providing the necessary amount of money to keep the family together when possible.

"Institutional care for homeless children was the only solution at the time the Arkansas Children's Home was established, but under the present concept of social service, it is rarely necessary and is generally considered a less desirable way of helping a child through the formative years into independent adulthood. The adoption of this policy by federal-state social agencies has almost eliminated the need for institutional child care.

"At the same time," she added, "we have had a tremendous increase in the need for hospital services and medical treatment for children. Emphasis on that part of the institution's work is not only logical, but is urgently needed. The hospital was built originally to provide correction of remediable defects for children in the home at a time when no hospital in the state was open to dependent children. Now it has become the most important part of our work, with continuing appeals for aid to children in every county in Arkansas."

Also in July 1954 Board member Bruce R. Anderson, a prominent Little Rock architect, was authorized to draw up master plans for a long-range building program for the hospital. The Board voted that Anderson was to receive the standard architect's fee for his services. The most immediate need was a new laundry and utility building.

In late October 1954 Anderson informed his fellow Trustees that although the initial cost would be higher, it would be cheaper in the long run to construct a new hospital building than to remodel the existing one. He estimated that remodeling as outlined in the Hamilton study would cost approximately $375,000, while the cost of erecting an entirely new structure was estimated at $557,356.

At this point it was revealed in a board meeting that John Gilbreath, administrator of the Baptist Hospital, had expressed an interest in the possibility of a joint operating agreement between the two hospitals. He stated that Baptist Hospital would be willing to provide ground for the relocation of the pediatric medical facility if such an agreement could be worked out. The board decided against this course of action.

On November 3, 1954, the Board of Trustees voted to go forward with the expansion of the existing hospital building along the lines recommended in the Hamilton and Associates study. They decided, however, not to spend more than the $200,000 already available for this purpose. Anderson was instructed to revise his architectural plans accordingly. Also, Beall was authorized to begin admitting black children to the hospital, and Ruby Rainwater, a native of Huttig in south Arkansas and a registered nurse with a degree in business administration from the University of California at Los Angeles, was hired as assistant superintendent.

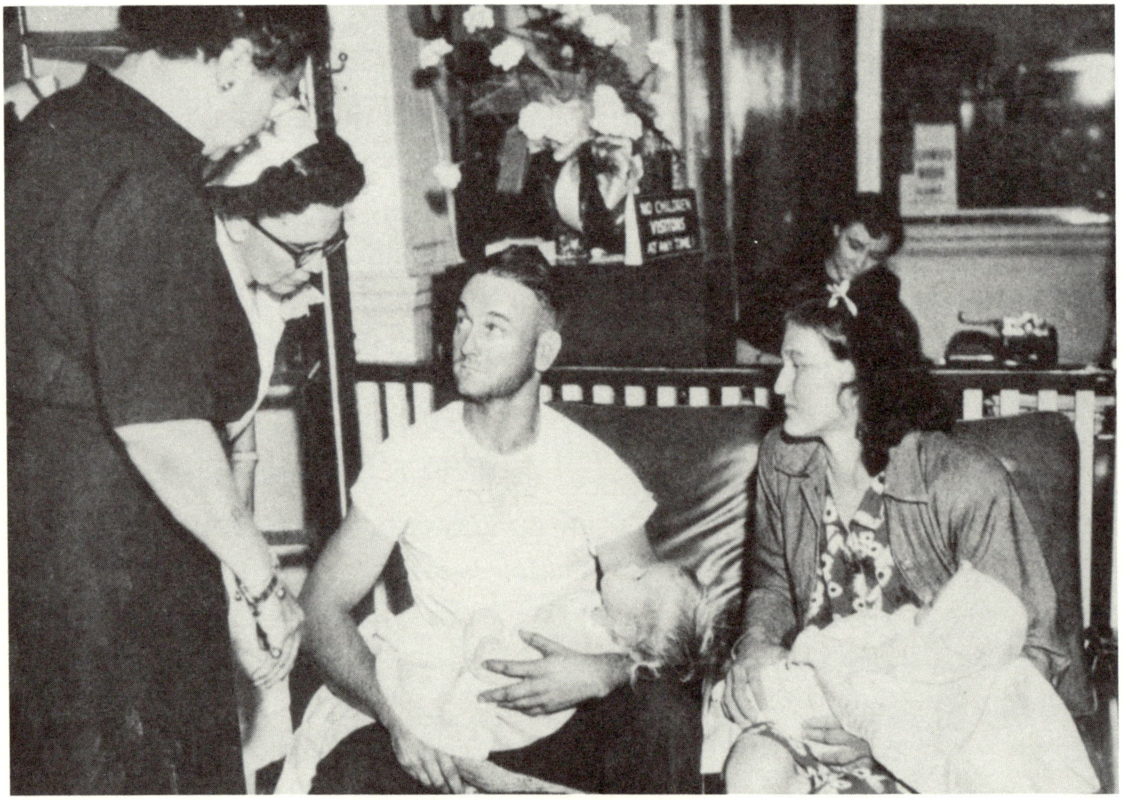

Ruth Beall talks to parents
about admitting their child, ca. 1951.
Courtesy of The Saturday Evening Post

The following month the Masonic Lodges of Arkansas presented the hospital with a check for $40,000, used to construct the new laundry and utility building. The G.W. May Construction Company of Little Rock was awarded the contract to erect the structure, which was completed in June 1955. The old laundry and utility building was razed to make way for the new west wing of the hospital.

The most important medical advance of the decade was the development of an effective polio vaccine by Dr. Jonas Salk of the University of Pittsburgh. The Salk vaccine was first used on a large scale in 1955. In April of that year, Chief of Staff Dr. Sam Thompson reported that the medical staff was enthusiastic about the polio vaccine, but he cautioned that no vaccine was 100 percent effective, and that even if it were, there would still be polio cases for some years to come. He estimated that reconstructive work on existing polio cases would continue for another fifteen or twenty years.

During the following year the Arkansas Department of Health as part of a nationwide effort underwritten by the federal government, was able to provide most of the state's counties with polio vaccine and the necessary supplies to administer it. By the end of 1956, more than 250,000 Arkansans—most of them children and expectant mothers—had been vaccinated. The vaccine proved so successful that within two years the rate of polio in the United States dropped eighty percent.

This celebrated triumph of science over disease would eliminate the need for the sixty-bed convalescent unit recommended in the Hamilton study, but many of its other recommendations would become a reality. On September 14, 1955, the necessary legal documents were signed in the Circuit Court

Polio patient receiving hydrotherapy, ca. 1955

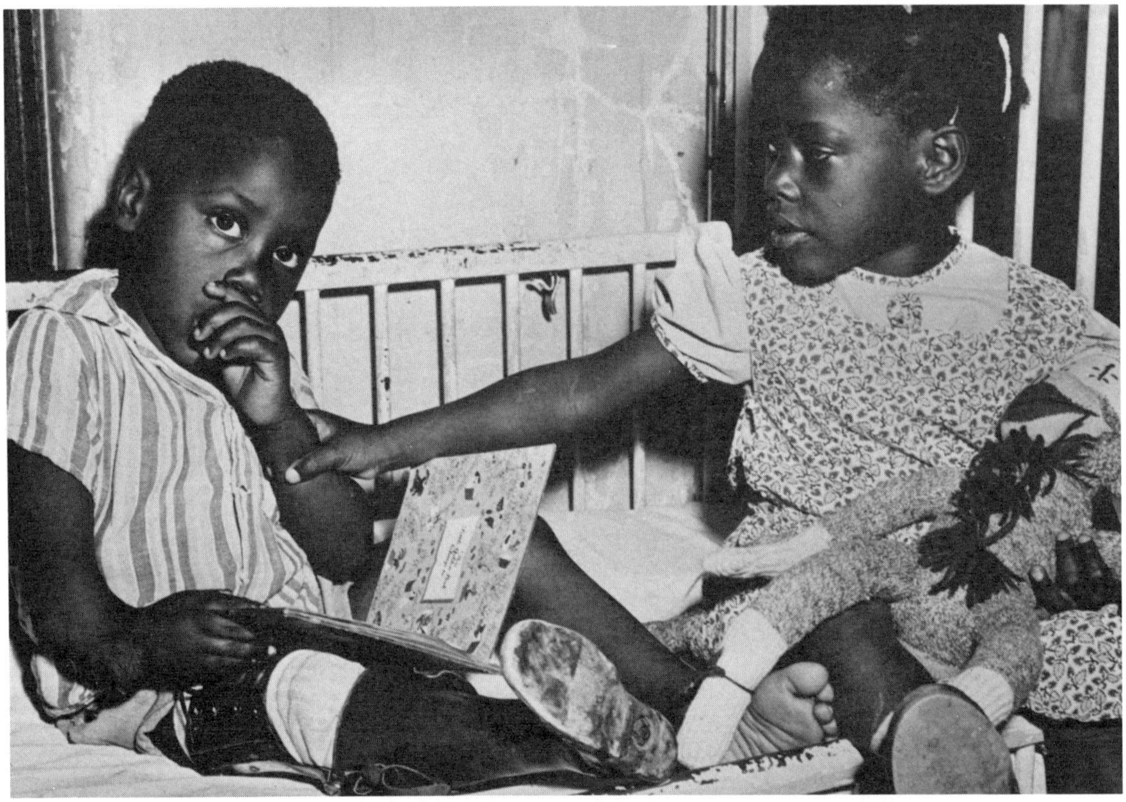

Patients visit in girls' ward, ca. 1956

Birthday party in boys' ward, ca. 1956

Danny Villarreal of Marianna
enjoys a comic book as Frederica Blankenship, R.N.,
and 13-month-old Alfred Michels look on, ca. 1956.

of Pulaski County to officially change the name of the institution to Arkansas Children's Hospital. Also, as recommended, the hospital's dental facilities were opened to private patients.

On January 17, 1956, the Board of Trustees discussed the possibility of moving to the old University Medical Center or the old St. Vincent Infirmary while the expansion and remodeling of the hospital was underway. Closing the facility for approximately three months would shorten construction time and thus save money. Board member Carroll Thomas presented this plan to the Little Rock city council and on February 21, Mayor Woodrow W. Mann informed the Board that the old city-owned University Medical Center at Eleventh and McAlmont Streets could be occupied by Children's Hospital for a period not to exceed six months. The move was scheduled for the first week of July.

In mid-June 1956 the Board voted to allow two local specialists, Dr. Frances C. Rothert, director of the Division of Maternal and Child Health of the State Board of Health, and Amy Key, an audiologist, to establish a Hearing and Speech Clinic in the former Girls' Home. The clinic staff was to include an audiologist, a speech pathologist and a speech and hearing therapist. While this clinic was to be considered a separate organization operating on hospital property, it was envisioned to eventually become a part of the hospital.

By the end of the month all necessary supplies and equipment had been moved to the old University Medical Center, and on July 5 and 6, the patients were transferred by ambulance from Children's Hospital to the temporary facility. The move went smoothly, with no disruption of any essential hospital services, including those of the outpatient clinics.

John Bale succeeded Louis Rosen as president of the Board of Trustees in November 1956. Bale was the owner of Bale Chevrolet, an automobile dealership located at Second and Broadway in downtown Little Rock. He had been on the panel for eight years.

The newly expanded and remodeled Arkansas Children's Hospital was opened on February 25, 1957. Among the many improvements were a new dental clinic and space within the hospital for the speech and hearing clinic. The operating room had all new equipment and both the boys' and the girls' wards had new patient beds. Also for the first time, each ward was equipped with a television set. As one staff member commented, "It just didn't look like the same place. It was like a whole new hospital." The total cost of this transformation was $321,900, far more than the Board had originally planned to spend, but everyone was pleased with the final results.

Ruth Beall regarded the expansion and remodeling of the hospital as the capstone of her career. Now sixty-one years old and in her twenty-third year as superintendent, she was among the best known women in Arkansas. The February 17, 1951 issue of the popular national weekly magazine *The Saturday Evening Post* had featured an article about her entitled "The Terrible-Tempered Angel of Arkansas," and in December of that year, she had been named "Arkansas' Woman of the Year" by the *Arkansas Democrat.*

"Miss Beall is a vigorous, buxom, middle-aged woman with a Tallulah Bankhead voice which can rage with authority or coo a baby to sleep. She has reddish-brown hair now turning gray, hypnotic eyes and vehement mannerisms," wrote journalist Hartzell Spence in the *Post.* "She is conceded to have more friends in Arkansas than the state chairman of the Democratic Party. She has no enemies, although she tromps heavily on the toes of anyone she considers inefficient, lazy or uncooperative. She even cusses people a little, which Arkansas ladies are not supposed to do. Her anger, her forthrightness, even her cussing, are known to be short cuts toward her objective, and they are forgiven."

She liked to take physical hold of a conversational adversary, clutching them by the shoulder in an iron grip until her point was made. "When you see Ruth Beall coming with that look in her eye," observed oilman Roy W.

Spence in the *Post* article, "there's no question of saying 'no,' you just pray hard that she'll be lenient, and pray harder that she won't lay hold of you!" Long-time medical staff member Dr. Joseph F. Shuffield reflected, "She's like a pounding surf; just keeps moving in until something crumbles. When she calls, you save time by complying immediately."

Once when a prominent doctor failed to check post-operatively on one of "her kids," Beall awoke him by telephone, "You get yourself down here," she thundered, "or I'll come and get you in your nightshirt! What do you think we're running, a pool hall?" On another occasion, she summoned Dr. J.B. Crawford, an eye-and-ear specialist, from a medical meeting where he was to deliver an address. "Anybody can make that speech," she told him, "but only you can save this child."

If she could be blunt and demanding, she could also be tender and caring, procuring oxygen for the sick husband of one of her nurses, or writing a letter to one of her former "home boys" serving in Korea. She often delved into her own pocket to aid the hospital. Once when Assistant Superintendent Ruby Rainwater mentioned this generosity Beall quipped, "If you never put ships to sea, you never get cargo back."

Ruth Beall and residents with elephant
ca. 1954

Shrine Circus performers
ca. 1954

Her colorful personality and creative solutions to problems made the Arkansas Children's Hospital a unique institution. Hospitalized children were often frightened and lonely. What could be more reassuring to them than a pet?

For years a mongrel dog named Susie fulfilled this need, visiting the wards and occasionally leaping happily onto a patient's bed. Examiners from the State Board of Health and the American College of Surgeons, annually scrutinizing procedures at the medical facility, raised their eyebrows at Susie. "If you want to get rid of Susie," declared the outspoken administrator, "you'll have to get rid of me! She helps to keep the patients happy and

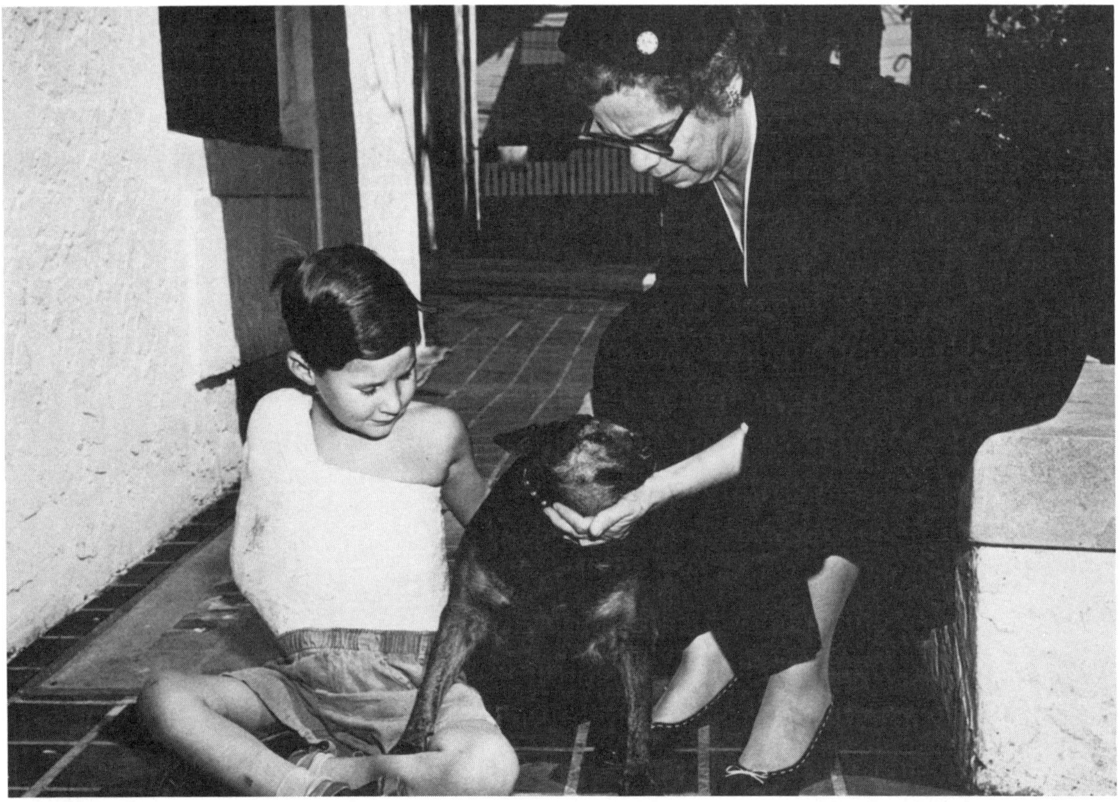

Ruth Beall with Susie
and an unidentified patient, ca. 1955

she's going to stay!" Thanks to this spirited defense, the canine comforter remained on the job.

Beall sometimes kept in touch with patients after they had returned home, and she took great pride in their accomplishments. One girl treated for five years after having been immobilized in both arms and legs by polio went on to graduate at the head of her high school class, marry and raise a family. A boy, so doubled up from burns that his knees and chin had grown together, walked again after thirty-two skin grafts.

One little girl, while a patient at Children's Hospital in 1950, received attention so much superior to that of her home environment that her mother threatened to sue Beall for alienation of her daughter's affections. Only an interview with a well-known Little Rock attorney dissuaded the woman from filing suit. When the story got around Arkansas, people who knew Beall were not surprised. "That's Ruth, all right," they declared. "She loves them as though they were her own."

As superintendent, Beall ran the hospital with the economy of a banker, bargaining with merchants to obtain the lowest price on day-to-day household items, yet freely spending thousands of dollars to establish a new burn unit or to improve premature baby care because she knew that these were life-giving options. She cast herself in the role of a fierce protective guiding mother, providing the best possible medical care for her young charges and then sending them forth into the world with healed limbs and restored health. "We walk into the future on the feet of our children," she often said, "and we must not limp on club-feet."

Nurse checks patient in baby unit, ca. 1959

In January 1958 Willis Johnson succeeded John Bale as president of the Board of Trustees. The owner of a food brokerage company, Johnson had served on the hospital panel for six years. Under his leadership the drive to improve the quality of medical care available to the children of Arkansas continued. In February, the Board appropriated $1,500 for the purchase of the new equipment for the dental clinic. Later that year, a total of $5,414.24 was spent on repairs and new equipment for the hearing and speech clinic.

On March 17, 1959, at the urging of the medical staff, the Board voted to participate in a proposed orthopedic residency program between Children's Hospital, the University Medical Center and the Veterans' Administration Hospital. Conceived by Dr. Dana Street, professor of orthopedics at the University of Arkansas Medical School, the program would provide Children's Hospital with two orthopedic residents. Half the salaries of these residents was to be paid by the participating institutions. This program was to begin on July 1, 1960.

In October 1959 the Board voted to retain Hamilton and Associates, the consulting firm which had made the 1954 study to undertake a new survey. The cost of this report was to be $2,000 plus $500 travel expenses. The board decided that no further steps should be taken by the building committee until this new study had been completed.

In May 1960 the conclusions of the second Hamilton and Associates survey were outlined to the Board of Trustees. The consultants pointed out that the number of admissions to the medical facility had peaked in 1950 at 1,167. The subsequent drop in admissions was attributed to a number of factors—chief among them:

- ❖ The remarkable success of the polio vaccine.
- ❖ The fact that more Arkansans had health insurance through their place of employment and were using their county hospitals for their children's surgery and other medical care.
- ❖ The continued decline in the population of Arkansas.

The report concluded that while the need for medical services to children from other parts of the state could be expected to continue declining if the state's population continued to decrease, the need for children's medical services in the Little Rock area could be expected to increase.

The principal recommendations of the new study were:

- ❖ That the hospital continue its present inpatient care program.
- ❖ That consideration be given to providing convalescent care for some of the orthopedic and other long-term patients rather than transferring them to another medical facility at the end of the acute phase of their illness.

- ❖ That consideration be given to providing additional outpatient services by expanding the present dental service to provide dental care to indigent children not now being cared for as inpatients.
- ❖ That consideration be given to providing space for a child guidance clinic to be located in the hospital.
- ❖ That if Arkansas Children's Hospital decides to provide the above described outpatient services, an addition to the present building should be constructed, the estimated cost of this addition being $70,000.
- ❖ That if the present inpatient care program should decline in the future to a point where it was no longer economically feasible to continue its operation, consideration should be given to converting the program to the long-term custodial care of severely handicapped children.

In the ensuing discussion, the members of the Board of Trustees expressed strong disagreement with most of the study's recommendations. All felt that it was unduly pessimistic in its outlook. At the request of Board president Willis Johnson, a committee was formed to look into the possibility of establishing a child guidance clinic.

The 1950s had been a decade of unprecedented change and growth for the institution. The orphanage had been closed and the hospital had been expanded in response to the changing needs of the society which it served. The new study made it clear that more changes lay ahead.

Hospital before remodeling in 1957

Hospital after remodeling in 1957

Six

THE DECLINE IN ARKANSAS'S POPULATION during the 1950s was primarily due to the mechanization of the state's farms. Machines had reduced the demand for hand labor. One man riding a two-row cotton harvester could do the work of more than 100 field hands. Mechanization had also reduced the number of farms. In 1935 there were 235,000 farms in Arkansas, but by 1960 the figure had fallen to 95,000. As their number decreased, the remaining farms grew larger. The average size of Arkansas farms increased from 103 acres in 1950 to 173 acres a decade later.

Agriculture was changing in other ways, too. The state remained a leader in cotton production, but by 1960 most of its cotton was grown in the eastern counties. As federal crop subsidies and soil conservation payments encouraged upland farmers to convert their cotton fields into pine forests, pastures and stock ponds, cotton gins were being replaced by livestock sale barns. Rice fields now dotted the Grand Prairie region, soybeans were becoming an increasingly important crop to many lowland farmers, and poultry production was spreading across the western counties. The modest level of industrial growth during the decade following World War II had not been sufficient to offset the impact of these changes, and the state's population continued to decline.

To reverse this trend, the General Assembly of 1955 had created the Arkansas Industrial Development Commission (AIDC), and Governor Orval Faubus had named Winthrop Rockefeller as its first chair. Rockefeller, a grandson of industrialist John D. Rockefeller, had moved to Arkansas from his native New York in 1953. During his nine years as head of the AIDC, Arkansas would undergo an industrial revolution. Over 600 new industrial plants would be built and many existing plants would be expanded. By 1970 about twenty-four percent of the state's work force would be employed in manufacturing, and Arkansas would find itself gaining rather than losing population.

The impact of these and other changes on Arkansas society was not fully apparent when the conclusions of the second Hamilton and Associates study of Arkansas Children's Hospital were presented to its Board of Trustees in May 1960. Even so, the trustees disagreed with most of the study's recommendations. Despite the prolonged decline in admissions, they were convinced that there remained a real need for the pediatric medical services offered by the facility.

In November 1960 Carroll Thomas succeeded Willis Johnson as president of the Board of Trustees. Thomas, an agent for the General American Life Insurance Company of St. Louis, had been on the panel for six years. He was also active in the local Red Cross and the Boy Scouts. In accepting the presidency, he expressed his conviction that the institution was headed in the right direction.

The 1960 annual hospital service report would strengthen this belief. According to the report, a total of 1,059 patients were admitted to Arkansas Children's Hospital in that year, and 629 operations were performed. It was the best report in ten years.

Architect Bruce Anderson submitted his plans for the proposed addition to the hospital on June 20, 1961. The addition was to have a ground floor and a basement. On the ground floor would be a schoolroom, a dental clinic, a physical therapy department and some office space. In the basement would be a large storage room, an enlarged dining facility and a private dining room. The estimated cost was $120,000. The building committee stated that $135,000 should be allocated for the project in case of contingent changes. Following Anderson's presentation, there was much discussion concerning the need for the proposed addition. When no consensus could be

Ruth Beall shortly before retirement, June 1961

Ruby Rainwater

reached, the board adopted a motion to table the question.

At the close of this meeting, Ruth Beall announced her intention to retire after twenty-seven years as superintendent. "Due to recurring health problems," she explained, "it would be impossible for me to continue at my normal pace." The members of the Board, most of whom had known her for years, understood what she meant. Beall, who loathed closed doors, appointments and formality, had spent little time in her small office. She had preferred instead to roam the corridors of the three-story hospital from eight in the morning until midnight, answering the phones on every floor, checking on workers and patients alike, detouring occasionally to the business office to issue orders or dictate a few letters while opening the latest mail. She had seldom sat down except to grab a bite to eat.

Her resignation was accepted with expressions of regret. The Trustees voted to provide a monthly retirement allowance of $300 per month, plus $56 per month—the amount of the monthly payment on her home. "It was a very challenging job and I loved it," reflected Beall. "But the only thing I will miss is my patients." Assistant superintendent Ruby Rainwater was named acting administrator. Three months later, on September 19, 1961, Rainwater was named administrator of Arkansas Children's Hospital, succeeding Beall, under whom she had worked for seven years.

A reception honoring Beall was held on October 29, 1961, at the Riverdale Country Club. Among the gifts she received was a set of keys. With a smile, Board president Carroll Thomas explained that these were the keys to a new car. Ordered the previous week, it had failed to arrive in time for the reception. The following day, Beall flew to St. Louis to visit relatives. Upon her return, her next-door neighbors, Mr. and Mrs. Leroy Brummett and their nine-year-old son, Don, met her at the airport. "My, this is a nice car," said

Beall as she climbed into the back seat of the white 1962 Chevrolet Impala. "Did you get a new car?" With a grin, the youngster replied, "No, Miss Beall. This is your car! This is your new car!" There were tears in her eyes.

The Child Guidance Committee issued its report on November 21, 1961, defining a child guidance clinic as one which "examines and suggests or supervises treatment for children with mental and emotional problems." Such a clinic would require the services of a psychiatrist, a psychologist, a social worker and a secretary. It would require a total salary budget of approximately $50,000, and an estimated 1,500 square feet of floor space, but would require very little specialized equipment. Its office needs were several small conference rooms, a reception room, a playroom and a record storage area.

The report concluded that "the state of Arkansas and the local community need a child guidance clinic," and it recommended that the board take the necessary steps to establish one. It cautioned, however, that such a clinic should be established "only after the community has expressed a desire for such a facility, and only after there is complete willingness by the United Fund to bear a fair share of the cost." A motion was made and carried that

50th Anniversary Sign, 1962

the committee's report be accepted, and that its recommendations be implemented. As a first step, Bruce Anderson was instructed to make the necessary revisions in the hospital's building plans.

The 1961 annual hospital service report disclosed that a total of 1,133 patients were admitted in that year, and 641 operations were performed. Income for the year was $467,614.02, while expenses totaled $438,957.81. The average cost per patient per day was $22.46. The medical staff now boasted sixty-five doctors and twenty-three dentists who donated more than $1 million worth of services to Arkansas Children's Hospital in 1961.

Mildred Ward, who was hired as business manager and chief accountant in April of that year, retained vivid memories of those years. "I remember one youngster—a boy about four years old—who rode his tricycle through the business office every morning. We would let him use the adding machine, and he liked that. Things were more informal in those days, and we all enjoyed seeing him." This routine continued for several months. Then one morning the bright-eyed little biker failed to appear.

"After that, the girls in the office visited him regularly in his hospital room until he died of leukemia," said Ward. "The day he died it was very difficult for us to keep our minds on accounting.

" ...I remember Ruby Rainwater, the hospital administrator when I came to work, as a plain-spoken, no-nonsense woman with a heart," she reflected. "I once saw her talking to a man who was holding his small son in his arms as he stood in the hospital hallway. The father and son were about to take a long bus trip home, and their bus fare had been paid by the hospital. Rainwater asked the father if he had money for food along the way, and he reluctantly admitted that he didn't. She had the kitchen staff prepare sack lunches for the two of them, and she brought the lunches out to them herself. That incident made me realize how much she really cared about the families there."

One day, when she saw a woman come in with four daughters, Ward became a character in one of her own stories. While the youngest girl was being treated by Dr. W. Thompson Dungan, a pediatric cardiologist, the other three sat in the waiting room just outside the business office. "They were dirty, their hair wasn't combed and their clothing was tattered. Well, I just couldn't stand to see those little girls like that," said Ward. "So I took them to the linen room where donated clothing of all sizes was kept. Another lady and I gave the girls baths, put clean clothing on them and ribbons in their hair. My, they were so pretty!"

By the time Dr. Dungan returned to the waiting room the three little girls were back in their seats, and Ward could not resist asking his opinion of the transformation. "He couldn't believe that they were the same children," she declared, smiling at the memory of that long-ago day.

"It was the committee's understanding," Child Guidance Committee Chair Cooper Jacoway reminded his colleagues as he addressed the Board on March 22, 1962, "that the Board voted to establish the child guidance clinic. The committee also investigated various sources from which they hope to get some revenue to operate the clinic. The committee is quite confident that the money will be forthcoming, but they cannot get a firm commitment until such time as we have something definite to offer." In response the Trustees voted to allocate $20,000 per year beginning September 1, 1963, toward the operating expense of a child guidance clinic.

Following this vote, Anderson reported that he was working on new plans which would include space for the child guidance clinic. The cost of the project was estimated at over $300,000. He also disclosed that he was surveying the hospital building to determine needed repairs.

Bruce Anderson, Herschel Friday, and George Alexander,
board members, break ground for the hospital's $1.3 million expansion, 1966
Courtesy of Lowell Staggs

Building Committee Chair George Alexander reported on September 11, 1962, that the Arkansas Department of Health could secure $205,540.30 in federal Hill-Burton funds for the proposed construction, if the Board would authorize President Carroll Thomas to sign documents stating that Arkansas Children's Hospital would set aside $103,000—one third the cost of the building. The Board granted Thomas the authority to sign the necessary papers.

Herschel Friday succeeded Carroll Thomas as president of the Board of Trustees in November 1962. The new president was a partner in the Mehaffy, Smith and Williams Law Firm (now Friday, Eldredge and Clark). He had been on the panel for ten years, and had served as treasurer and vice-president. He shared his predecessor's conviction that there was a vital need for the hospital's services.

"We need to begin thinking along a different line," the new president advised his fellow Trustees on December 18, 1962. He explained that after conferring with officials from the State Board of Health, the building committee had concluded that the Board should reconsider the building plans which had been recommended in the first Hamilton and Associates study in 1954. The report had advocated removing the medical facility's two wings and going into a more elaborate overall program.

Bruce Anderson stated that as an architect he felt this was the best possible alternative, because with only a few slight modifications, such as space for the child guidance clinic, the 1954 proposal would answer all the institution's needs. He added that it would also bring the facility up to the standards set by the United States Public Health Service. President Herschel Friday cautioned that further study was needed, as they were now talking about a $600,000-plus building program. It was agreed by all that further study was indeed warranted.

At the request of Long-Range Planning Committee Chair Jack Lynn, a subcommittee was appointed in January 1963 to undertake a study of admission trends during the past decade, and of what might be anticipated for the next one. Five weeks later, this subcommittee reported that the average number of service days for the sixty-five-bed pediatric medical facility had dropped from around 20,000 in 1952 to around 16,400 a decade later.

While no specific area of operation could be singled out as the primary cause of this decline, the report noted that the Salk vaccine had greatly reduced the number of polio cases. It also pointed out that the absence of isolation facilities often meant that children who had not had measles, mumps or chicken pox could not be admitted. The study concluded that the reduction in the number of referrals to Arkansas Children's Hospital was due in large measure to a lack of information in outlying parts of the state. The principal recommendations of the subcommittee were:

- ❖ That steps should be taken to provide isolation facilities, so that during outbreaks of communicable disease, admissions to the hospital could continue as usual.
- ❖ That through the Public Relations Director, the facilities and services offered by Arkansas Children's Hospital should be made known in every corner of the state.
- ❖ That steps should be taken to redesign the operating rooms to provide the surgeons more space and greater efficiency.

Two months later, on May 8, 1963, at a joint meeting of the long-range planning and building committees, Jack Lynn urged the Board to think in terms of a $1 million construction program. He suggested contacting the State Board of Health to find out how much money could be obtained through the federal Hill-Burton program.

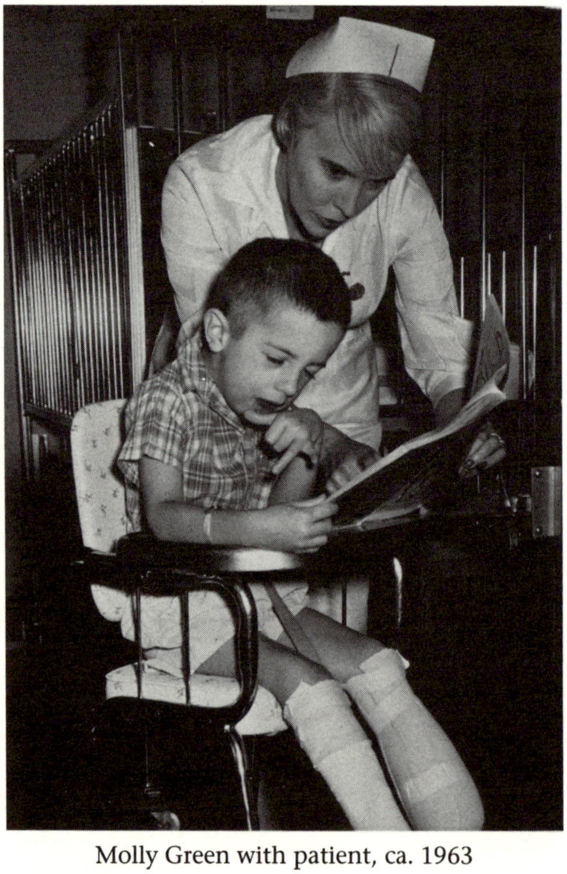

Molly Green with patient, ca. 1963

Anderson reported in mid-December 1963 that several physicians had approached him about the possibility of accepting paying patients—those who could pay all or part of their expenses—on a limited basis. Administrator Rainwater stated that the medical staff favored doing so. Asked if his plans could be revised to include a limited number of private rooms, Anderson replied that such a revision was feasible. President Friday inquired as to whether the hospital would still be entitled to federal funds if such patients were accepted. Anderson stated that as long as the institution was nonprofit it would be eligible for federal aid.

Following this discussion, Friday asked Public Relations Director Calvin Collier to make a survey of children's hospitals around the country to determine how many were accepting such patients and under what circumstances. The overwhelming majority of pediatric hospitals responding to this survey reported long-established policies of admitting paying patients based primarily on bed availability. After much debate, the Board voted to authorize the admission of a limited number of paying patients when space was available.

Building plans and the proposed change in the admissions policy were discussed in detail on February 25, 1964. Herschel Friday opened the discussion, declaring that the building plans should be finalized as soon as possible. In response to questions, Bruce Anderson stated that the estimated cost of construction was $1,200,000. Two-thirds of this sum was available in the form of a Hill-Burton grant. It was mandatory, he explained, that the first phase of construction be under contract by June 30. This first phase—the South Wing—would consist of two twenty-bed wards, the child guidance clinic, public relations office and dental clinic. The second phase would have to be under construction within two years. This phase would consist of tearing down the old east and west wards and constructing two new wings. The board decided against adding any private rooms for paying patients.

Asked about the possibility of building a completely new hospital at a new site, Anderson pointed out that the net worth of the present facility was estimated at $100,000 while the cost of rebuilding at a new site—i.e. near the University of Arkansas Medical Center—was estimated at $4 million. In view of this fact, the Board decided that Arkansas Children's Hospital should remain at its original 804 Wolfe Street location and go forward with Phase One of the building plan.

Bids for the first phase of construction were read on June 23, 1964. The lowest bid—that of the Baldwin Construction Company of Little Rock—was $412,200. The expansion was soon underway. In August, Anderson reported that work could begin on Phase Two as soon as the necessary papers were signed. He stated that this second phase could be completed in about eighteen months.

One final change was made in the building plans after construction was underway. The space originally set aside for the child guidance clinic was changed to an isolation area. The Board apparently believed the latter to be the more immediate need. The need for a child guidance clinic would be addressed in the future.

Jack T. Lynn succeeded Friday as president of the Board of Trustees in November 1964. Lynn was president of Parkin Printing and Stationery Company. A member of the hospital's governing body for sixteen years, he was also active in the Chamber of Commerce and the Little Rock Rotary Club. Friday would remain on the Board, and in 1992 would mark forty years of continuous service to the children of Arkansas.

"Despite the tragedies at this hospital," observed a visitor in early December 1964, "the Christmas spirit is apparent in every ward. All four wards—girls' ward, boys' ward, infant and premature baby ward—are decorated with *Merry Christmas* signs strung across their doors. Windows sport Christmas candles, bells, sleighs and religious scenes. Large Christmas trees glitter with lights, ornaments and tinsel."

Nowhere was the spirit of the season more evident than in the letters to Santa Claus written by the younger patients. Many wanted something not for themselves, but for a brother, a sister, a mother or father. One five-year-old boy, explaining that there was not enough milk at home for his baby sister, asked for a cow for his father. Another wanted "something" to help his brother walk again. A little girl whose clothing had caught fire when her sister accidentally pushed her into a gas heating stove, asked for a doll, as she had never had one. On Christmas morning her wish was fulfilled.

"Toys were given to us by the Amalgamated Workers Union, the Ottenheimer Company and numerous church and civic groups," explained Public Relations Director Calvin Collier. "We try to sort them out according to what the children said they wanted in letters to Santa. What we buy for them are things like watches, jewelry and transistor radios with money given to us. For some of these kids," he added, "this will be the only Christmas they get.

Clyde S. Nevill

They won't really have one when they get home."

On August 17, 1965, Clyde S. Nevill was named administrator of Arkansas Children's Hospital, succeeding Ruby Rainwater, who resigned to assume an administrative position with the University of Arkansas Medical Center. Nevill had attended the University of Texas and had graduated from the University of Iowa with a degree in business administration. While serving in the navy during World War II, Nevill's duties had included the commissioning and decommissioning of Navy hospitals. After the war, he became administrator of the S. B. Allen Memorial Hospital in his hometown of Bonham, Texas. He came to Little Rock from Paragould, Arkansas, where he had served as administrator of the eighty-five-bed Community Methodist Hospital for eleven years.

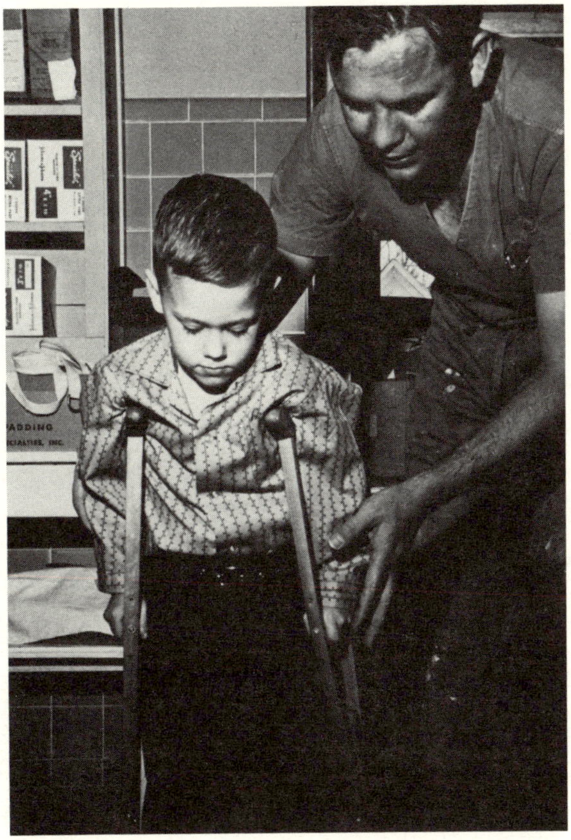

Youngster learns to walk with crutches, ca. 1962

At the same time as Nevill's hiring, Dr. W. Thompson Dungan was named to the newly created post of medical director. A native of Little Rock, Dr. Dungan had received his bachelor's and medical degrees from Vanderbilt University, had served his internship and pediatric residency at Vanderbilt Hospital and had received a fellowship in pediatric cardiology at the University of Chicago.

This new position was to be part-time, with Dr. Dungan dividing his time between Arkansas Children's Hospital and the University of Arkansas School of Medicine where he served as assistant professor of pediatrics. The medical director was to oversee the care of patients, act as a liaison with the medical staff and with other hospitals and supervise the training of medical interns.

Amid these changes, the day-to-day routine of caring for the patients continued. John Ward, a reporter for the *Arkansas Democrat* who visited the hospital in April 1965, was impressed with the dedication of the staff. "Compassion is like a moving current at Arkansas Children's Hospital," he observed. "It is in the faces and voices of the nurses and doctors and other helpers of children there.... They have to love these youngsters to do what they do for them—extra things like fixing little girls' hair, giving boys haircuts, playing with them, crying with them and getting fiercely angry over neglect that brought some of the children here."

The journalist found the boys' ward to be a lively place. Many of the youngsters—arms or legs in casts—were up and playing. One freckle-faced little boy raced up to him. "Take my picture," he pleaded, and then, in the same breath, confided, "I'm going home today!"

Despite their illnesses, the patients often brought smiles to the faces of those who cared for them. A new nurse was once asked by a five-year-old named Donnie, "Did you know Miss Smith?" Receiving a negative reply, he complacently stated, "Well, she worked here till we drove her crazy." Another youngster, a six-year-old burn patient, upon being served his lunch tray looked at the Fritos and demanded, "Where's the dip?"

A Hot Spring County resident who was a patient in the late '60s remembered the kindness of a staff member. "The last time I was a patient at Children's I was fifteen years old. When I was admitted for orthopedic surgery there was only one other boy in the ward my age. After he went home, I had no one to talk to. To pass the time I read a lot, mostly paperback westerns and adventure stories. Being confined to bed, I quickly ran out of anything to read. One morning a staff member—Mr. McWhorter I think his name was—brought me a grocery bag full of paperback westerns. 'I've read these,' he explained, 'and I thought maybe you could use them.'"

In January 1966 Board president Jack Lynn reported that specifications for the second phase of construction—the new building—would be ready in time to be under contract by the deadline of June 30, 1966. He estimated that it would take from eighteen to twenty-four months for the old building to be demolished and the new one erected. The contract was once again awarded to Baldwin Construction Company.

John Harvey Baird succeeded Jack T. Lynn as president of the Board of Trustees in November 1966. Baird, a successful advertising and real estate executive, had been on the panel for nine years. He was a leader in numerous other organizations including the Salvation Army and the Boy Scouts, and was a member of the Little Rock City Planning Commission.

At the urging of Administrator Clyde Nevill, the Board voted on November 17, 1966, to establish an auxiliary to aid the hospital. The institution had been without such support since 1945. By mid-January of the following year, approximately 125 women had received letters regarding the auxiliary. On March 7, 1967, Board member Robert Douglass addressed the organizational meeting of the Arkansas Children's Hospital Auxiliary. "The main functions of a hospital auxiliary," he declared, "are to provide volunteer services, to raise funds in various approved ways and to promote public awareness of the hospital." Officers were elected for the year, and a set of bylaws and regulations were formulated. The auxiliary's governing document was approved by the Board at its April meeting.

The new building was scheduled to be completed in December 1968. In May of that year, the new dining room and kitchen were opened. "It's like going from a Model-A to a limousine," declared Geneva Jackson. Jackson—"Geneva" to three generations of hospital staff and patients—had been in charge of the institution's kitchen for thirty-seven years.

"Hamburgers are number one with the children," Jackson told an interviewer. Other favorites were hot dogs, fried chicken and french fries. Potatoes, English peas and green beans were the only vegetables on the list. Desserts were almost exclusively fresh fruit, ice cream and cookies. "They won't eat pie or cake, except birthday cakes, and prefer 'finger foods.' They don't like anything fancy and will not eat things they can't identify, like casserole." Topping the list of unwanted foods were liver and asparagus. "The most nutritious food in the world," she pointed out, "won't do the children any good if they won't eat it."

Hospital dietitian Geraldine Getty agreed. "We try to make the hospital as homelike as possible," she explained. "And so we strive to serve appetizing food that will be to the sick child a link with home. It may be the square of hot cornbread or the sugar cookies—or Geneva's fried chicken. A glorified dessert or a complicated casserole would only add to the children's homesickness, bewilderment and inability to cope with their physical problems. Younger children particularly prefer simple foods.

"At least once a week a picnic style 'sack lunch' is served," said Getty. "Sometimes we do a 'somersault,' serving orange juice, bacon, pancakes and maple syrup for supper rather than breakfast. One of the ways we arrive at our menus is by talking with the patients individually and in small groups. They unhesitatingly state their likes and dislikes. Our job is to go along with them and at the same time remember their nutritional needs."

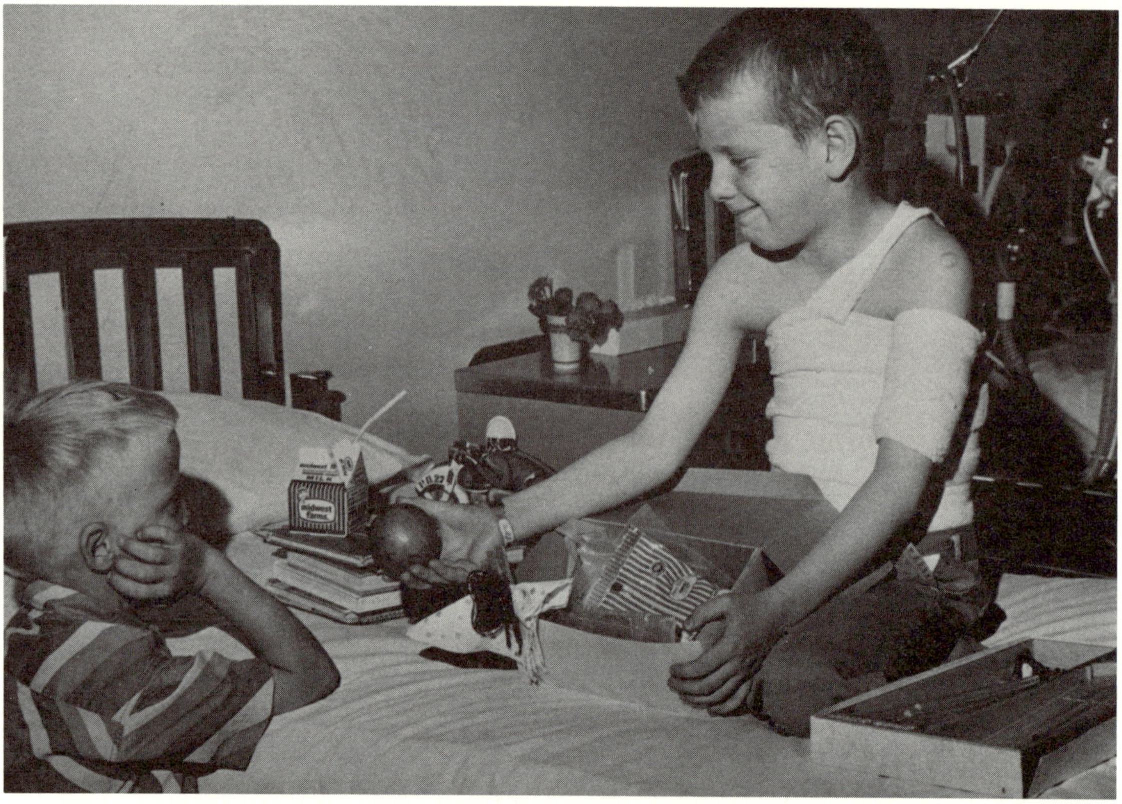

Patient enjoys box lunch, ca. 1962

Board president John Baird presented a resolution to his fellow Trustees in November 1968 requesting the creation of an ophthalmology clinic. He stated that the Lions Club had been contacted and had expressed an interest in the project. The equipment necessary for such a clinic would cost an estimated $15,000. This resolution was adopted with only one dissenting vote.

Administrator Clyde Nevill reported in February 1969 that four private patients had been admitted to the hospital. These were the first paying patients admitted under the hospital's new policy. He also disclosed that a letter had been sent to each member of the hospital's regular medical staff urging them to send their private pediatric patients to the facility.

The new wing was completed in March 1969. "The Arkansas Children's Hospital has a few touches ... that one may not find in other hospitals," observed Bob Ferguson, an *Arkansas Democrat* reporter who toured the expanded facility. "The dental chair is a special type designed in a manner to accommodate children wearing casts. In the recovery room, small children who have undergone surgery come out from under sedation and receive the gift of a new toy to help ease the experience."

Students in schoolroom with Eula Jones, ca. 1962

A special service which delighted some patients—but was less than delightful to others—was school. "The daily parade to classes," noted Ferguson, "usually includes a few who skip along ... and others in wheelchairs." Two teachers handled the teaching of grades one through twelve, allowing students to keep up with their classes while hospitalized.

"No day is the same. It's a new day every time because you have different pupils," observed Eula Jones, who taught at Arkansas Children's Hospital for nearly twenty-five years. "Patients are encouraged to attend school if they are to be in the hospital for more than one week. I don't force them to go to school," she declared, "they want to go." For hesitant youths, however, she had subtle methods of persuasion. "With boys, for instance, I might show them a book about snakes and teach them the four poisonous snakes found in Arkansas, and before you know it they are wanting to learn more!"

One student, an eighteen-year-old boy with clubfeet, came to the hospital on his own initiative and stayed for more than a year while his feet were amputated and prosthetic devices were fashioned for him. He explained to the teachers that he had quit school in the second grade because his twisted feet had made regular attendance impossible. During his hospitalization he completed the requirements for the third, fourth, fifth, sixth and seventh grades. He later continued his schooling, married and raised a family.

When the new wing was opened, hospital admissions had been down for eight months. A major reason for this decline was increased competition from other Little Rock area hospitals for pediatric patients. In addition, more parents were making use of the small county hospitals around the state for their children's medical care, especially surgery. These trends, combined with construction costs, triggered a financial crisis. Treasurer Louis Lanford reported in June 1969 that the institution would have only $20,000 left after all construction-related expenses were paid. Clearly, expenditures would have to be cut. Lanford offered four alternatives:

- ❖ That Arkansas Children's Hospital accept only those patients receiving assistance from the Crippled Children's Division of the State Welfare Department.
- ❖ That all or part of some services be eliminated.
- ❖ That the new wing be closed.

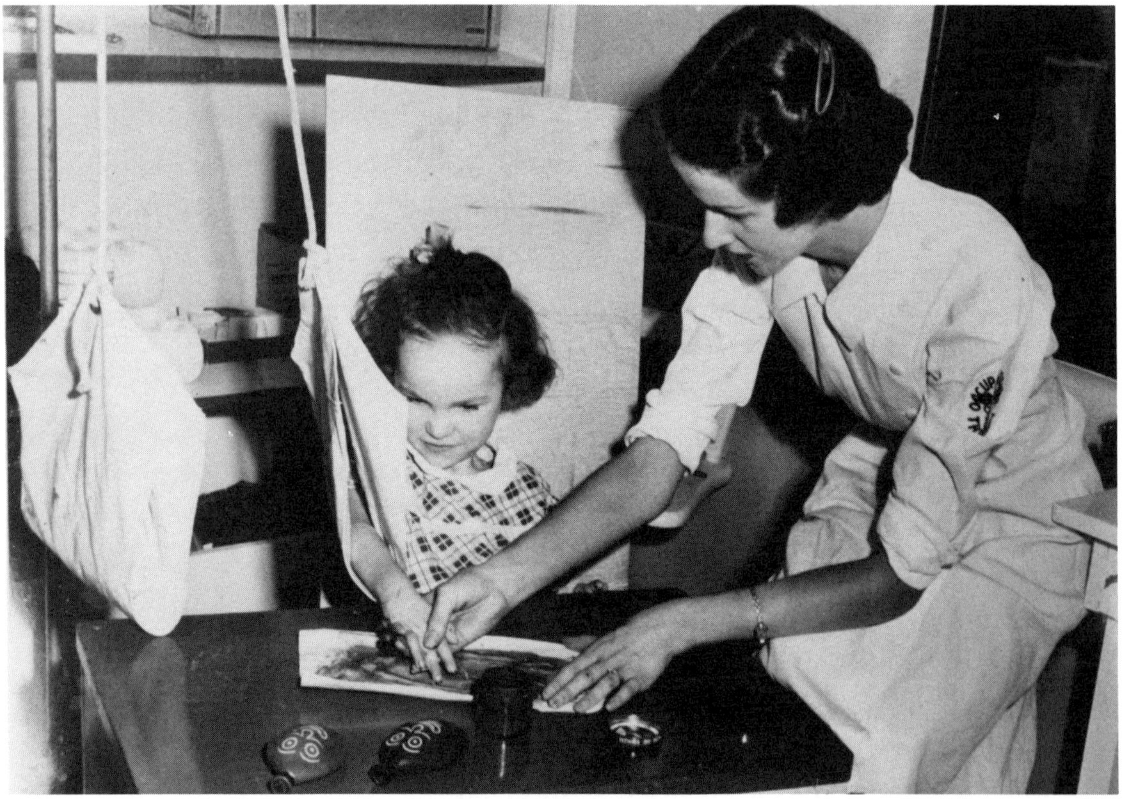

Occupational Therapist Betty Sorensen
with polio patient, ca. 1961
Courtesy of Betty Sorensen

❖ That Arkansas Children's Hospital be closed and its assets—the building and the surrounding land—be sold.

During the sometimes heated discussion which followed, Chief of Staff Dr. William Steele suggested the possibility of a contractual agreement with the University of Arkansas Medical Center to strengthen the ties between the two institutions. Dr. Dungan, who was resigning as medical director in order to devote full time to cardiology at the Medical Center, stated that he would talk with officials there about the matter.

A contractual agreement between the University of Arkansas Medical Center and Arkansas Children's Hospital was signed on October 1, 1969. Drafted by Dr. Dungan and Dr. Theodore C. Panos, Chair of the Department of Pediatrics at the University Medical Center, and approved by officials of both institutions, the agreement outlined ways in which they were to work together to provide treatment for patients and education to medical students, interns and residents. The major provisions of the agreement were:

❖ That Arkansas Children's Hospital was to maintain its separate identity.

❖ That the medical director of Arkansas Children's Hospital was to be selected by the chair of the department of pediatrics at the University of Arkansas Medical Center. The person chosen was to be acceptable to the hospital's Board of Trustees and its medical staff.

❖ That officials of the two institutions were to meet annually—or as often as deemed necessary—for the purpose of discussing matters of mutual interest relating to the operation of Arkansas Children's Hospital.

❖ That the chiefs of the various departments at Arkansas Children's Hospital were to be members of the faculty of the University of Arkansas Medical Center. They were to be selected by the Chair of the respective departments of the University and acceptable to the hospital's Board of Trustees and its medical staff.

❖ That the University of Arkansas Medical Center was to provide interns and resident physicians to be rotated through Arkansas Children's Hospital in such numbers as agreed upon.

❖ That medical residents, interns and students were to be responsible to the chiefs of the various departments at Arkansas Children's Hospital.

When Board president John Harvey Baird died suddenly in November 1969, Louis Lanford was named to the top post. Lanford was president of

Hill, Crawford and Lanford Inc., a Little Rock investment securities firm. A member of the hospital's governing body for eleven years, he was also active in the Metropolitan YMCA and the Little Rock Rotary Club. Reversing the decline in admissions was clearly his number one priority.

On February 17, 1970, the possibility of moving the hospital to a new location was again discussed. Several local pediatricians voiced their views. St. Vincent Infirmary, Baptist Hospital and the University Medical Center had all expressed an interest in forming a partnership with the pediatric medical facility. Following this exchange, President Lanford instructed the long-range planning committee to undertake a study of the relocation question.

The decade which had dawned with such promise was ending in a cloud of uncertainty. Not since the depths of the Great Depression had the institution faced such a crisis. While few doubted that a solution would emerge, none could have imagined the triumph which lay ahead.

Occupational Therapy stages puppet show, ca. 1961
Courtesy of Betty Sorensen

Shrine Circus clown visits ACH, ca. 1963

Seven

IN 1970 AMERICA WAS DEEPLY divided by the seemingly endless fighting in Vietnam. Spiraling inflation—a side effect of the conflict—along with increasing unemployment and soaring oil prices, was threatening the nation's prosperity. In addition, after years of exploiting and polluting the country's natural resources in the name of progress, Americans realized that their resources were not infinite. Millions were pessimistic about the future.

Caught up in the turmoil and confusion of the times, Arkansans shared this pessimism. Even so, the 1960s had, in many respects, been a decade of great progress for Arkansas. Industrial development had reversed the state's population decline, but had proven to be a mixed blessing. Many new plants locating in Arkansas were attracted by the state's low wages and undereducated labor force. Most new plants were small, with an average of fifty workers, and few employed more than five hundred. Still, industrial development did much to bring Arkansas into the nation's economic mainstream.

This industrial growth was aided by the system of federal hydroelectric and flood-control dams completed in the mid-60s. These dams also created fifteen man-made lakes, which became popular vacation and recreation areas, boosting the state's growing tourist industry. The most ambitious federal project in Arkansas during the post-war era—the effort to tame the Arkansas River—was completed in the early '70s. When water traffic was opened from the Gulf of Mexico to Tulsa, Oklahoma, in 1968, Little Rock, Pine Bluff and Fort Smith became ports for international cargo. This diversification and other changes helped free Arkansans from their long-held sense of isolation.

Arkansas Children's Hospital, like the state it served, stood at a crossroads in 1970. On April 21 of that year, the long-range planning committee recommended that the hospital remain at its original 804 Wolfe Street location for the next three years. Committee Chair Jack Lynn urged that if the Board of Trustees approved this recommendation, a letter should be sent to

St. Vincent Infirmary, Baptist Hospital and the University of Arkansas Medical Center informing them of the decision and thanking them for their invitations to pursue a joint operating agreement. No action was taken on this recommendation.

Administrator Clyde S. Nevill submitted his resignation on June 16, 1970, in order to assume a position with the Blue Cross-Blue Shield Insurance Company. Two weeks later, in a letter addressed to his fellow Trustees, Board President Louis Lanford reported on the action of the executive committee during the panel's summer recess. He stated that an agreement had been reached with the Medical Center whereby Dr. Roger Bost, interim Chair of that institution's Department of Pediatrics, would be named acting administrator and medical director of Arkansas Children's Hospital. "The committee," asserted President Lanford, "is quite impressed with Dr. Bost." He added that this arrangement was temporary, and that anything permanent would require the approval of the Board.

Dr. Roger Bost

The following month, Dr. Bost, who had served part of his medical internship at Children's in the 1940s, submitted two initiatives. First, he proposed that the Children and Youth (C&Y) Project, of which he was executive director, be moved from the Medical Center to Children's Hospital. This federally-funded program provided comprehensive services ranging from medical, dental and psychological care to secretarial and administrative support.

"This move," stated Dr. Bost, "would enable Children's Hospital to provide medical care to approximately 15,000 children from low-income families living in Little Rock, North Little Rock and adjacent areas." He also disclosed that Robert L. Holliday, administrator of the C&Y Project, would be assisting him in the administration of the hospital.

Robert L. Holliday
Courtesy of Mrs. Bobbie Holliday

Second, he advocated a financial classification system whereby a patient's bill would be discounted according to the family's ability to pay. "Several benefits would be derived from this financial classification system," explained Dr. Bost. It would increase the hospital's income, and in so doing would provide the matching funds required by the C&Y Project. It would also allow the hospital to maintain an accurate total of the amount of care provided each year. This information would be useful in fund raising and in creating the matching funds required for other programs in addition to the C&Y Project. Both proposals were approved by the Board's executive committee.

On October, 28, 1970, Dr. Bost called for an expansion of the outpatient service. "As ACH builds the outpatient service," he reasoned, "the inpatient load will follow." The sewing room was soon remodeled, providing a new treatment room and four examination rooms for the outpatient clinic. In January of the following year, the Well-Baby Clinic was moved from the Medical Center to Children's Hospital. This clinic offered routine checkups, nutritional information, immunizations, developmental screening and referral services to children from birth to age four.

The pediatrician's administrative ability did not go unnoticed. In March 1971, shortly after Governor Dale Bumpers won legislative approval of his plan to reorganize state government, Dr. Bost was named director of the new Arkansas Department of Social and Rehabilitation Services. In order to accept this position, he resigned as interim administrator and medical director of Arkansas Children's Hospital and was granted a leave of absence from his post at the Medical Center.

While administering the agency, Dr. Roger Bost was one of the initiators in expanding the state's Medicaid program, bringing community centers for the aging and retarded to every county in Arkansas, and beginning the state's prescription drug program. In 1976, Dr. Bost resigned the state post, returned to the Medical Center and accepted a position on the ACH medical staff where he remained until his retirement in September 1993.

The Board of Trustees voted on June 15, 1971, to name Dr. Neil H. Sims to the post of medical director. A native of Fort Smith, and a 1950 honors graduate of the University of Arkansas School of Medicine, Dr. Sims had served as an associate professor of pediatrics and director of pediatric ambulatory services at Johns Hopkins University Hospital in Baltimore, Maryland. Following the Board's vote to approve Dr. Sims, Robert Holliday reported that in its first month of operation, income for the new eye clinic had totaled $2,797, and that since moving to Children's Hospital the C&Y Project had purchased $65,000 in services from the medical facility.

These figures reflected the success of the expanded outpatient service. Admissions to the hospital, however, remained well below capacity. It was for this reason that Chief of Staff Dr. Robert Stainton recommended that the number of beds be reduced from ninety-four to eighty-three. Such a reduction, he pointed out, would tend to increase the occupancy rate. With Holliday's endorsement, this recommendation was unanimously adopted.

Dr. Robert E. Merrill was named Chair of the Medical Center's Department of Pediatrics in July 1971. A graduate of Vanderbilt University School of Medicine, Dr. Merrill came to Arkansas from the University of Virginia where he had served as professor of pediatrics and had been in charge of a program for children with multiple handicaps. Following several discussions with the Board of Trustees, Dr. Merrill was named director of Arkansas Children's Hospital and Holliday was named administrator. Holliday, a native of Casper, Wyoming and a retired air force officer with a master's degree in hospital administration from the University of Pittsburgh, was to be responsible for the day-to-

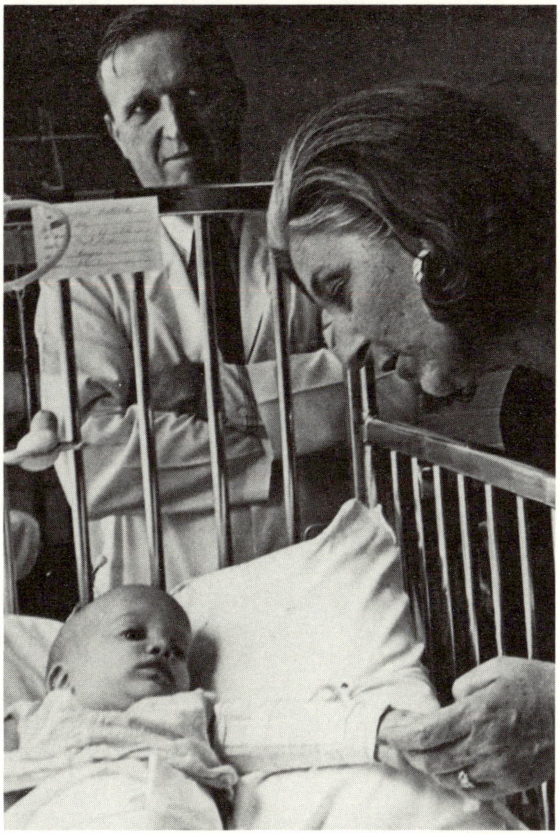

Betty Bumpers and Dr. Robert Merrill, ca. 1972

day operation of the facility, allowing Dr. Merrill to devote more time to his duties at the Medical Center.

Medical Director Dr. Neil Sims reported in October 1971 that plans had been developed to better utilize the dental facilities by procuring the services of a dentist on a part-time basis to treat both inpatients and outpatients. He also outlined a plan to provide 24-hour-per-day outpatient service. Under this plan, a storage area within the hospital would be remodeled, providing nine new examination rooms. The additional staff necessary for this expansion would be obtained from the Medical Center. The Masonic Lodges of Arkansas had offered to underwrite most of the expense. The trustees voiced their approval of these proposals and construction was soon underway.

In November 1971 Robert Douglass succeeded Louis Lanford as president of the Board of Trustees. Douglass was a vice president and sales manager of Coleman Dairy in Little Rock. A Board member for nine years, he was also active in the Arkansas Epilepsy Foundation.

The following month, the Board's executive committee recommended that a chapel be constructed within the hospital. President Douglass was

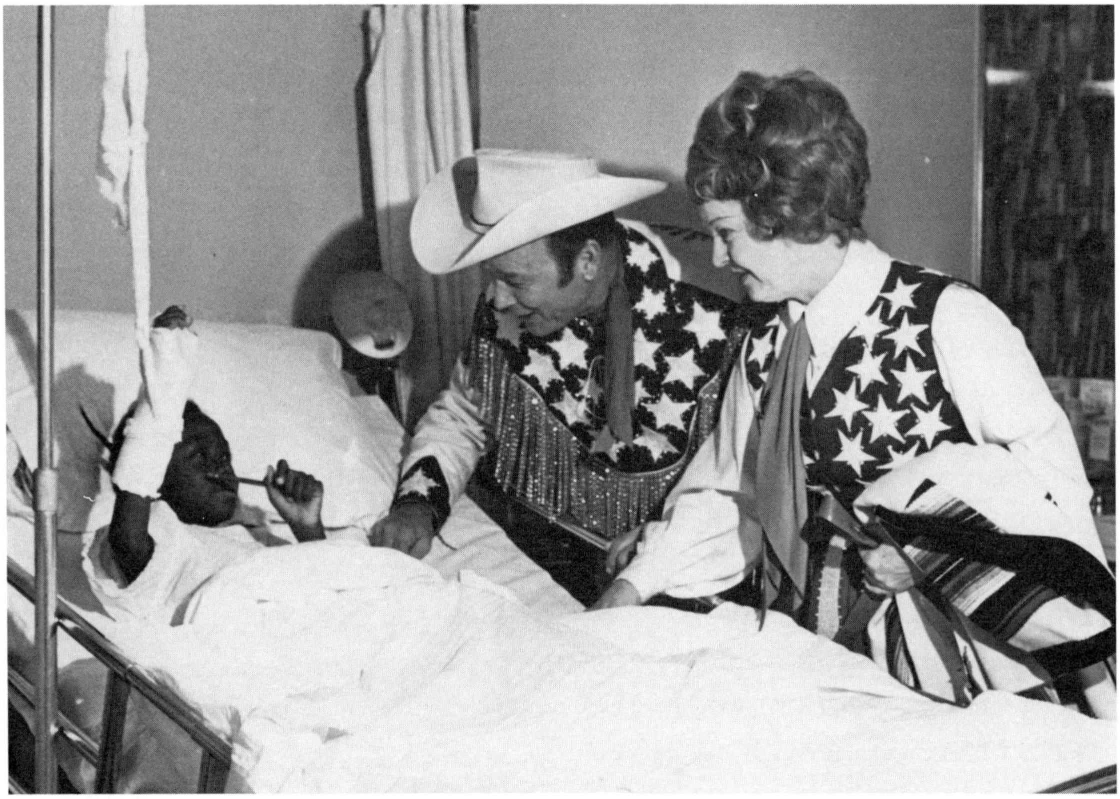

Roy Rogers and Dale Evans, October 1970
Courtesy of Lowell Staggs

authorized to contact the Greater Little Rock Ministerial Alliance concerning whether or not that organization would be willing to provide chaplains on a volunteer basis.

According to the 1971 annual hospital service report, a total of 1,990 patients were admitted to Arkansas Children's Hospital in that year, and 2,461 operations were performed. The number of outpatients totaled 16,314. This was more than double the figure from the previous year. Income for the year, however, was only $14,067 above expenses.

In his medical director's report for January 1972, Dr. Sims suggested that the boys' and girls' wards be converted into a ten-bed ward and three triple-bed rooms, respectively. A motion was approved that this matter be turned over to the building committee. Dr. Sims also noted that 24-hour-per-day outpatient service would begin on January 31. This "walk-in clinic" would provide acute health care to children from birth to age twenty-one. Its services would range from routine checkups and immunizations to nutritional information and referrals.

Leland McGinness, who had succeeded Holliday as director of the C&Y Project in August 1971, remembered, "The 24-hour clinic was an effort to provide easily accessible, high quality, comprehensive health care to the central Arkansas area. The response was absolutely overwhelming. We found that of those children examined between the hours of 7 A.M. and 11 P.M., one in forty-two required hospitalization, while of those examined between 11 P.M., and 7 A.M., one in eleven required hospitalization.

Leland R. McGinness

McGinness further stated, "It was conceived as a clinic, not an emergency room. We didn't have the staff or equipment required for an emergency room, but we treated a great many emergency cases. The 24-hour clinic became our front line in the delivery of acute health care for children. The need was just so great. I felt that the children of Arkansas were depending on me to keep the clinic open for them."

Treasurer Robert Cress reported in April 1972 that income for the first nine months of the fiscal year was higher than anticipated. This increase was primarily due to the initiation of 24-hour outpatient service. Following this report, Executive Committee Chair Louis Rosen urged the purchase of a piece of residential property located at 1914 Maryland Avenue, just west of the hospital building. After some discussion, the trustees authorized $15,000 for this purpose.

Administrator Robert L. Holliday died suddenly on June 10, 1972, at the age of fifty-two. After consulting with the Board of Trustees on the question of a successor, Hospital Director Dr. Robert Merrill offered the job to McGinness, who accepted. He reported for duty on June 14, 1972. Six days later, he was officially named administrator of Arkansas Children's Hospital.

His first day on the job was a baptism of fire. "When I came in and looked at my old friend Bob Holliday's desk," McGinness reflected twenty years later, "it was piled high with obligations and responsibilities. Well, when I sat down I couldn't see over that mountain of paper. That's when Mildred Ward came in. Mildred ran the business office, the purchasing department and the switchboard; she ran everything in those days. She told me, 'Mr. McGinness, no one should have to come in and take on this responsibility. Payroll is due tomorrow, and we can't meet it.'" Income, she explained, had been down for over three months, while expenses were up sharply.

McGinness spent the remainder of the morning reviewing the institution's financial situation with Ward. That afternoon, he met with the Board of Trustees. Following a sometimes heated discussion, he was authorized to transfer $10,000 from an account which had been set aside for another purpose in order to meet the payroll.

The new administrator of Arkansas Children's Hospital was no stranger to adversity. Leland Robert McGinness had been born on February 19, 1930, in Burlington Junction, Missouri, the oldest of seven children of Dale Joseph and Thelma Deneen McGinness. "We were poor—the poorest family in the community," McGinness would later say of his early years. "But our parents loved us and taught us the value of hard work, ambition and honesty."

At the of age thirteen, McGinness left home to work on a neighboring farm. "I knew that if I was going to get an education, if I was going to have clothes like other kids my age, I had to go to work," he later reflected. "In some ways I missed a lot—missed being with my folks, missed going hunting with my father and having long talks with him."

During his sophomore year in high school, the ambitious teenager worked in a restaurant in his hometown of Maryville, Missouri, for one dollar a night and his evening meal. The following year, he managed the local movie theatre. After graduating from high school in 1947, McGinness enrolled at Northwest Missouri State College. "I was thinking of becoming a physician, a dentist or a veterinarian," he reminisced forty-six years later. "But I soon realized I was ill-prepared for the study of science."

He was also hard-pressed financially. Determined to continue his education, McGinness lied about his age and enlisted in the air force. "I was seventeen and had not lived at home since I was thirteen. And I was confident that I could make good in the service."

Following basic training, McGinness enrolled in school at Brook Army Medical Center at Fort Sam Houston in San Antonio, Texas, to become a laboratory technician. He was intrigued by the idea of being able to help the physician make a diagnosis and decide on a course of treatment.

In 1950, Staff Sergeant McGinness was transferred to Korea and then to Japan where he helped establish a field hospital. While there, he met Yachiyo Urata, the twenty-year-old daughter of a candy maker from Kumamoto City on the island of Kunshu. After less than three months in Japan, he was transferred back to the United States.

"As soon as I got back to the States, I put in for a transfer back to the Far East. I didn't know whether I'd be sent to the Philippines, Korea or Japan, but whatever the outcome, I would be closer to the girl I'd met in Japan." McGinness was transferred back to Japan in November 1951. On February 27, 1952, he and Yachiyo Urata were married.

For the next three-and-a-half years, he served as chief medical laboratory technician in a 500-bed military hospital and as a staff technician in a 210-bed civilian hospital. He studied pre-medicine at Phillips University in Enid, Oklahoma, for a time after leaving the air force in 1954, but rejoined the service in 1958. By 1960, he was back in the Far East, and in January 1962, Second Lieutenant McGinness received a Bachelor of Arts Degree from the University of Maryland, Far Eastern Division. During this tour of duty, McGinness met Robert Holliday. Impressed with his determination to excel, Master Sergeant Holliday urged him to pursue a Master's degree in hospital administration.

Returning to the United States, McGinness earned a Master's Degree in Hospital Administration from the Graduate School of Public Health at the University of Pittsburgh in June 1966. In 1967, he was named Chief of Plans and Hospitalization Division for the surgeon, Fifth Air Force. Returning to the United States in 1970, he was assigned to Lockbourne Air Force Base in Ohio, where he served as administrator of the base hospital. In July of the following year, Major McGinness retired from the air force after twenty-one years of service.

At the urging of Robert Holliday, he accepted the position of director of the Children and Youth Project at the University of Arkansas Medical Center. Holliday had resigned the post to become administrator of Arkansas Children's Hospital. Although the job was the lowest paying of several he was offered, McGinness decided to accept it because of a desire to work with children.

In the aftermath of the fiscal crisis, the possibility of moving the hospital to a new location was again considered by the Board. Modification of the boys' and girls' wards was postponed pending a decision on this much-debated option.

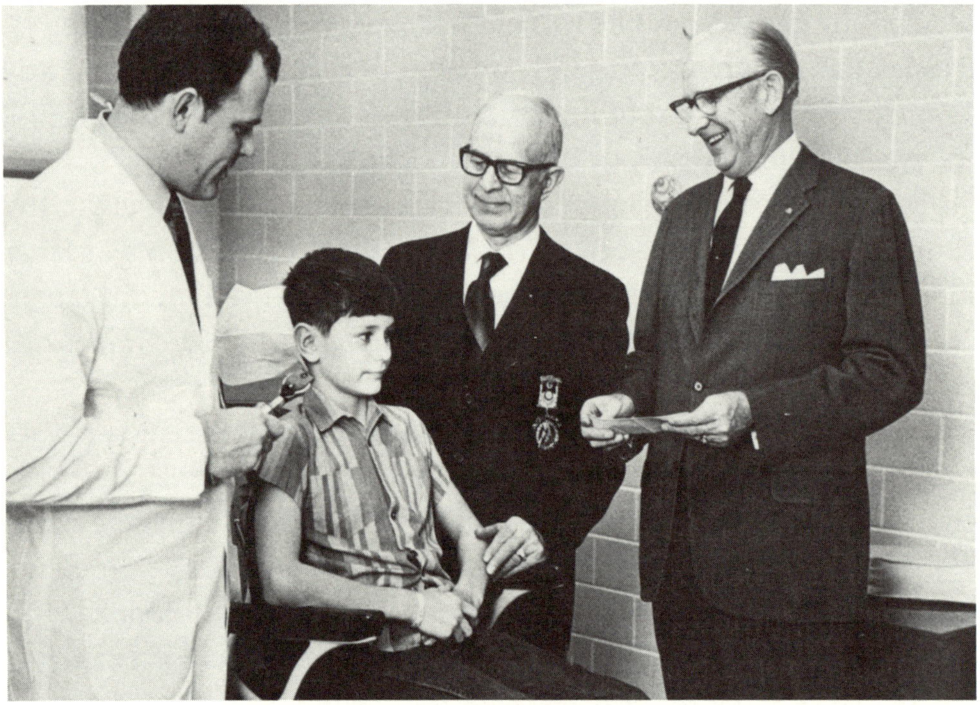

Dr. F. Hampton Roy examines a patient
as Claude Collie, Grand Master of the Masonic Grand Lodge and
Louis Lanford, president of the ACH Board of Trustees, look on.
Donations from the Grand Lodge helped make the eye clinic a reality. May 1971.

Work, however, would continue on a new Infant Care Unit. This unit—made possible by a $10,000 donation from long-time supporter Stella Boyle Smith of Little Rock—would serve infants who did not require intensive care.

Louis Lanford reported in September 1972 that over $3,000 had been contributed thus far toward construction of a chapel. McGinness stated that he wanted to develop a special waiting room in conjunction with the chapel for the families of surgery patients.

In November 1972 Stanley M. Bauman Jr. succeeded Robert T. Douglass as President of the Board of Trustees. Bauman was vice president of Sterling Stores, Inc. A member of the hospital's governing body for eleven years, he had served as secretary and vice president. He was also on the board of the Metropolitan National Bank and was active in the West Little Rock Rotary Club.

Also in November 1972 the Board's executive committee voted unanimously to retain the Careage Corporation Hospital Consultants of Bellevue, Washington, to study the feasibility of relocating and constructing a new Arkansas Children's Hospital. The cost of this study would be $20,000. The following week, Ken Burress, president of the Careage Corporation, addressed the Board. He stated that local firms would be utilized on a subcontracting basis to assist in the design and creation of an institution which would reflect the present administrative autonomy. The Board of Trustees voted to retain the Little Rock architectural firm of Wittenberg, Deloney and Davidson Inc. to work with the Careage Corporation.

Five months later, on April 10, 1973, the conclusions of the study were outlined to the Board by Gene Lynn, Chair of the Board of the Careage Corporation. It was the opinion of the consultants that a new Arkansas Children's Hospital should be constructed. The principal recommendations of the study with regard to the proposed new pediatric medical facility were:

- ❖ That the new Arkansas Children's Hospital consist of a 153-bed teaching hospital with complete facilities including neonatal intensive care unit, eight operating rooms, four diagnostic x-ray rooms, laboratory, pharmacy, psychiatric nursing and treatment floor, central stores, receiving, housekeeping and central plant.
- ❖ That the new Arkansas Children's Hospital be located at the southwest corner of the University of Arkansas Medical Center campus.

❖ That the new Arkansas Children's Hospital be financed through a combination of state and federal funding programs, public fund-raising efforts and through disposition of the existing facility.

Louis Lanford stated that while the members of both the executive and finance committees favored relocation, there was a consensus that the study had failed to address several key issues—chiefly those relating to disposition of the existing facility, which had been appraised at $2.9 million. Gene Lynn responded that the Careage Corporation planned to continue efforts to resolve these issues without requiring any additional monetary commitment from the hospital. He added that it was the opinion of both the Careage and Wittenberg firms that relocation was financially feasible at the time.

Despite Lynn's remarks, the Board of Trustees decided that disposition of the existing facility must be assured prior to making a firm relocation decision. A special committee was established to work with the Careage and Wittenberg firms to resolve the various financial aspects of the relocation endeavor.

Whatever the ultimate decision concerning relocation, Administrator McGinness was determined that Arkansas Children's Hospital would become a pediatric medical center of excellence. "At that time families with sick children who could afford to do so traveled to children's hospitals in Boston, St. Louis or Houston," he observed. "Seriously ill children whose families couldn't afford to travel were treated locally or at the pediatric wing of the Medical Center. There, they either responded to the level of care available, or they died. I asked myself why any child should ever have to go out of state for medical treatment? Why can't we do better? Because of the things I'd achieved in the military I had a certain self-esteem, a certain pride. I was determined to be associated with the best. I told the Board of Trustees, 'We can, we will, we must make this facility a children's medical center of excellence.'

"The idea, the concept, was so good that no one could be against it. And I wasn't the only one who had this dream. Every person here felt that they could make a real difference. We felt that there was no problem too great for us to overcome; this belief was inherent in our quest for excellence."

Dr. Gordon H. Green was named medical director on November 15, 1973, succeeding Dr. Neil H. Sims, who resigned in order to devote more time to his academic responsibilities at the Medical Center. A graduate of the University of Texas Southwestern Medical School, Dr. Green was Assistant Professor of Pediatrics at the University of Arkansas Medical Center. He had served as Associate Medical Director of the C&Y Project prior to coming to Children's.

"Our goal," he told the governing body, "must be to develop a pediatric medical center which can respond to the needs of children to the extent that no child will ever again have to go out of state for any type of treatment. We must move to establish services as quickly as possible whenever we determine that there is a definite need within our state for a particular type of treatment."

The Ruth Beall Chapel—named in honor of the former superintendent—was dedicated on Sunday, July 15, 1973. Despite failing health, Beall attended the dedication and heard words of praise for her years of unselfish devotion to the children of Arkansas. Three chaplains of different denominations would be provided on a volunteer basis by the Greater Little Rock Ministerial Alliance.

Nine months later, on April 18, 1974, former superintendent Ruth Beall died at the age of seventy-eight. Her innovative leadership and colorful personality had transformed the near-destitute and demoralized Arkansas Children's Hospital into one of the best-known and most respected institutions in the state. "Ruth always managed to get what she wanted, because it was always something for someone else," observed an old Benton County friend. "We walk into the future on the feet of our children," Beall had often said, "and we must not limp on clubfeet." She was buried at Roselawn Memorial Park in Little Rock.

On December 7, 1974—a date that he would refer to as his "personal Pearl Harbor"—Leland McGinness was told by Dr. Merrill that most of the hospital's medical residents were threatening to walk out of the 24-hour clinic if conditions were not improved. McGinness met with the physicians-in-training in an effort to avert a crisis. "They told me they felt exploited—overworked and undertrained," he reminisced years later. "They pointed out the lack of proper supervision and instruction. In that respect, they felt like students in a classroom without a teacher. They felt that they weren't being trained in current pediatric techniques."

The residents remained adamant; they were going to walk out on January 1, 1975, if working conditions did not improve. A few days before this deadline, McGinness made a second attempt to persuade them to remain on the job. This time, he offered to compensate them for their professional services. To his relief, they accepted. "They left work on December 31, 1974, as medical residents," he observed, "and they came back on January 1, 1975 as private contractors."

The bold initiative averted a walk-out. "I knew that if the residents quit, the 24-hour clinic would have to be closed," McGinness reflected in a 1993 interview. "And I was determined to do whatever it took to keep it open."

Dr. James O. Cooper agreed to fill in on weekends or whenever a resident was not available. An Arkansas native, Dr. Cooper was a 1942 graduate of the University of Arkansas School of Medicine. Following an internship at the San Diego County Hospital in California, he had served as a lieutenant in the Navy Medical Corps. In 1948, he had completed his pediatric residency at Washington University in St. Louis. Dr. Cooper had joined the Pediatric Department of the University of Arkansas Medical Center in 1965, following seventeen years of private pediatric practice in El Dorado.

"Dr. Cooper refused to accept any pay for his services," said McGinness. "He would always read the charts to review what the residents were doing. He was always willing to do whatever needed to be done."

Dr. Robert H. Fiser, Jr.

Dr. Robert H. Fiser Jr. was named Chair of the University of Arkansas Medical Center's Department of Pediatrics in April 1975, succeeding Dr. Robert E. Merrill, who resigned to accept a similar position at Texas Tech University. At thirty-two, Dr. Fiser was the youngest chair of a pediatrics department in the nation. A native of Morrilton, Arkansas, and a 1966 *Summa Cum Laude* graduate of the University of Arkansas School of Medicine, he came to Little Rock from the University of California at Los Angeles where he had served as Assistant Professor of Pediatrics. Dr. Fiser was quick to embrace McGinness' dream of a first-class pediatric hospital.

"I'd spent part of my medical residency at Children's and I had a good feeling about the hospital. That's one of the main reasons I accepted the chairmanship at the University," recalled Dr. Fiser in a 1993 interview. "And I was in total agreement with Leland McGinness and his steadfast determination to create a pediatric medical facility which would be able to care for every child regardless of the nature of their illness."

In June 1975, at the urging of McGinness, who felt that the Careage Corporation study had been biased in favor of relocation, the Board's executive committee voted to retain Ross Laboratories Hospital Consultants of Columbus, Ohio, to undertake a new study with regard to the question of whether or not the hospital should relocate. Ross Laboratories had made themselves available at no charge in exchange for receiving credit as the planners of the new Arkansas Children's Hospital. Completed in less than four months, the Ross study would prove to be the most important in the history of the institution.

Also in June 1975 another vital professional agreed to sign on. Dr. Betty A. Lowe, a highly regarded Texarkana pediatrician, was appointed to the joint position of Director of Pediatric Education at Arkansas Children's Hospital and Professor of Pediatrics at the Medical Center. A native of Texas, and a 1956 *Cum Laude* graduate of the University of Arkansas School of Medicine, Dr. Lowe had been a junior and senior assistant resident at Children's Medical Center in Boston and had served as an instructor at Harvard Medical School. She came to Little Rock largely because of McGinness and his steadfast conviction that "we ought to make Children's a real hospital or call it quits."

Dr. Betty A. Lowe

"I had as busy a practice in Texarkana as there was anywhere in Arkansas—and I loved it," she later explained. "But in that practice, I spent countless hours finding places around the country for my patients who needed secondary and tertiary care. Leland McGinness and Dr. Tom Bruce, Dean of the School of Medicine, were convinced that the potential was here at Children's to develop a pediatric medical center which would address the needs of Arkansas children. That's what hooked me."

Stressing the advantages of getting in on the ground floor of a fast-rising young medical center, McGinness and his new-found allies set about recruiting an array of pediatric specialists. "We told them, 'If you have any pioneering spirit left, this is the last frontier,'" remembered McGinness.

Dr. Raymond T. Morrissy, a specialist in pediatric orthopedics, was the first to come aboard. A native of Chicago and a 1967 *Magna Cum Laude* graduate of the Stritch School of Medicine at Loyola University, Dr. Morrissy had served in the air force prior to coming to Children's. While assigned to the David Grant Medical Center at Travis Air Force Base, California, he had initiated a program for surgical correction of scoliosis (curvature of the spine) and had started a clinic for pediatric residents.

Over the next few years, Dr. Morrissy would be followed by specialists in pediatric pathology, hematology/oncology (cancer), pulmonary services, radiology, otolaryngology (ear, nose and throat) surgery, burn surgery and others. McGinness often referred to these young professionals as his "All-Americans."

When Dr. Terry Yamauchi, a nationally known specialist in infectious diseases, accepted the post of Director of Pediatric Ambulatory Services in September 1975, his colleagues at the University of California at Los Angeles and the Los Angeles County Hospital were puzzled. "Little Rock, Arkansas! Are you crazy?" they asked. "Have you lost your marbles?"

Within six weeks of arriving in Little Rock, Dr. Yamauchi, a 1967 honor graduate of the University of Oregon Medical School, was convinced he had made a wise decision. "I couldn't ask for a better place to be, or better people to be with.... Everything's been just perfect for me so far," he told the *Arkansas Gazette*. "And I look forward to the day when people around the country are going to say, 'Gee, the Children's Hospital at Little Rock, the University of Arkansas Department of Pediatrics—that's a crackerjack group.' I think we have the potential to develop that type of program."

"Our whole effort," asserted McGinness, "was a throw of the dice. We certainly didn't have much in the way of buildings, not even private rooms for our patients, but what we did have was a group of people chomping at the bit to build a pediatric medical facility which would be recognized by their peers in Boston, St. Louis and Houston as one of the best."

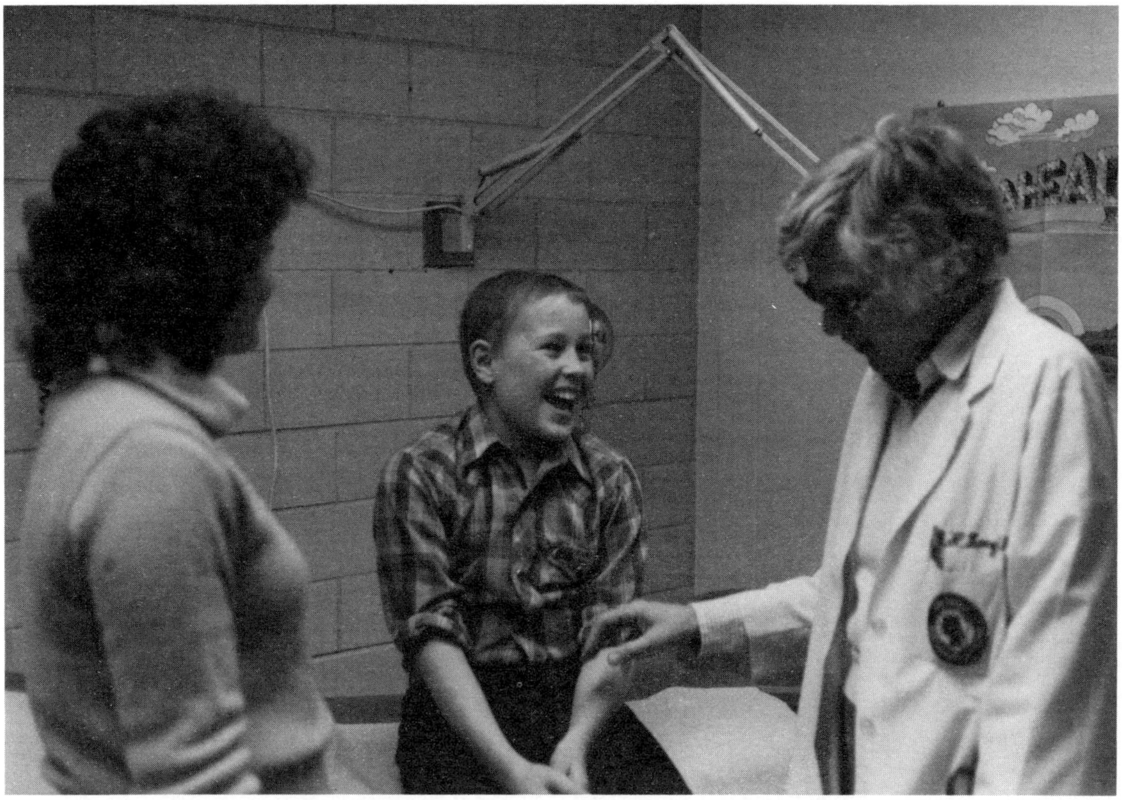

Dr. Daisilee L. Berry chats with 11-year-old Shane Childress
as his mother, Fran, looks on. Dr. Berry was the first pediatric hematologist in Arkansas.
ca. 1983

The Hematology/Oncology Clinic, which began treating patients in January 1976, exemplified the hospital's growing medical expertise. Under the direction of Dr. Daisilee L. Berry, the first pediatric hematologist in Arkansas, this clinic provided diagnosis, evaluation and treatment of childhood problems relating to blood and/or tumors, such as anemia, leukemia and other malignant diseases. Dr. Berry and her staff were also involved in laboratory research on white blood cells in an effort to find new methods of treatment.

"There are no guarantees in life," stressed Dr. Berry, "just good preventive care. Ten years ago, the majority of children diagnosed as having cancer died, but today there's hope. We can't control life and death, but we do believe that every child with cancer deserves a chance to be a long-term survivor...and we see a lot of survivors in this clinic."

The inpatient wards soon felt the impact of the new Hemotology/Oncology Clinic. "Due to the very nature of the diseases treated by this service," reported Medical Director Dr. Gordon Green in February 1976, "we've sustained several patient deaths, none of which were unexpected.... However, it is a fairly new experience for some of our staff, particularly those of long standing, to have such intensive exposure to critically ill and dying patients. It is a mark of the maturing process of this hospital that these changes are going well."

In March 1976, with the aid of the Arkansas State Spinal Cord Commission, the first Spina Bifida Clinic was held. This clinic, under the direction of Dr. Raymond Morrissy, provided multidisciplinary care for children with spina bifida, a congenital birth defect involving damage to the spine and nervous system. Its long-term effects usually include paralysis of the legs, problems with bowel and bladder control, hydrocephalus (accumulation of fluid surrounding the brain), and a number of other health problems. Services available through the new specialty clinic included orthopedics, urology, neurosurgery, nutritional and genetic counseling, occupational and physical therapy and others as needed.

As these and other specialty clinics increased the hospital's expertise, physicians in Pulaski County and around the state began referring patients there. Faced with the need to house all the new medical professionals and the flood of patients they generated, the facility's physical limitations soon became intolerable. Dr. Lowe remembered recruiting physicians knowing that there was no office space for them. "They'd arrive and someone would say, 'Oh, you can put your things over there in the corner of my office for the time being.' Three weeks later, when they complained we'd say, 'Oh, that's nothing.' And then we'd tell them about whoever held the record and how long they'd had to wait for an office."

Inpatient admissions rose substantially, and the hospital's budget climbed from $1,200,000 in 1970-71 to $4,900,000. in 1975-76. Fortunately, as the hospital's reputation grew, so too did its level of fund raising. "During these years of development we were often worried about money," remembered Leland McGinness. "The business community was wonderful to us. They were very generous in allowing us extra time to pay our bills when we needed it. We went to the people for support—sending out thousands of letters asking them to contribute money—and they too were very generous. Our most precious commodity at Children's Hospital has always been the good will of the people of our state."

McGinness remembered a child from Searcy, who was referred to Dr. Watson Arnold, the hospital's new pediatric nephrologist, only to have his parents change their minds when they saw the hospital. They wanted a private room for their son and Children's could offer only a twenty-bed ward. "So they took him home to Searcy. It was a great failure," McGinness later told *Arkansas Times* magazine. "It was something that needed to be pointed out to us. Here we had the only pediatric kidney specialist in Arkansas, but because our facility didn't meet the parents' expectations, the child was deprived of this expertise."

The conclusions of the Ross Laboratories study were outlined to the Board of Trustees on September 28, 1976. Noting that the recently announced plan to relocate the Veteran's Administration Hospital from East Roosevelt Road to the University Medical Center campus would leave too little room for the Arkansas Children's Hospital, and that no buyer had been found for the existing facility, the consultants recommended that Children's remain at its original 804 Wolfe Street location and undertake a long-range plan of development.

The study then outlined a long-range plan to develop Arkansas Children's Hospital into a major regional pediatric facility with close ties to the University of Arkansas Medical Center Department of Pediatrics. Children's was envisioned as providing the kind of sophisticated medical services not available elsewhere in the state—a tertiary level of care for the treatment of major burns, cancer, genetic anomalies such as spina bifida and other medical problems that most general hospitals were not equipped to treat.

The consultants estimated that under this plan the demand for pediatric beds would grow to 230 and the total bed need to 400 if the development of a neonatal intensive care unit was accomplished. Therefore, the physical space needs of the hospital were identified with three time frames: by 1981 (160 bed level); by 1986 (180 bed level); and the long-range future to the year 2000.

Phase One of this plan (by 1981) would include the development of a twenty-two-bed neonatal intensive care unit which would serve as a tertiary care referral center for the state of Arkansas. In conjunction with this unit, the consultants urged that a seven-bed pediatric intensive care unit be developed. Both of these specialized units would require many support elements—pulmonary technology, respiratory therapy, cardiac catheterization and micro-laboratory technology—all directed toward the specific care of pediatric patients.

In the area of general pediatric beds, the consultants recommended that the boys' and girls' wards, which consisted of forty beds in two twenty-bed rooms, should be replaced by two new thirty-two-bed units composed of private and semi-private patient accommodations. They also urged the establishment of an inpatient psychiatric program. This proposed fifteen-bed unit would serve as a short-term diagnostic and therapeutic unit.

Changes to take place in the second phase (1981-86) would include the addition of a sixteen-bed general pediatric unit and the expansion of the pediatric intensive care unit. As for Phase Three (1986-2000), it was predicted that this fourteen-year period would bring substantial changes in the institution's physical structure as existing buildings began to age and utilization increased. There would be bed increases in the pediatric intensive care unit, psychiatric unit, and neonatal intensive care unit, as well as a need for additional general pediatric beds.

Phase Three also urged construction of a research laboratory along with several support functions and offices. "Such facilities will serve as an attraction to competent physicians who are also interested in research," asserted the consultants. "It is very difficult...to estimate how much space will be desired. For this reason, we recommend that a separate research building be constructed on the hospital campus providing for vertical or horizontal expansion when monies and desirability coincide. We believe that in the long range there could be as much as 20,000 square feet of research space developed in the Arkansas Children's Medical Center complex."

The study concluded that there were three key factors which indicated to the consultants the true growth potential of the Arkansas Children's Hospital. "The increase in these factors—inpatients discharged, outpatient visits and radiology and laboratory diagnostics—indicate that the Board of Trustees...had better make a commitment and agree upon a master plan of development before physical space problems become insurmountable to the extent that they cause a severe decline in the quality of care which the institution is capable of delivering."

In the exchange which followed the Ross Laboratories presentation, Board member Walt Bennett stated that he could see no justification for relocating. Louis Lanford voiced agreement, declaring that more parents would bring their children if the existing facility were updated. Robert Douglass asserted that he had read the Ross study and was "sold" on its recommendations. Garnier Puryear made a motion that the hospital remain at its original 804 Wolfe Street location. The motion passed unanimously.

Robert G. Cress succeeded Stanley M. Bauman Jr. as president of the Board of Trustees in November 1976. Cress was president of the J.A. Riggs Tractor Company. A member of the Board for eleven years, he had served as its treasurer and vice president. He was also active in the Pulaski County chapter of the Red Cross and the Little Rock Rotary Club.

The following month, Administrator Leland McGinness and several of the Trustees met with members of the news media. Board President Cress confirmed that there was no longer any question about the long-range objective of developing Arkansas Children's Hospital into a major regional pediatric medical center. As a first step, he announced, the Board had acquired the block to the east of the hospital, half of the block to the south and most of the block bounded by west Ninth, Marshall, Wolfe and west Tenth Streets along with additional space for parking west of Battery Street, the institution's western boundary.

"Arkansans should understand that children are not merely small adults," observed McGinness at this press conference. "They have different medical problems which require different approaches to treatment. Contemporary practice is to bring together all children with catastrophic diseases in one place where complex equipment can be acquired and specialized skills can be pooled and developed."

Throughout its history—even in its darkest hours—when operating expenses threatened to close its doors, the hospital had maintained a policy of treating all children, regardless of the family's inability to pay. On February 22, 1977, the Board of Trustees adopted a formal statement of philosophy affirming this policy. "The philosophy of the Arkansas Children's Hospital is to provide continuous, easily accessible, high-quality comprehensive health care for all the children of Arkansas without regard to financial status, religious preference or ethnic background."

The document also spoke of the future. "In conjunction with patient care, which shall be given the highest priority, it is recognized that educational and research programs comprise integral parts of a comprehensive health care program and these shall be incorporated in the total program to the extent that supportive funding is available. The hospital will continue as an independent not-for-profit institution governed by a Board of Trustees serving without compensation and responsible for the development of professional policies consistent with a complete child health care center and of fiscal policies to assure a continuing sound financial posture."

Dr. Green's February 1977 medical director's report reflected the growing enthusiasm of the medical staff. "Reye's Syndrome is a disastrous though uncommon condition, and we have felt some satisfaction in bringing one young patient through a bad time indeed. Our work with children with leukemia will withstand comparison with any institution in the country. And the Spina Bifida Clinic offers a new dimension in comprehensiveness of care for this catastrophic illness.

"We are anticipating the addition of new skills and talents to our medical staff. Within the next few months you will be hearing about gastroenterology, nephrology, immunology and pediatric surgery. All of these represent new and previously unavailable services for the children of Arkansas. I believe we will all be proud to have a role in this children's medical center."

Arkansans from every walk of life voiced their support for the institution during these years of development. "Our statement of philosophy could in no way equal the eloquence of many of the letters which we received," said McGinness. A parent of one former patient wrote to express her gratitude "for the good you have done in the past and for the wonderful things you will do in the future."

A pediatrician's letter praised the care that one of his patients had received. "This young child had a rare tumor of the central nervous system which required meticulous neurosurgery therapy. This type of surgery and follow-up on this level is really only done in two or three other centers in the country. It makes me extremely proud that Arkansas has an institution now that can carry out this type of care."

In March 1977 Arkansas Children's Hospital was notified that it would be the major beneficiary of the estate of Durbin Bond, a Little Rock investments manager who had died in October 1976 at the age of eighty-four. Following completion of the bequests to designated beneficiaries, Children's would receive over one million dollars from the Bond estate. This sum—the largest ever bequested to the hospital up to that time—would be used for the building program. "Mr. Bond's gift came to us at a time of great need," McGinness later reflected, "and it became the foundation upon which a children's medical center of excellence was built."

Dr. Betty A. Lowe was named Medical Director in May 1977, succeeding Dr. Gordon H. Green, who resigned to accept a position with the regional office of the United States Department of Health, Education and Welfare in Dallas, Texas. Along with her new duties, Dr. Lowe would continue serving as Director of Pediatric Education and also as director of the Rheumatology Clinic.

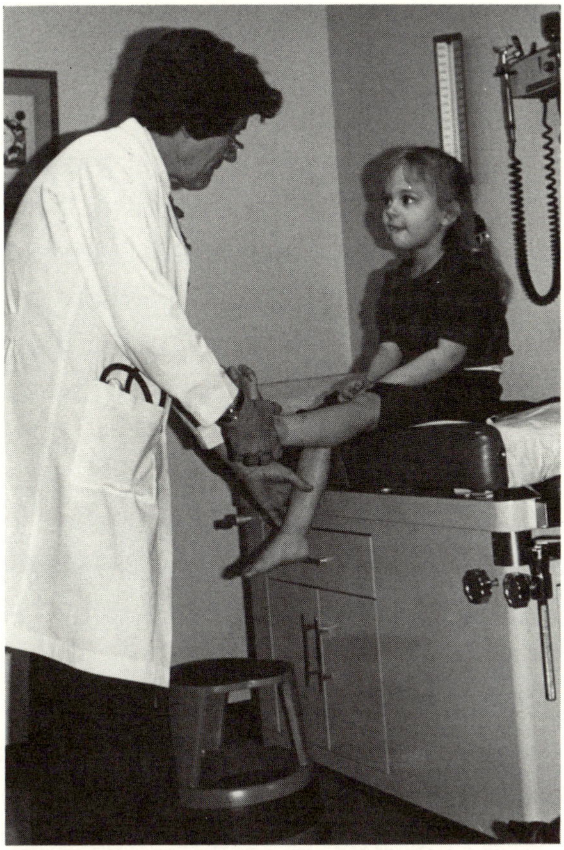

Dr. Betty Lowe examines three-year-old Misty Beck of Morrilton in the Rheumatoid Arthritis Clinic, ca. 1981.

Established with the aid of the Arkansas chapter of the National Arthritis Foundation, the Rheumatology Clinic provided evaluation and/or follow-up treatment for children with juvenile rheumatoid arthritis (JRA) and other connective tissue diseases. "Most people think of the elderly—never of children—having rheumatoid arthritis," asserted Dr. Lowe in a 1981 interview. "It truly is a disease of adulthood, and a major cause of disability in adults. But it does happen to children—about 250,000 in this country, with approximately 300 of those in Arkansas.

"Maintaining as normal a lifestyle as possible during bouts with JRA is one of the most important treatments," stressed the former Harvard Medical School instructor. "These children must go to school, must continue their education and they must have fun—that's all part of growing up.... It's always hard for children to see their way through a chronic disease—and sometimes it's even harder for the parents. But if they understand the disease, if their questions are answered, and if they are encourged to maintain their activities and goals, most of these children do very well."

In addition to providing check-ups, medication, physical therapy and other services for its young patients, the Rheumatology Clinic offered education and support for the entire family. "Children's Hospital wouldn't be doing what they're doing if it weren't for Dr. Betty Lowe," asserted Donald Riggin, former director of the Arkansas Arthritis Foundation. "She has the respect of every pediatrician in Arkansas. When you want someone to carry your banner, you pick the best, and that's what we did. You can't visit with Dr. Lowe without getting hyper about wanting to help kids."

Margaret Bogle, R.D. (Registered Dietician), joined the hospital staff in July 1977, as its first full-time nutritionist. Prior to coming to Children's, the Arkansas native had served as Professor of Nutrition at Texas Woman's University (TWU) at Denton and had worked as a registered dietician at several pediatric facilities in Texas and Oklahoma. She would earn a Ph.D. in nutrition from TWU in December 1989.

Under her leadership, the Nutritional Services Department conducted a one-year study to determine which foods children preferred. A menu was then developed which met nutritional requirements and at the same time let the children select foods which they were familiar with and would eat.

"We allow patients to choose their foods, even letting them write in items of their choice which do not appear on the menu. We get a lot of write-ins and many dieticians ask how we can keep all the different types of foods," Bogle told an interviewer in 1993. "Usually the children's choices are simple and easily filled, but for some children we do have to make special purchases. One child who was on chemotherapy wanted Tang breakfast drink and would not drink anything else. So we went out and bought a jar of Tang.

"I remember once we had two sisters in the Burn Center who wouldn't eat. They were young children—one was nine and the other six—and their parents had been killed in a fire. When I went to see them, they wouldn't talk to me, wouldn't tell me what they liked to eat. Nutrition is so critical to the healing process, we knew we had to get them to eat."

The following Saturday when the children's grandmother came to visit, Burn Center Director Dr. Fred T. Caldwell, Jr., phoned Bogle at home. "I came in and talked to the grandmother," Bogle remembered. "She told me that the youngsters liked biscuits and gravy. Well, Geneva Jackson got busy and 'whipped-up' some biscuits and gravy. When we took it to those kids, they were so excited! Their grandmother being there helped, but still they were so excited about having biscuits and gravy. They ate it and from then on they would talk to me about what they liked to eat.

" ...Another patient—a very articulate youngster—would always tell the staff what he wanted to eat, but when they brought it, he would eat very little. When I asked him why, he replied, 'It's not like my mother makes.' The next time his mother came I got her to go to the kitchen with me and cook a meal for her son. I watched how she did it. This made a real difference in getting him to eat.

" ...Eating habits and foods serve psychological and emotional as well as physical needs," Bogle explained. "And proper nutrition is so important to growth—especially in pediatrics—that we attempt to meet all nutritional requirements for each patient through innovative combinations of food or specially formulated tube feedings and formulas. We have special foods for a child having a birthday. We also celebrate Thanksgiving, Christmas and the Fourth of July with parties in the cafeteria for patients and their families. It helps alleviate some of the disappointment of being away from home on these special days."

A new twenty-bed Infant and Toddler Unit (ITU) was opened on the first floor of the hospital in August 1977. The girls' ward was moved to new facilities on the second floor in order to make space for this unit, whose cribs were situated around a large room in easy view of a central nurses' station. This unit, which served children from one to five years of age, had two "isolation" areas for patients with communicable diseases. In addition to cleaned and soiled utility rooms, the new ITU was equipped with a "bathing" room, specially designed to facilitate bathing of pediatric patients. A waiting room was also added across the hall from the ITU for the convenience of parents.

Bright green graphics decorated the walls of the new eight-bed girls' ward. Color television sets were suspended from the ceiling in view of each patient, and individual beds could be curtained off to allow for privacy when desired. Associate Administrator Russell Tolman told a group touring the rapidly expanding medical facility, "We used to think of space in terms of square feet, now we're utilizing square inches!"

In September 1977 Administrator McGinness announced that the Cosgriff Company, a fund-raising consultant firm headquartered in Omaha, Nebraska, had been retained to undertake a study to determine how much money could be raised from the private sector toward construction of a children's medical center of excellence.

Completed in December 1977, the Cosgriff study estimated the total cost of expanding the facility to 170 beds at $18 to $20 million. Of this sum, it was estimated that $3 million could be raised through a statewide fund drive. A portion of the remainder could be secured through various state, federal and private foundation grants. The consultants noted that Congress had recently voted to provide $1 million in federal funds for the first phase of the expansion—a three-story addition to the south wing of the hospital. Arkansas Senator John L. McClellan, Chair of the Senate Appropriations Committee, had placed these funds in an appropriations bill for the Labor and Health, Education and Welfare Departments.

Board approval of a major expansion program for Arkansas Children's Hospital was announced on January 24, 1978. "Arkansas lags behind other states in providing a complete range of services for its infants and children," asserted Leland McGinness. "To begin with, we do not have adequate space for our more than thirty clinics which annually serve about 60,000 outpatients. We have the expertise on our medical staff to perform the most delicate heart surgery, but neither we nor any other institution in Arkansas has the appropriate pediatric heart catheterization lab and cardiac surgical unit to permit prompt, accurate diagnosis and indicated surgical procedures. At the urging of physicians and health agencies throughout the state, the ... Board of Trustees, after a series of studies by outside consultants, has authorized ... a major expansion to meet these and other indicated needs."

In June 1978 long-time Board member Herschel Friday was named Chair of the "Children's Crusade," the hospital's $3.2 million public subscription campaign, which was scheduled to begin in early 1979. Dr. Roy B. Shilling, Jr., president of Hendrix College at Conway, had agreed to serve as State General Chair of the fund drive; Betty Bumpers, wife of United States Senator Dale Bumpers, had accepted the position of Honorary Chair; and Wayne Cranford, president of Cranford Johnson Hunt and Associates, Inc., a Little Rock advertising and public relations firm (now Cranford Johnson Robinson Woods), would serve as Chair of the campaign's public relations committee.

A petition was filed with the Pulaski County Clerk in August 1978 to place a proposal on the November 7 general election ballot for a one-mill county tax. If approved by voters, the increase would be used to help finance the operation of Arkansas Children's Hospital. Board member Frank D. White, president of Little Rock's Capitol Savings and Loan, who served as co-chair of the millage drive, explained, "The tax money is needed to help the hospital defray the estimated $800,000 in non-compensated medical care given annually and to allow it to continue adding services not now available in the state."

The proposed one-mill tax was approved by an overwhelming sixty-eight percent of Pulaski County voters. In the aftermath of this vote, the Pulaski County Quorum Court unanimously approved a resolution authorizing County Judge Roger Mears to accept the transfer of hospital properties, thus making the facility a county-owned hospital. The hospital was then leased by the county to the independent not-for-profit corporation which currently operated it. Under the terms of this agreement, the institution would continue to be known as Arkansas Children's Hospital.

Often, when children were admitted to Arkansas Children's Hospital from out of town, parents had to arrange for their own overnight accommodations. If they had friends or relatives in Little Rock, they might stay with them, or if they could afford it, stay in a local hotel or motel. Most parents, however, did not have access to friends' homes, and many could not afford to stay in commercial lodgings. And even if they could, the nearest accommodations were some two miles away, further than many parents wanted to be, especially if their child was in critical condition. Thus many parents slept in hospital waiting room chairs or in their cars.

Parents and Friends of Children, Inc. (PFC) was formed in July 1978 to raise funds for the purchase of a patient-parent guest house near the hospital. Little Rock attorney Sam Perroni was elected president of the organization. Fellow attorney Bruce Bethell of Fort Smith was secretary, and Barbara Lasley, a Little Rock homemaker, was treasurer. Judy Thurman, a member of the hospital's Development and Public Relations staff, served as the group's liaison with the hospital.

"With the exception of Judy, all of us are volunteers," Perroni told the *Arkansas Gazette*. "Actually, she's a volunteer, too, because all the work she does with us is in addition to her regular job with the hospital. Most of the rest of us have either had experience with one of our children being in the hospital or have been close in some way to a situation like that."

Contributions came from individuals and from organizations such as the Candlelighters, a support group for parents of children with leukemia and other forms of cancer, the American Association of Retired Persons, the Knights of Columbus, the Catholic Youth Organization, and the Second Presbyterian Church of Little Rock. By October, about $8,000 had been raised or pledged.

A suitable house was found in September 1978 at 1009 Wolfe Street, only a block and a half from the hospital. The two-story brick structure was owned by Lee and Linda Longstreet of Little Rock, who agreed to sell it to PFC for $120,000, with $5,000 taken off the purchase price as a donation to the organization. The house was on a quarter-block tract that also included two smaller frame houses, both of which were included in the sale.

"We were able to purchase the house, thanks to a loan from the First Commercial Bank of Little Rock," Perroni later told an interviewer. "Loaning us that money was an act of faith on the part of the bank. After we purchased the house, people could see what we were doing and donations increased.

"We're not planning anything opulent," said Perroni, "but we want it to be homey and comfortable. There will be roll-away beds for children to sleep on in their parents' rooms, and the living room will be a place for the parents and children to get together and talk. Parents will be invited to use the kitchen to cook their own meals. The resident managers won't be doing any cooking for the guests. Guests will buy their own food to cook, but cereal and sandwich makings will be kept on hand for snacks."

Progress was also being made in other areas. In August 1978 the hospital became the home base of a Neonatal Intensive Care Transport Service. Purchased with the aid of the State Health Department, the transport vehicle—a new van on a Ford chassis with a removable module equipped to care for two newborn infants—was available for use by referral nurseries throughout the state. It had wall-mounted oxygen, compressed air and suction, and was equipped with infant ventilators, IV pumps, warming beds, a blood gas machine, heart monitors and routine laboratory capabilities.

In its first six months, the neonatal transport logged over 9,000 miles transporting fifty-five newborns to hospitals across the state. In addition, it made fifteen transports in support of St. Vincent's Infirmary, which also maintained a neonatal transport service. Transport Coordinator Phillip J. Mains projected, based on these statistics, that it would be transporting twenty-five newborns per month by December 1979. "As physicians across the state are made aware of the service, more and more transports will be requested," said Mains. "We hope eventually to see a reduction in Arkansas' infant mortality rate.

"The people who serve on the transport van team are hand-selected for training," said Mains. "The stress level on those runs is tremendous. There are no back-up people as in a regular hospital situation, so the whole load is on the shoulders of those four people. Even the drivers are specially selected. Despite the stress, the work is rewarding," he asserted. "Like the time we had just completed one run, and were immediately called to El Dorado for another newborn. The baby's condition worsened just as we got there, and we spent four or five hours stabilizing the baby at the hospital there. When we finally got back to the van, there were buckets of fried chicken, soft drinks, and a pie inside. The local pediatrician knew we hadn't had a chance to eat all day, and he had gotten the food for us.

"Once when the transport van stopped for gas," recalled Mains with a chuckle, "the station attendant came out making comical remarks about 'such a big stork.' Another time, a guy brought out cigars for everyone, including the nurses!"

Medical Director Dr. Betty Lowe shared Mains' concern about the state's high infant mortality rate. "It was the era of level-three pediatric care," she remembered. "Medical science had developed technology which could warm, feed and even breathe for a newborn during its first critical weeks of life, but such advanced technology wasn't available in Arkansas. Dr. Bob Fiser and I were determined to change this situation."

In December 1977, Arkansas Governor David Pryor had appointed a "Special Committee on Maternity and Newborn Care." Chaired by Dr. Lowe, the committee's report, issued in June 1978, noted that in many areas of the state, expectant mothers could not receive the specialized care which they needed to ensure good health for themselves and their unborn infants.

"We have found that pediatricians, obstetricians, family practitioners and parents regard the inability to get care for critically ill infants as a major health care problem," asserted the report. "Therefore, it is submitted that an expenditure of $3.1 million per year to reduce maternal and newborn deaths and stillborns, to decrease the number of damaged newborns and to enhance the quality of life in Arkansas through improved perinatal health services is a justified financial request to the taxpayers of Arkansas."

Governor Pryor's decision not to convene a special legislative session in August 1978 had prevented immediate action on the committee's recommendation. When Bill Clinton was elected Governor in November of that year, the hospital quickly attracted the attention of his wife Hillary Rodham Clinton, who was already well known for her interest in child health-related issues. The Clintons, like thousands of their fellow Arkansans, became enthusiastic supporters of the state's only pediatric medical facility.

House Bill #972, sponsored by the Clinton administration during its first regular legislative session in February 1979, appropriated partial funding for the operation of a level-three neonatal intensive care unit (NICU) at Arkansas Children's Hospital. The bill provided $595,000 during fiscal year 1980, and $1,233,600 in fiscal year 1981. A separate administration bill appropriated $1,318,170 for construction and equipping of the NICU during the next biennium. As a result of this legislation, the hospital would have a ten-bed NICU in operation by early 1980, and a full twenty-bed unit in operation by mid-1982.

"We as Arkansans are fortunate to have elected such a conscientious group of lawmakers," wrote McGinness in the March/April 1979 issue of *The Achiever*, the hospital's bimonthly publication. "The very intensity and determination with which they have acted for the welfare of Arkansas' children is deserving of high praise. In passing this legislation, each member of the legislature has accepted the role of 'advocate' for Arkansas' children with unquestionable vigor and conviction.

"Regionalized perinatal health care was one of Governor Clinton's priorities when he took office last fall," asserted McGinness. "By calling for legislation that increased the availability of perinatal health care for children, he has fulfilled one of the earliest commitments he made to the people of Arkansas."

The Children's Renal Dialysis Center was another example of modern, high-tech pediatric medical care. Opened in January 1979, the center provided a full range of services to children with kidney disease. Treatment depended on the nature of the disease and its effects on kidney function. One form of treatment—the artificial kidney machine—was a lifesaving device for patients whose kidneys had failed to function. While it could not match the performance of the natural kidney, it helped preserve the lives of many patients.

"Since blood waste products would be fatal if allowed to accumulate for a few days, the artificial kidney machine provides the blood-washing which the human kidney usually performs," explained Dr. Watson Arnold, director of the clinic and Assistant Professor of Pediatrics at the University of Arkansas Medical Center from 1976 to 1988. "The blood slowly migrates over a cellophane membrane. On the other side of the machine is a salt cleansing solution which filters out body wastes.

"The patient is connected to the machine by a tube inserted in an artery of the arm or leg to conduct the blood into the machine and over one side of the cellophane filter. When cleansed, the blood is then routed back by another tube to a vein in the body. During the entire period of treatment, the blood flows through the machine, back through the patient's body, back through the machine, making the round trip about twice an hour, filtering out impurities each trip. Chronic dialysis patients usually require two or three treatments a week which last from four to eight hours each."

Noting that concern over duplication of medical services had led some to question the need for a specialized pediatric dialysis facility when adult facilities were available, Dr. Arnold pointed out that smaller coils and lines were essential for pediatric patients. Also, due to a child's small size and age, more supervision is required. "But the most important reason," he asserted, "is that children need to be with other children."

Among those attending the Little Rock Country Club on the night of February 15, 1979 to help kick off the "Children's Crusade," the statewide campaign to raise $3.2 million for the expansion of the hospital were United States Senator Dale Bumpers and his wife Betty as well as Governor Bill Clinton and Hillary Rodham Clinton. Senator Bumpers, the featured speaker for the evening, recalled that he and Betty had taken their daughter Brooke to Boston Children's Hospital in 1966 because there was "no center of pediatric excellence in Arkansas. Now," he declared, "the standards at Children's are excellent and the progress over the past eight years has been dramatic, but it is only an embryo of what we can and must do."

L to R: Sara Albertson, RN and Mildred Ward, Medical Library Director, along with Board of Trustees president Robert G. Cress and Administrator Leland McGinness. The oversized check for $51,306.17 represented the amount contributed by hospital employees to the Children's Crusade. May 1979.

By May 1979 the fund drive had passed the $2 million mark on the way to its goal of $3.2 million. At a press conference, Dr. Roy Shilling, state general Chair of the effort, disclosed that most of this sum had been raised in Pulaski County. "Our goal in central Arkansas is $2,679,000. So naturally this is the area in which we will concentrate our efforts before turning to our outstate areas in force," he explained.

Ed Penick, Jr., Chair of the "Crusade" in North Little Rock, and Jerry Crowley, Jacksonville Chair, reported that activities in their regions were well underway. Saline County Chair Ron Keumer reported five major gifts totaling $13,050. In response to reporters' questions, Dr. Shilling stated that gifts had ranged as high as $500,000, and thirty-three gifts of $10,000 or more had been received to date.

Dr. Shilling also noted that three groups had already met or surpassed their goals for the campaign. Members of the hospital's Board of Trustees and their friends had given $886,825, $11,625 above their goal. Hospital employees had given $51,306, $1,306 above their goal, and the hospital auxiliary had met its goal of $50,000.

In August 1979, the Arkansas Children's Hospital Developmental Center was opened. Established in cooperation with the State Health Department, the center provided diagnosis, evaluation and recommendations for follow-up treatment of children with developmental disabilities (cerebral palsy, mental retardation, etc.), learning disabilities, hyperactivity, delayed speech and other speech disorders, behavioral and emotional problems, general developmental delays and genetic disorders.

The Developmental Center's multi-disciplinary team included pediatricians, nurses, speech/language pathologists, social workers, psychologists and psychological examiners. Emphasis in this new program was on children between birth and five years of age. "Eventually we hope to increase the center's effectiveness," stated Assistant Administrator Bob Burton. "We hope to serve as an educational day school, offering special training, treating patients on a regional basis, and conducting workshops throughout the state."

Former Patient Leah Lasley at Ribbon-Cutting Ceremony
September 1979, with ACH Board President Robert Cress
and Leland McGuinness

"Within the next seven weeks, the South Wing addition of the hospital should begin to look finished," reported Associate Administrator Russell Tolman in June 1979. "The construction crews are making good progress." Despite inclement winter and spring weather which had caused Nabholz Construction Company of Conway to fall behind schedule, work was again on target, and the three-story addition to the South Wing of the hospital would be completed by August 1979 as originally planned.

Medical staff members, employees, volunteers and supporters were invited to attend open house activities on Sunday, September 23, 1979, at the new South Wing. Following a dedicatory prayer offered by Administrator McGinness and a brief welcome by Medical Director Dr. Betty Lowe, the guests looked on as Leah Lasley, the ten-year-old daughter of Mr. and Mrs. James Lasley of Little Rock, used a pair of oversized scissors to ceremoniously cut a wide white ribbon extending across the doorway to the new wing.

Two days later, following a final inspection by State Health Department officials, eleven-year-old Renee Routhier, daughter of Mary Routhier of Little Rock, became the first patient admitted to the new wing. Later in the day, other patients from within the hospital were transferred to the new addi-

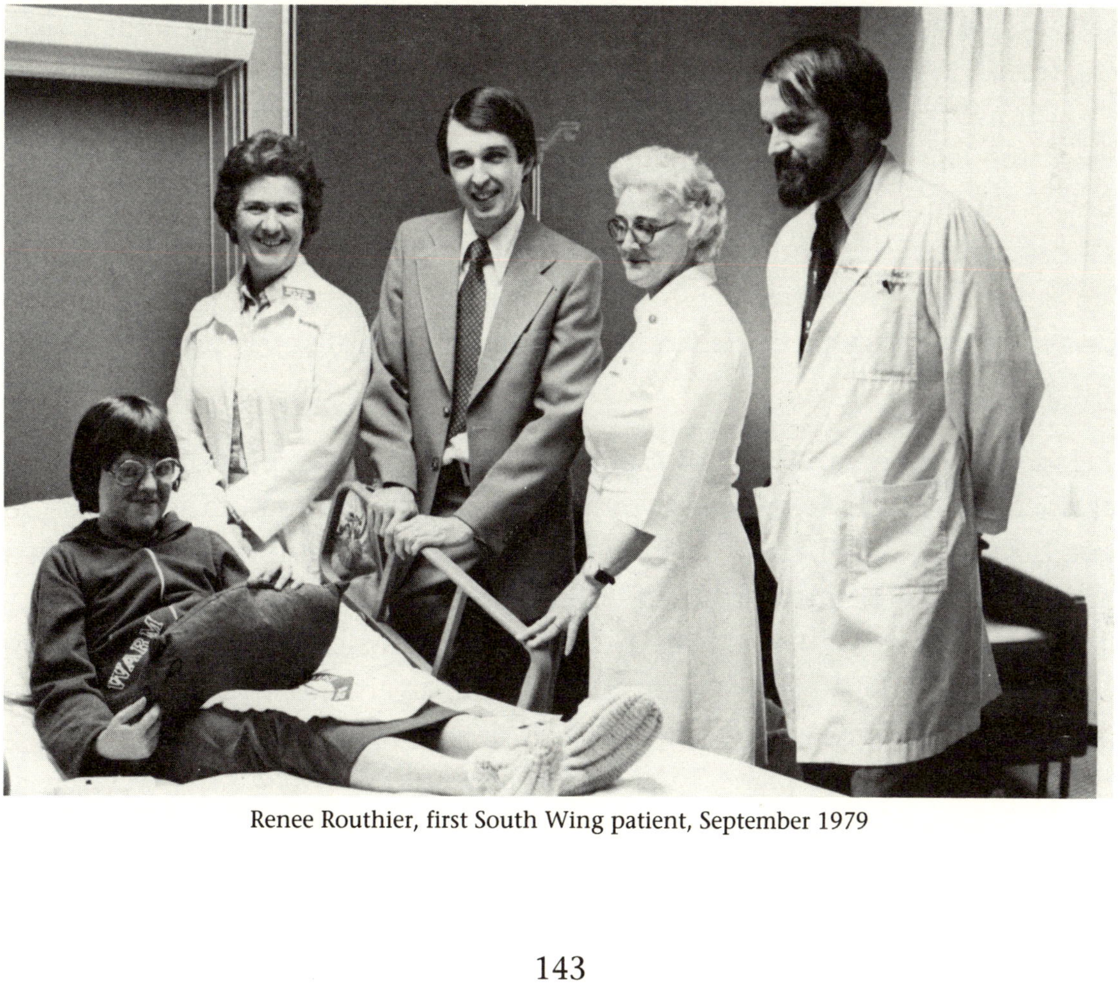

Renee Routhier, first South Wing patient, September 1979

tion. The $1 million expansion added twenty-four beds—four private rooms and ten semi-private rooms—giving the hospital a total of 126 beds.

Governor Clinton proclaimed Monday, October 1, 1979, as "Arkansas Children's Hospital Day" to coincide with the national "Child Health Day" proclaimed by President Jimmy Carter. In his proclamation, the Governor stated that the hospital's Board of Trustees, medical staff, administration and employees had proven their dedication to providing top-quality comprehensive health care. "Children's Hospital is sincere in its goal of providing the best possible health care to all children," he declared. "And it is committed to giving all Arkansas children the chance to lead healthy, productive lives."

Guy Amsler, Jr., succeeded Robert G. Cress as president of the Board of Trustees in November 1979. Amsler was a partner in the Barber, McCaskill, Amsler, Jones and Hale Law Firm. A former member of the State Board of Law Examiners, Amsler was at that time president of the Pulaski County Bar Association. He had served on the hospital panel for ten years.

On December 14, 1979, for the first time in its fifty-three-year history, Arkansas Children's Hospital exceeded the 100 mark in patient admissions. On that date, 101 children from throughout the state were hospitalized at the pediatric facility. Sixty-five percent of these patients were admitted from outside the Pulaski County area, and were treated for a variety of ailments ranging from low-back pain to leukemia and congenital heart defects.

During the 1979 holiday season, 169 groups—more than 800 persons—took time out of busy schedules to remember the patients at Arkansas Children's Hospital. A group of American Airlines flight attendants called on Christmas morning and asked if they could visit with the patients. Since their flight was not scheduled to leave until late that afternoon, they were away from their families and wanted to share their Christmas spirit with the hospitalized children.

Leland McGinness and his "All-Americans" knew that the creation of a pediatric medical center of excellence would hinge on whether or not the institution could secure a bond rating high enough to enable it to borrow money at a reasonable rate of interest. It had never before had a bond rating. In January 1980 McGinness, Dr. Lowe, Hillary Clinton, Guy Amsler, Board member James Foster and Dr. Harry Ward, Chancellor of the University of Arkansas School of Medicine, flew to New York City in an effort to secure one.

"Here we get on a plane," McGinness later told the *Arkansas Times* magazine, "Hillary is visibly pregnant. It's icy. We land in New Jersey and drive into the innards of Wall Street, to the offices of Moody's and Standard and Poor's, and we make our presentations.

"... I mean when it's a bad day, and when the First Lady of Arkansas is there, big with child, and she stands up and speaks, with no notes, about how this is the only children's hospital in the state and about how everybody supports it.... Well, we received a bond rating that was probably higher than we merited."

"Jim Foster, one of our Board members was there," remembered Dr. Lowe. "He worked for Stephens Inc., the ones who were going to float our bonds, and one of the men we were talking to challenged him on that. 'Isn't it a conflict of interest,' he asked, 'for you to work for Stephens and also be here representing Children's Hospital?'"

"Well, that may be," replied Foster, who was vice president of Municipal Underwriting for Stephens Inc. "But I'll tell you what. I owe my life to that hospital.... "

Jim Foster had no memory of his stay at the Arkansas Children's Home and Hospital in 1938. He had been only a few weeks old—an abandoned baby suffering from severe malnutrition—when a Columbia County sharecropper had brought him to the big brick building on Wolfe Street.

"The woman who brought me to the hospital had been trying to take care of me, but I was in pretty bad shape," said Foster. "Children's Hospital restored me to health and then, when I was six months old, found me a permanent home with wonderful parents."

He knew from the time he was old enough to understand that he had been adopted from the Arkansas Children's Home and Hospital. His adoptive parents told the story of visiting the Home desiring to adopt a child. They asked the woman who met them at the door if they could speak to Ruth Beall. Saying that Miss Beall was busy, the woman took the couple on a tour of the facility herself. Not until the Fosters had been thoroughly "checked out" did the woman introduce herself as Ruth Beall.

As a youngster, Jim Foster remembered driving by the institution and seeing the swings on the front lawn. "I've watched the hospital through the years and seen it grow into a first class medical facility," said Foster. "I was able to fulfill my desire to help the hospital when I was asked to become a member of its Board of Trustees."

"When Jim Foster told that story, ... well ... I can assure you that was the end of that particular discussion," said Dr. Lowe. "Finally, the guy we were talking to said, 'You know, you people don't really have a very sound financial base. But we've not heard such an enthusiastic presentation from such a broad spectrum of the community in a long time.' We got—what was it?—an A-rating for our bonds!"

Without formal ceremony, the long-awaited neonatal intensive care unit (NICU) opened on March 11, 1980. "Our neonatal ... nursery is unique in the state," Dr. Rick Nestrud, director of the new NICU, asserted in the *Achiever*. "Its uniqueness is not because we alone offer intensive care for newborns; other hospitals in the Little Rock area, particularly, are equipped to provide some level-three care. Instead, we are unique because we can provide the maximum level of specialized care for every possible health problem that a critically-ill newborn might encounter.

"To date six bassinets are in constant use," said Dr. Nestrud. "And the availability of specially-trained nurses will enable us to increase to eight in July. The nurse at the bedside is probably the most important member of the baby's health care team, and special training and experience are required. We are in the process of training these dedicated people ... and by fall we plan to open the entire twelve-bassinet unit."

Ground was broken on Sunday, March 30, 1980, for a $14 million addition which would double the size of the hospital. The event's featured speaker, Governor Clinton, reflected on the importance of health care services. "We don't need a facility of this type in every town in the state, or even in every major urban area, but having this center for referrals is something that Arkansas can be proud of," declared the future President of the United States, adding that it would be "penny wise and pound foolish" to forego expenditures on health care programs.

"If we can keep our hearts and heads together in public policy and private giving, then in the future politicians won't have to cite dismal statistics about Arkansas' health problems. One of my most cherished goals is to see the day when the infant mortality rate in Arkansas drops below the national average."

Following the governor's remarks, three young children wearing construction hard hats—each a former patient at the hospital—used oversized toy construction vehicles to "move the dirt." The youngsters were assisted by Governor Clinton.

On August 26, 1980, Leland McGinness announced the appointment of Randall L. O'Donnell, Ph.D., as administrator and chief operating officer of Arkansas Children's Hospital. McGinness would continue to serve as the medical facility's chief executive officer. "During the past few years, Children's has experienced dramatic growth and development, and the position of administrator/CEO once handled by one person, now demands the attention of two people," explained McGinness in making the announcement.

Dr. O'Donnell, a native of Gary, Indiana, came to Little Rock from Buffalo, New York, where he had served as Associate Administrator of Buffalo Children's Hospital for three years. He held a Ph.D. in hospital and health administration from the University of Iowa, where he had also served as an instructor.

"When I was sixteen," recalled Dr. O'Donnell in a 1993 interview, "I got a job as a surgery orderly at the hospital where my mother worked as a nurse. I enjoyed the work, especially working with children. When I entered graduate school, I knew I wanted to concentrate on children's health care."

In his new position, Dr. O'Donnell would have administrative responsibility for the day-to-day operation of the hospital—its fiscal affairs, nursing and patient services, personnel, physical facilities, special procedures and support services. He would report to the CEO, along with Medical Director Dr. Lowe and Larry Woodard, President of the Arkansas Children's Hospital Foundation. This change in administrative structure would allow McGinness to devote more time to the institution's expansion program and to strengthening its relationship with the University Medical Center and other outside agencies.

The Parents and Friends of Children, Inc., Guest House also opened its doors in August 1980. In its first four months of operation, more than ninety families stayed in the facility—families from throughout Arkansas as well as Missouri, Texas, Louisiana, Oklahoma and Arizona. Arkansas Children's Hospital was the first pediatric hospital in the nation to sponsor a parents' guest house without a major corporate backer.

On November 18, 1980, a special "Victory Celebration" was held in honor of the successful completion of the "Children's Crusade." Thanks to the leadership and hard work of hundreds of dedicated volunteers, the pediatric medical facility had surpassed its $3.2 million goal—raising more than $3.3 million.

"The crusade's success," declared honorary Chair Betty Bumpers, "was possible because each of you in your own special way has become involved. You have been willing to give of yourself for the benefit of others. And your participation will be reflected in the happy smiles of healthy children for many years to come."

As a result of the fund drive and the availability of additional interest from the tax-exempt bonds sold to finance the expansion, the Board of Trustees was able to approve several additional construction projects. A two-story addition to be located on the north side of the hospital—the largest single project approved—would house an enlarged cafeteria and nutritional services area as well as a purchasing department, offices and storage areas.

Construction of thirty-two additional patient rooms on the first floor of the new wing was also approved along with a neurosurgery operating room to be located in the surgical area of the new wing. In addition, the Trustees authorized the purchase of a cost-saving heat recovery system for the hospital's new physical plant.

No one was more pleased with this remarkable progress than Leland McGinness. In eight years as administrator of Arkansas Children's Hospital, the former air force officer and his "All-Americans" had converted retreat into advance. And it was only the beginning.

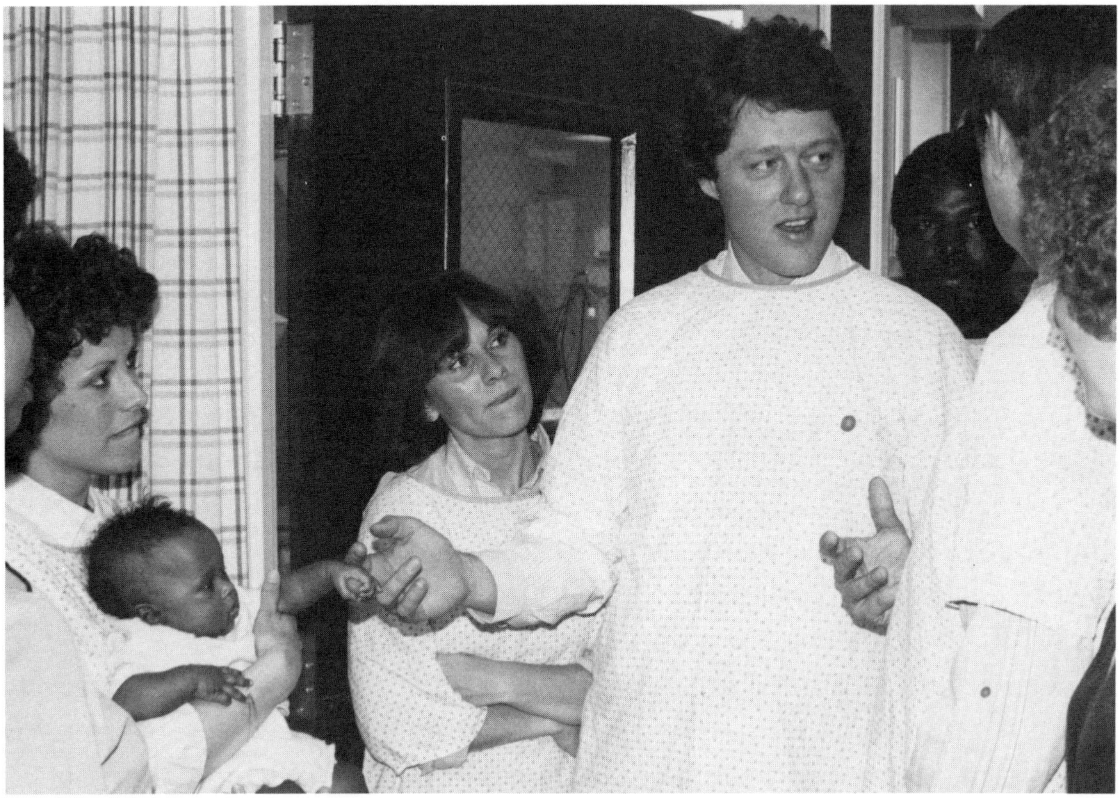

Governor Bill Clinton with nurses, March 22, 1981

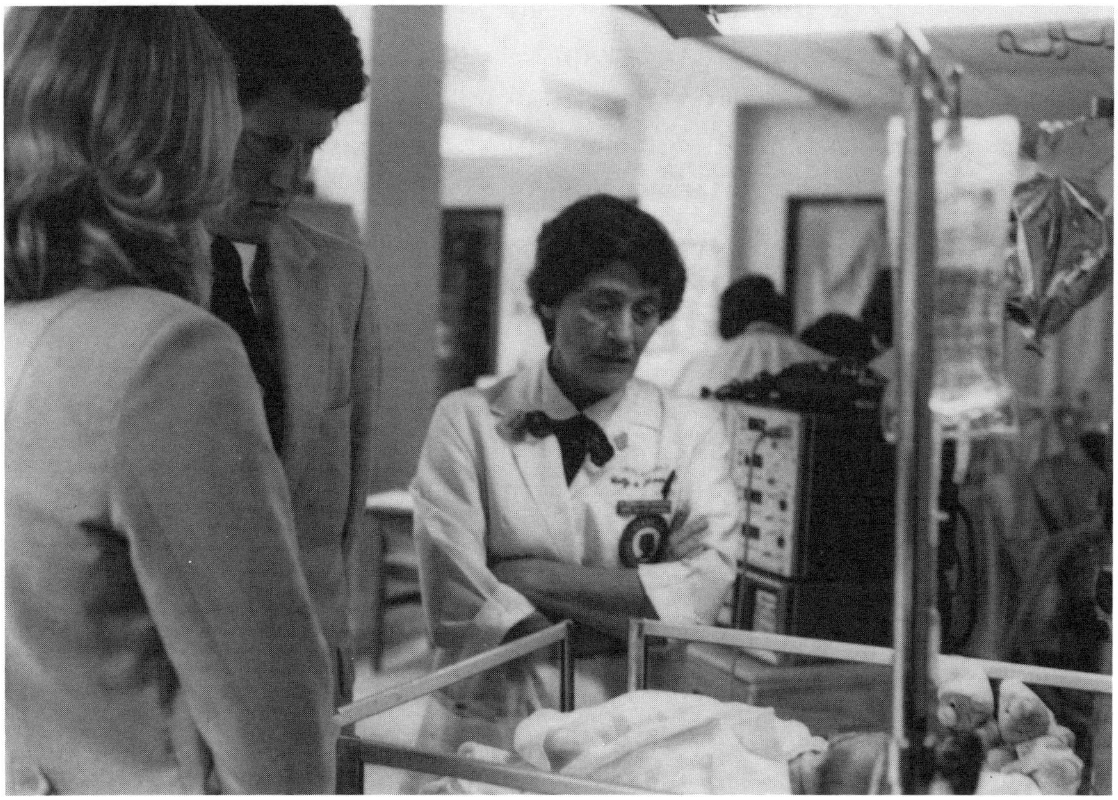

Dr. Betty Lowe with Governor Clinton, ca. 1980

Eight

ARKANSAS HAD A POPULATION OF ALMOST 2.3 million in 1980, about one percent of the nation's total population. The so-called "sunbelt migration"—the movement of people and industries from the northeastern United States to the South and Southwest—was a major factor in this population growth. The South's lower taxes and land costs made the region attractive to industry. Between 1955 and 1980, more than 4,000 industries had moved to Arkansas.

Agriculture continued to be an important factor in the state's economy. While the number of farms continued to decline, the average size of farms grew as small farms were sold to make larger ones. By 1980, more than one-third of Arkansas' agricultural production was being exported to other countries. In 1980 egg production alone exceeded the state's cotton crop in value—a fact which would have astounded earlier generations of Arkansans.

By 1980 more than half of Arkansas' population lived in towns of over 2,500 people. Tourism had become a major industry as visitors discovered the state's natural beauty. Many counties—especially those around the man-made lakes and in the northwest corner of the state, were experiencing some of the nation's highest population growth rates.

The decade would see increased state funding for public schools, accelerated highway construction and a greater emphasis on the conservation of natural resources. Nowhere was this new spirit of optimism and progress more apparent than at Arkansas Children's Hospital.

Eighteen healthy babies and their proud parents—from Fort Smith, Helena, Dumas and even as far away as Bokoshe, Oklahoma—returned to the hospital on Sunday, March 22, 1981, to show off their progress to the people who had cared for them during the first critical weeks of the children's lives, when they had been patients in the neonatal intensive care unit (NICU). "They're the most heartwarming sight I've ever seen," declared a nurse at this first anniversary reunion. "It makes it all so worthwhile."

It was often hard for the nurses and doctors to recognize their former patients—many of them now learning to walk—as the two- or three-pound premature infants whom they had cared for. "Can you guess who this is?" one NICU staff member, holding a baby, would ask another.

A special "diploma" of graduation from the NICU was presented to each former patient and their parents by former Governor Clinton, his wife Hillary and Dr. Rick Nestrud, the unit's medical director. As Governor, Clinton had been instrumental in helping to establish the unit. Since its opening in March of 1980 the NICU had cared for more than 175 critically ill newborns.

The Clintons enjoyed a tour of the facility by Dr. Robert Arrington, Director of Neonatology. The future president of the United States remarked that it was incredible that babies so small could be kept alive. "It's almost unbelievable," he added, "that they'll one day be as large as you and me."

In pointing out the highly advanced nature of the unit's equipment, Dr. Arrington called attention to an instrument capable of feeding an infant as little as a half-teaspoon of milk over a 24-hour period. "We didn't know how to feed them before," he asserted.

Asked what the hospital did before the unit opened, Dr. Arrington replied, "We did the best we could and we saved some of them." He pointed to a baby brought to Children's by the NICU transport van from Texarkana who weighed only nineteen ounces. "He wouldn't have made it. He would have died in Texarkana."

Two days after the NICU reunion, the traditional evergreen tree was lifted to the highest point of the hospital's new east wing during "topping out" ceremonies when the final beam of the structure was lifted into place. More than 100 guests attended the ceremony, a centuries-old tradition which signifies the completion of a major phase in a building project. The beam was signed by everyone present before being lifted into place to become a permanent part of Arkansas Children's Hospital.

Topping Out Ceremony, March 24, 1981

In August 1981 the hospital's intensive care unit, general pediatric clinic, outpatient registration and renal dialysis clinic moved into "Area B," a two-story area linking the existing facility with the new three-story addition which was still under construction. "This initial move," declared CEO Leland McGinness, "represents the beginning of the achievement of our goal to progress and grow as a pediatric medical center of excellence."

Two months later, in early October 1981, the hospital's new 24-hour emergency room opened in the new addition. Later that month, the radiology department completed its move to the new addition. "The main advantage of our move is that all of us are now located in the same area," said Charlene Arnold, technical director of radiology. "Before we were spread down three corridors and the physicians' offices were in another building."

Groundbreaking for expansion, March 30, 1980

Also in October, the new Ambulatory (one-day) Surgery Center opened. One-day surgery programs—a growing trend in hospitals nationwide—were designed to cut health care costs and to free additional bed space for other patients. "Our ambulatory surgery program provides these advantages, but maintains the same high quality medical standards for which Children's Hospital is known," said Dr. Walter Guinee, the program's medical director. "It's designed for children who are basically healthy and are going to have low-risk elective surgical procedures."

Only procedures which required less than one hour of surgery and three hours of recovery time, such as inserting ear tubes for infections, hernia repairs, circumcisions and cast changes requiring anesthesia were done at the Ambulatory Surgery Center.

On the day of surgery, the patient and parents arrived forty-five minutes to an hour before the time the surgery was scheduled. A nurse took the patient's vital signs and gave him or her a pair of hospital pajamas. After changing, the patient was then taken to the surgery area.

Following surgery, one parent was allowed in the recovery room until the patient was ready to go back to the Ambulatory Surgery Center. There, both parents could be with their child for two to three hours before returning home.

A nurse made follow-up phone calls to the family twenty-four hours after surgery. If everything was going well contact with the family ended. If there were problems, the child's physician was notified. "The Ambulatory Surgery Center helps everyone involved," declared Dr. Guinee. "And we expect the number of outpatient surgeries to double in the next few years."

In November 1981 the Central Arkansas McDonald's Hamburgers Co-Op announced a long-term financial commitment to assist Parents and Friends of Children Inc. (PFC), the organization which had established and maintained the patient-parent guest house. McDonald's sponsored patient-parent guest houses near pediatric hospitals in thirty-two cities around the nation. Arkansas' First Lady Gay White and Philadelphia Eagles football great Bill Bergy—a former All-American at Arkansas State University—were among those present on January 8, 1982, when the guest house was officially renamed the Ronald McDonald House of Arkansas. Governor Frank White was a former member of the hospital's Board of Trustees. The PFC's Board of Directors would continue to operate the guest house which, since its opening, in 1980 had hosted the families of 385 children.

By 1980 Children's was a major teaching hospital, a "school" where the pediatricians of the future—as well as other physicians, nurses, and a variety of paramedical professionals—all received "hands-on" training in pediatric medicine. Often, a child who was a patient at Arkansas Children's Hospital would be seen by a number of different physicians. Groups of doctors and medical students made daily rounds through the hospital, discussing the various cases and examining the patients involved.

"It may be disconcerting at first to have four or five different people examine a patient," said Dr. Robert Fiser, Chair of the department of pediatrics at the University of Arkansas Medical Center and chief of pediatrics at Children's. "But one advantage of a teaching hospital is that a doctor is in-house twenty-four hours a day, and can be at a child's side immediately, providing the necessary treatment and reassuring worried parents."

The immediate availability of a physician was only one of the advantages provided by the educational aspects of the hospital. "Many health care institutions have found that doing patient care in a teaching facility results in better patient care," reflected Dr. Lowe. "In trying to explain things to students, your thought processes will turn up more ideas."

Most members of the hospital's regular medical staff also held teaching positions at the University Medical Center. Thus they taught medical students and residents in the classroom as well as in a clinical setting. "The best teaching tool, the best role model for students," declared Dr. Fiser, "is to see the excellence in patient care given by the staff at Children's Hospital.

"The students and residents are here to learn, as well as to question, to explore and to provide care. I've always felt that you should have a continual questioning of everyone so you can obtain the widest possible variety of opinion. When a patient has a problem," he asserted, "the greater the number of people who know about it, the greater the fund of knowledge from which to draw in seeking a solution. And the best opinion may be presented by that junior medical student."

"Our patients and their parents generally appreciate the increased attention they get from more people seeing them," said Dr. Lowe. "Most parents appreciate the fact that the residents are in-house 24 hours a day—and they like that. Many times they find it easier to converse with a medical student than with the attending physician, because they may feel less intimidated and the student may have more time to spend with them."

This education in patient care did not come only from the regular staff physicians, however. The nurses and paramedical professionals played an important role in the educational process. "Their obligations and commitment at Children's goes beyond just patient care," observed Dr. Fiser. "They've all been supportive of this concept for a long time."

"After seeing the excellent patient care provided, and the enthusiasm and commitment of the students, very few parents ever complain about having a medical student caring for their child," said Dr. Fiser. "All students and residents," he added, "are supervised by staff physicians who have the final responsibility for each patient. It's just a matter of educating the public as to what a teaching hospital is."

Arkansas Children's Hospital had made a major financial commitment to the education of these future physicians—with more than $500,000 earmarked for residents salaries in 1981-82. "This commitment is one way in which our Board of Trustees has accepted the responsibility to help assure quality health care for children across the state," said Leland McGinness. "We are extending our commitment, through these students and residents, to children throughout Arkansas today—and to future generations by contributing to a quality education for the physicians who will care for them in the future."

In 1981, 138 junior medical students came to Arkansas Children's Hospital for their basic clinical pediatric training. Senior medical students could return for an elective rotation, or in a specialized area such as pediatric ophthalmology, surgery or orthopedics. A student who chose pediatrics as a primary care specialty could apply for a house position at the hospital.

"The residency program at Children's has become more popular, and more of our residents end up staying in Arkansas afterwards," observed Dr. Lowe in a 1981 interview. "And we are getting better and better applicants from all over the United States. We're becoming recognized as one of the best residency programs in the South. And almost all of them will tell you that they came here because of the commitment to excellence at all levels."

While the residency program at Children's is now recognized as one of the best, the life of a resident is far from easy. "They must deal with long hours of hard work while trying to understand and retain an incredible amount of knowledge," reflected Dr. Fiser. "But the thing that really gets to most of them is the dying child. When there's one that they've worked with for weeks and been closely involved with, and then the bottom falls out, it's hard. The constant question is always, 'Is there anything else I could have done to save that child's life?'"

"It's a tough grind," he added. "They've got three intensive years to prepare for the rest of their lives, so we can't coddle them. We're very straightforward with them. But we also try to show an attitude of care and concern for them. Knowing that we realize their worth is very meaningful to them at this special time in their lives."

Nurses from six Arkansas nursing schools also receive their practical experience in pediatric care at Arkansas Children's Hospital. "It gives us a chance to show future nurses what acute care nursing is all about," said Jewell Mainard, associate director of nursing from 1972 to 1984. "And we hope many of them like pediatric nursing well enough to come back after they graduate."

Board of Trustees member James Penick, Jr. (left) and Administrator Leland McGinness (right) talk with Governor Bill Clinton and First Lady Hillary Clinton following groundbreaking ceremonies for a $14 million expansion of the medical facility. March 30, 1980.

In addition, the hospital provides training in pediatric nutrition for dietetic interns. "They learn how pediatric nutrition differs from adult nutrition," said Dr. Margaret Bogle, director of nutritional services from 1978 to 1990. "They also learn the role of food service in patient care as well as how to counsel parents and work with members of the medical team."

Pharmacy students also do rotations at Children's, both in the pharmacy and in working with drug therapy in patient care. Other students in respiratory therapy—forty of them in 1981—rotate through the institution each year, learning how the care of newborns and children differs from adult care, especially with regard to the unique equipment needed for pediatric respiratory patients.

"The function of a teaching hospital ultimately becomes a two-way street," asserted Dr. Fiser. "The students provide new ideas and enthusiasm and the staff provides an education to the physicians and medical professionals of the future. And it all results in better care for the children. We're going to be at the forefront in a leadership role. That's what Children's Hospital is striving for. Just because kids are born in Arkansas, they shouldn't have to settle for second-rate medical care."

A miracle of modern medical science saved young Caleb Adcock from a life of sterilized isolation when in November 1981 he became the recipient of the first bone marrow transplant ever performed at Arkansas Children's Hospital. Caleb's case was particularly unusual because his mother served as the donor. This mother-to-son procedure had been attempted only a few times previously.

Caleb and his parents, Steve and Peggy Adcock of the Miller County community of Doddridge, came to Children's Hospital when their nine-month-

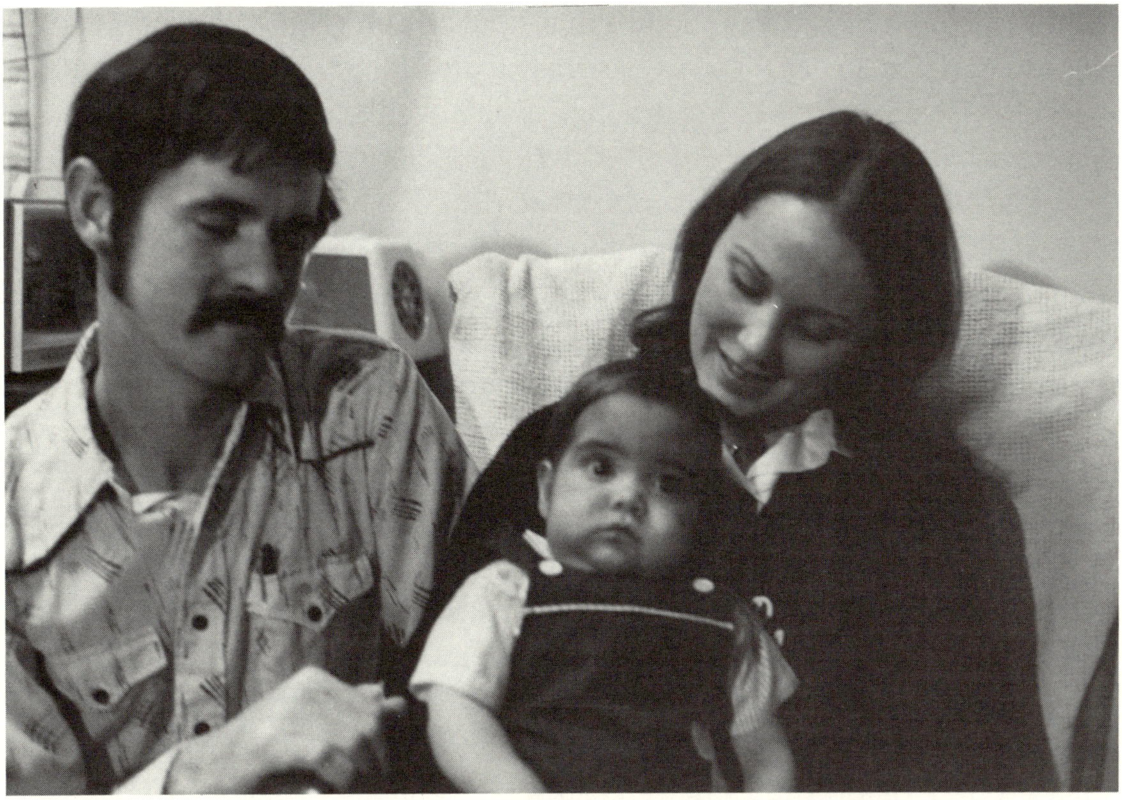

Steve and Peggy Adcock with their son Caleb, December 1982

old son was transferred from Texarkana where he had been treated for weight loss and a lung infection. Five days later, Caleb's condition was diagnosed by immunologist Dr. Russell Steele as severe combined immunodeficiency—a rare disease marked by the absence of functional white blood cells. Young Caleb had no natural immunities to disease.

The preferred treatment for severe immunodeficiency is bone marrow transplantation. Brothers or sisters usually are the best donors, but because families are smaller and because the genetic disease often causes the death of other siblings, appropriate donors are usually not available.

An alternative treatment was to keep Caleb in an isolation unit similar to that of the much-publicized "bubble boy" in Houston. However, medical and social problems during long-term support made this approach less desirable. This option was discussed with the Adcocks and the decision was made to attempt a bone marrow transplant at Arkansas Children's Hospital.

"The new pediatric intensive care unit and the presence of Dr. Debra Browning, trained in pediatric critical care, influenced my decision," said Dr. Steele. "We also have specially-trained nurses, residents and laboratory personnel who are as good or better than any in the country." Preparation for the transplant also involved the hospital's pulmonologist, Dr. Robert Warren; surgeon, Dr. Steve Golladay; gastroenterologist, Dr. Arthur Euler; and specialists from other pediatric disciplines—all available at Arkansas Children's Hospital.

Dr. Steele informed the Adcocks of the risks of a bone marrow transplant. The chance of success was only one in a thousand and there was a possibility that the procedure would prove fatal. But the Adcocks also knew there was a strong possibility that the knowledge gained in treating their son could benefit other children. "Faith in God was a big factor in our decision for Caleb and in our acceptance of the things he had to endure," reflected Steve Adcock. "Without that faith, without drawing on the Lord, we would have come apart."

The search for the best bone marrow donor for Caleb began with his four-year-old brother Josh since siblings are usually the best tissue-type matches. But Josh was not a good match. Further testing determined that his mother was the closest match and the best donor. Before the transplant Caleb's lung infection had to be cleared up and a feeding tube was placed in a main vein to allow intravenous feeding.

"Caleb had to be in an optimal nutritional state prior to the transplant," explained Dr. Steele. "His nutrition was monitored closely and after three or four weeks he looked like a 'Gerber baby.'" As the youngster was being prepared for the transplant, his physicians and nurses were preparing for the weeks after the procedure. Caleb would face dangerous graft-versus-host reactions when his body received the cells from his mother, therefore it was important to anticipate those reactions and plan possible treatments.

Since a bone marrow transplant had never before been performed at Children's, nurses worked with other hospital departments to develop an isolation procedure and arrange for the sterile equipment necessary to set up a special isolation room. Lisa Solls, R.N., and others worked to develop a nursing care plan to meet the patient's unique needs.

On November 24, 1981, Caleb's mother was taken to an operating room where, with a large bore needle, bone marrow was aspirated from her pelvic bone. The procedure took about an hour. This bone marrow was then processed in the hospital laboratory to isolate "stern cells" which were transplanted to Caleb by a simple technique resembling a blood transfusion.

"The stern cells seek sites in the body where they can grow," explained Dr. Steele. "That place was Caleb's bone marrow." Though the transplant itself was an unspectacular procedure, everyone involved knew the worst was yet to come. The graft-versus-host disease was expected in seven to eight days, and it appeared on schedule. It caused a rash which turned Caleb's skin lobster-red, as well as causing liver disease, lung disease and problems with his gastrointestinal tract.

Pediatric subspecialists treated these problems while the toddler continued to be kept in strict isolation so that no other diseases could further complicate his plight. Caleb's nurses and doctors were the only people allowed in his isolation room. The nurses performed housekeeping functions and procedures such as changing out oxygen equipment which would normally be done by respiratory therapists. His parents could see him only through the glass wall of his room. "For two weeks we could only walk to the window and look," remembered his mother. "We were afraid that he would forget us."

They were reassured and cheered by Caleb's nurses. The first time the Adcocks saw their son's bright red rash, nurse Debbie Dorman held up a sign reading *Palm Springs Vacation.* "I was there when his mother got to come in for the first time," said Dorman. "It was the most excited Caleb had been in three weeks."

Because of the limited number of persons allowed to enter Caleb's room, his primary nurses often came in on their days off to care for him. "I'll never say anything bad about a nurse," declared his mother with a smile. "To show you how much faith we had in them, we left Caleb over Christmas Eve to give our son Josh as normal a Christmas as possible."

Caleb's physicians regulated his drug dosages in an effort to depress the graft-versus-host disease, but not prevent engraftment (growth) of the new cells. "That was the tricky part," remembered Dr. Steele. "Since Caleb's circumstances were unique, the dosages were experimental." Another experimental portion of his treatment was the use of transfer factor made at Arkansas Children's Hospital. This transfer factor, which only three immunological centers in the nation were studying at that time, was extracted from white blood cells. It gave Caleb's white blood cells "memory capacity," the ability to remember how to fight off infection.

While the blood cells transplanted from his mother were growing in Caleb's bone marrow, Dr. Steele monitored the baby's blood. The patient was in a steady graft-versus-host reaction for about a month after the transplant. He was transferred out of intensive care the week after Christmas 1981—almost ten and a half months after undergoing the bone marrow transplant.

Gradually he was weaned from the oxygen and intravenous feeding. Drug dosages also were decreased gradually. In late January 1982 Caleb Adcock went home to the family farm near Doddridge. Dr. Steele would see him regularly and for the first few months he would be treated as a newborn who has not fully developed immunities. "The main concern is for him not to contract chicken pox," said Peggy Adcock. "And we'll have to keep him at home away from crowds."

During their long stay the Adcocks had lived at the Ronald McDonald House, making periodic quick trips to their parents' homes to visit their other child. "The people at the Ronald McDonald House have been a blessing," declared Steve Adcock. "We wouldn't have made it without their friendship and support in addition to a place to stay. We think the Lord worked a miracle through the doctors and others at Arkansas Children's Hospital."

On February 14, 1982—Valentine's Day—the first patients were transferred to the new patient rooms on the third floor of the new east wing. Four new nursing stations, new private and semi-private rooms providing sixty-two beds, and a playroom made up the new floor. The individual nursing units were called *Three-Blue, Three-Green, Three-Gold* and *Three-Orange*—with the colors of the rooms and nursing stations corresponding to the names. The playroom was located in the center of the new floor.

"The nurses were so excited about the new facilities," recalled Jewell Mainard, associate administrator of nursing from 1972 to 1984. "The new areas were so cheery, with big windows and bright colors. They enabled us to put all the

Jim Ed Brown visits with hospital patients, November 1981

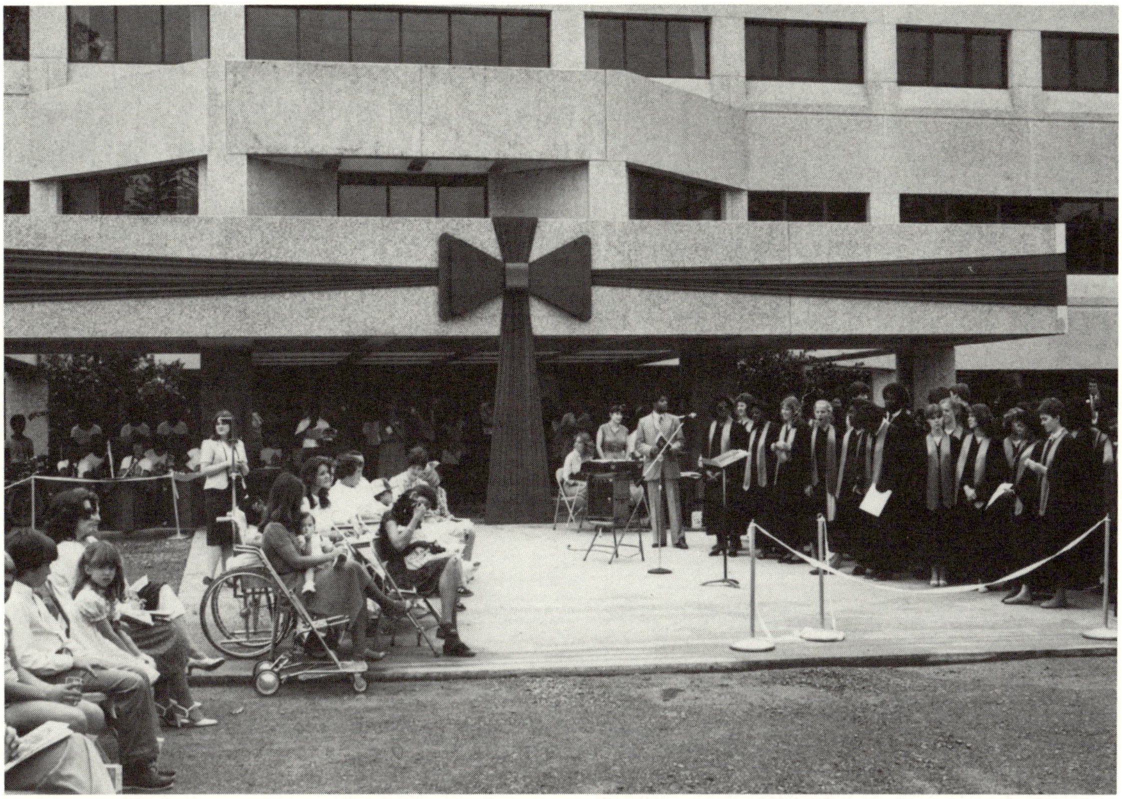

East Wing "gift-wrapped" for dedication, May 22, 1982

children in private or semi-private rooms. And having the parents able to stay comfortably with their child was so much better."

A new chapel was completed in April 1982. Located on the second floor across from the NICU waiting room, it had been built with an anonymous donation in memory of Pamela Friday Freeman, daughter of long-time Board member Herschel Friday.

Governor Frank White and First Lady Gay White, United States Senator Dale Bumpers and his wife Betty and hundreds of other hospital employees and supporters were on hand on Saturday, May 22, 1982, for the formal dedication of the new east wing. The night before the dedication, country music star Jim Ed Brown—a native Arkansan—had joined the Arkansas Symphony Orchestra for a concert, with all proceeds from the event going to the hospital. "God works in mysterious ways. He certainly has in my life," said Brown, explaining that he had been wanting to get involved in something outside of music. "I don't know how Children's Hospital knew I was looking for something like that, but it's just what I wanted. What could be better than helping children?"

Completion of the new east wing expanded the hospital's capacity to 169 beds plus twenty level-three NICU bassinets—making it one of the twenty largest pediatric medical centers in the nation. In addition to fifty-nine new private and semi-private patient rooms, it included six new surgery suites, a new and expanded burn center, and a new 24-hour emergency room as well as new facilities for pediatric intensive care, cardiac catheterization, radiology, kidney dialysis and numerous other support services.

A unique three-story-high motorized sculpture decorated the hospital's new lobby. Created by Hot Springs artist Harry Loucks, this sculpture featured an "elf society"—dozens of tiny figures hand-crafted by Little Rock artists Jane Hankins and Kathy Porterfield. Different elements of the artwork were visible at each level of the lobby. Hanging from wires at all levels of the structure were elves at play—a carousel, a tightrope walker, a Raggedy Ann riding in a bucket—and these elements were continually moving up and down between the second and third floor levels.

The dominant element, which hung on the second floor level, was a clock surrounded by dozens of rays, "like the rays of the sun, to symbolize light and health," explained Loucks. The theme of this artwork was ex-

ACH in 1982 following East Wing completion

pressed in a phrase conceived by Administrator Dr. Randall O'Donnell and lettered over the new main entrance: "Fear not illness ... this place of care, love and hope is for you."

In conjunction with the dedication of the new wing, the Playaway Gift Shop opened its doors for the first time. The gift shop, located near the hospital's main entrance, had been designed, stocked and would be run by the Arkansas Children's Hospital Auxiliary.

Jane Miller, a former president of the auxiliary, had spearheaded the drive to establish the shop. The organization's fund-raising efforts were boosted by an anonymous $5,000 challenge gift which it was able to match through private donations. "This is the first time we've had to solicit funds," said Miller. "It's not something any of us likes to do, but it's just to get the shop started. Once Playaway is off the ground, all proceeds will go to the hospital."

Because of the confines of a hospital bed, all games and toys had to be carefully selected. "All games in Playaway are self-contained and don't have separate pieces which can roll on the floor so that the nurse has to be called in to pick things up," explained purchasing manager Casey Holbert. There were also no bean bags or bean-stuffed items in the shop because beans could be swallowed or end up in a child's ear or nose. All figurines and toys were non-toxic, durable and usually unbreakable.

The emotional impact of items stocked in the shop was also carefully weighted. "There's no Snow White and the Seven Dwarfs with spooky wicked witches, and you won't find Hansel and Gretel here," asserted Holbert. Instead, the shop was filled with colorful little furry animals, books, smiling dolls such as Raggedy Ann, Little Orphan Annie and the family of Smurfs, stars of the popular Saturday morning cartoon. "Puppets are favorite items and one of our biggest clientele for them is the doctors," noted Holbert. "Kids are sometimes frightened of the doctors at first. A puppet can ask questions and get answers when a doctor might not be able to."

Eight-year-old Tommy Castleberry, Jr. of the Bradley County community of Hermitage became the first patient ever to undergo a kidney transplant at Arkansas Children's Hospital in September 1982. (Earlier transplants on ACH patients had been performed at the University Medical Center.) Thanks largely to its recently completed surgery facilities, Children's had been approved as a renal transplant center.

Three times a week for almost two years, Tommy and his mother, Mabel, had made the trip to Little Rock where Tommy underwent dialysis at the Children's Renal Center. Tommy had been born with only one kidney and when it had stopped functioning it became necessary to start dialysis—the process of mechanically cleansing the blood—which allowed him to live without a functioning kidney.

When the decision was made for Tommy to undergo a transplant, his remaining kidney was removed. At eight years of age, Tommy was a good candidate for a transplant, but he was younger and smaller than any child who had ever received a kidney transplant in Arkansas. "Because of Tommy's size, we decided to do the transplant here at Children's," explained Dr. Watson Arnold, chief of pediatric nephrology from 1976 to 1990. "We had the equipment and the expertise to handle someone Tommy's size and an excellent Pediatric Intensive Care Unit."

The Immunology lab did a series of tests to determine the best donor from among Tommy's living relatives. His father was the closest tissue match. Leslie Dinwiddle, transplant coordinator at the University Medical Center, gave an inservice for Children's Hospital personnel who would be working with the Castleberrys.

Tommy was admitted to Children's a week before the transplant to make sure he was in the best possible condition for surgery. During this time he continued dialysis and took medication which prepared him to receive his father's kidney. His father was admitted to the hospital three days before the transplant. The forty-four-year-old brick mason had never been hospitalized before and could not recall ever having been sick.

Tonda Bowen, a nurse on Three-Green, recalled the adjustment of treating an adult. "I went to pick up his breakfast tray one morning and said, 'Did you eat all your breakfast?' before I realized I was talking to an adult."

Tommy underwent dialysis for a final time and the last laboratory tests were completed just one day before the transplant. On the morning of September 28, 1981, Tommy and his father were taken to adjacent operating rooms. There, a team of surgeons worked to remove one of the senior Castleberry's kidneys, while at the same time other members of the transplant team prepared his son's body to receive the organ.

Following the operation, the senior Castleberry was returned to his room on Three-Green and Tommy was placed in isolation in the Pediatric Intensive Care Unit (PICU). Because rejection is more common in the first few days after a transplant, PICU nurses watched closely for changes in the

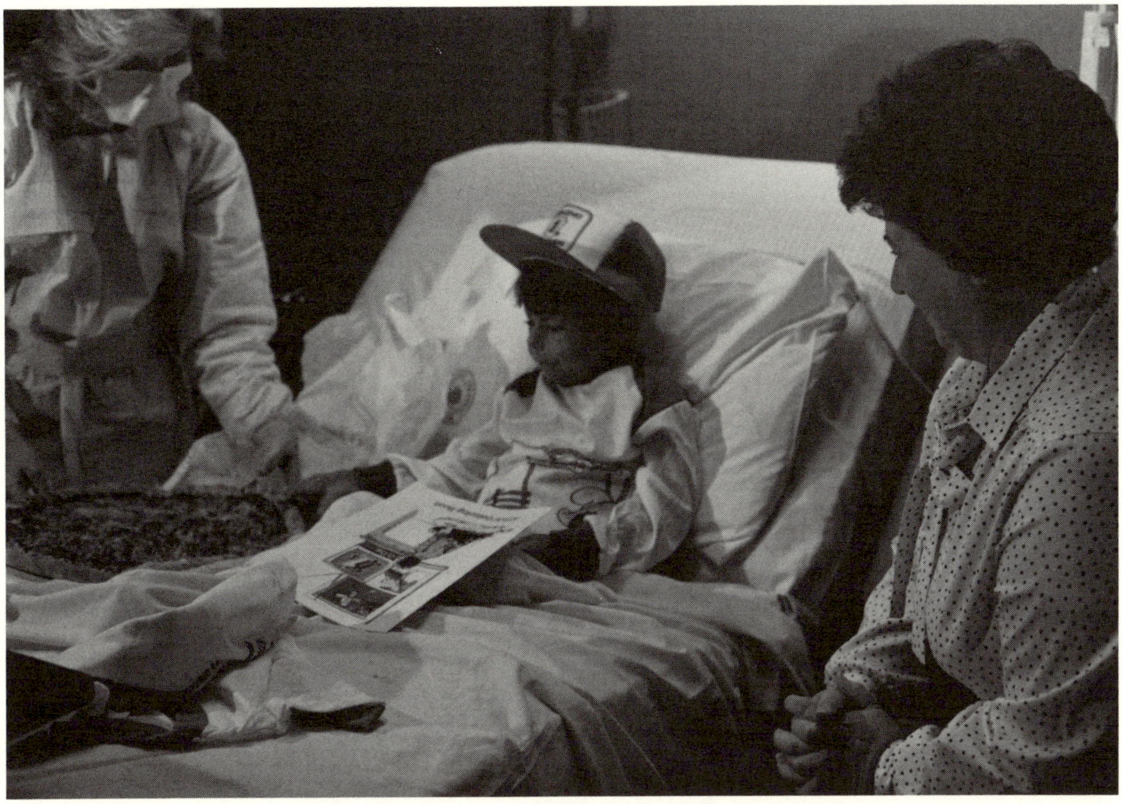

Tommy Castleberry enjoys a pizza, September 1982

youngster's condition. His mother stayed at his bedside and his father was able to come to PICU for a visit a couple of days after the surgery.

Tommy was kept in isolation because his immune system had been weakened by immunosuppressant drugs. These drugs were administered to suppress the reaction of his body's immune system to the foreign tissue of his new kidney. He would continue taking these drugs, in decreased dosages, for the rest of his life.

Although Tommy was listed in serious condition immediately after surgery, he recovered at the expected rate and by the sixth day after surgery, he was eating solid foods and was transferred to Three-Green. "He's doing just great and there's no sign of rejection," said Dr. Arnold. "He'll be able to do just about anything when he recovers, except play contact sports."

Tommy was able to eat just about anything too—a big switch from his former low-salt, limited-liquids diet. To celebrate, Dr. Arnold and the staff on Three-Green arranged a pizza party in Tommy's room. The delighted youngster enjoyed his first pizza in three years.

"It's hard to believe I don't have to worry about food and fluids now," said Mabel Castleberry. "We lived with dialysis for nearly two years and it's hard to get used to the change. But it is wonderful. It's such a miracle that they can do this."

The Arkansas Children's Hospital Adolescent Stress Unit was opened in October 1982. This seventeen-bed unit provided medically-supervised inpatient treatment for teenagers thirteen to eighteen with emotional, psychological and behavioral problems. The unit—the first of its kind in the state—would be operated in conjunction with Comprehensive Care Corporation, the largest operator of hospital-based psychological and alcoholism treatment units nationwide. Teenagers with a primary diagnosis of alcohol or drug dependency, however, would not be admitted to the unit at Children's Hospital.

"We are not here to *cure* a child as such," emphasized Dr. David McCray, medical director of the unit during its first year of operation. "We get teenagers when they're on a path that's self-destructive or maladaptive, and we try to help them change that direction to one of more fulfillment and positive growth."

When teenagers were admitted to the unit—usually for a four-to-six-week stay—they found a highly-structured program. Each patient had an individualized treatment approach which was reevaluated on a weekly basis by all members of the unit's multi-disciplinary team. In addition to the medical director, who was a child psychiatrist, the team included a psychologist, nurses, a social worker, an adolescent therapist, an occupational therapist and a schoolteacher.

"We employ an approach in which youngsters automatically gain more privileges by fully participating in the daily program or lose privileges by negative behavior," explained Dr. McCray. "This provides an avenue for directly approaching them in their problem areas, but it is not meant to be a forced behavior modification program."

Parent education and family therapy involving the entire family were also essential parts of this new program. After patients were discharged, they and their families would return on an outpatient basis for six to twelve weeks of follow-up reinforcement. During its first year of operation, sixty-two teenagers completed the program.

"Most of our kids are really neat kids. They've just been in bad situations or unstable family situations," observed Christine Slikker, the unit's program director from 1982 to 1986. "Their problems aren't that different from those of other adolescents—it's just their circumstances, or not having gotten the support they need, or not knowing how to ask for it. They all think their problems and feelings are unique, but in the group here they find that others have the same problems."

James T. Dyke succeeded Guy Amsler, Jr., as president of the Board of Trustees in November 1982. Dyke was Chair of the Board and CEO of Dyke Industries, a Little Rock-based building materials distributorship. A member of the hospital's governing body for twelve years, he had also served as Chair of the Arkansas Industrial Development Commission and as president of the Arkansas Arts Center Foundation.

A Beechcraft King-Air twin-engine airplane was added to the NICU transport system in February 1983. "For the first time," observed transport coordinator Phillip J. Mains, "Arkansas Children's Hospital is truly a statewide hospital because our transport system now makes the hospital readily available to any child in the state." The specially-equipped airplane was leased from Central Flying Service of Little Rock.

"Everything that might have caused a problem for our first air transport happened," recalled Mains. "The call from Paragould came in late at night. The weather was so bad we didn't think we'd be able to land at the Paragould airport, but things cleared up and we changed our destination in mid-flight. The patients needing transport were twin girls. When we got to the hospital in Paragould, their condition was far worse than had been reported.

"Our return flight took only forty-six minutes; a trip to Paragould by transport van would have taken over three hours. We got there, spent an hour and a half stabilizing the twins and got back—all in less time than it would have taken the transport van to arrive in Paragould."

Although newborn infants were the most frequent patients brought to Children's by air transport, the plane was also used for older babies and children whose condition was considered too unstable for travel by ambulance. An eighteen-month-old who had swallowed furniture polish and a five-year-old with spinal meningitis were among the patients flown to Little Rock in 1983.

Also in February 1983 a new eleven-bed Cardiovascular Intensive Care Unit (CVICU) was opened. Staffed with specially-trained nurses and sophisticated equipment, the new CVICU provided care for infants and children with heart defects. More than 250 heart surgeries were performed at the hospital in 1983—ranking it among the top ten pediatric medical centers in the nation.

"We have an average of four surgeries a week," said CVICU head nurse Mary Jo Whaley in August 1983. "And we have had as many as seven in one week." Whaley also noted that the nurses on the unit did preoperative teaching with parents and patients. "We answer questions about the surgery and about care in CVICU. A scrapbook with pictures of former patients also helps parents and older children understand what they will look like immediately after surgery and a few days later.

"So that parents and older patients can became familiar with the unit, they are taken on a tour by the child's primary nurse," she added. "Often the children recognize this same nurse when they wake up after surgery. During the tour, parents and patients have a chance to talk with others in the unit who are having similar experiences and this helps them cope with their fears and concerns."

The hospital's cardiology service had also been expanded through the establishment of satellite clinics in Jonesboro and Fayetteville. Additional clinics were scheduled to open in Lake Village, Texarkana, Fort Smith, El Dorado and Mountain Home. "It's been very gratifying to see the hospital administration respond to our needs," said Dr. J.B. Norton, Chief of Cardiology. "We appreciate the willingness they've shown to move aggressively in meeting our needs. That's the spirit that has enabled Children's to progress so dramatically in recent years."

The idea of taking the clinic to the patients was not new. Arkansas Children's Hospital had pioneered the concept in the 1930s. In the late '70s when Leland McGinness read about a Michigan hospital which sponsored satellite clinics, he and pediatric cardiologist Dr. W. Thompson Dungan decided to revive the concept in Arkansas.

By early 1986 two Arkansas Children's Hospital cardiologists and a nurse practitioner were traveling to various parts of the state—a total of forty-six separate trips a year—to examine pediatric heart patients. "There's an obvious logistic advantage in having two physicians going to Fayetteville, for example, instead of having twenty families coming to Little Rock," said Dr. Dungan, who had launched the satellite-clinic program in 1981.

"The families love it and are very appreciative," he added. "And our doctors like it because we get to visit with people in the clinics and hospitals around the state, and they are always very cordial to us. It's been a great experience for all concerned.

"Youngsters with heart disease generally fall into two categories," explained Dr. Dungan. "There are those who are very sick, usually babies, who need to get to Children's as quickly as possible. The others may have some symptom or sign, but the case is not urgent, and our outreach clinics are designed for this second group of patients."

The satellite clinics were also convenient for follow-up visits for children who had already undergone heart surgery at Children's Hospital. Patients were referred to these regional clinics by local physicians and other health professionals. Appointments were scheduled through the Cardiology office at Children's.

When more extensive tests or a heart catheterization were required, the patient was scheduled for admission to Arkansas Children's Hospital where surgery was also performed if necessary. "In many cases when a child is discharged after surgery," said Dr. Dungan, "they may never have to come back to Little Rock again. We do all our follow-up during outreach clinic visits in their home area."

Although most of these clinic visits were routine, there were a few unusual moments: a flat tire, a tornado the physicians saw as they were driving into Jonesboro, a dying baby brought into one hospital just as Dr. Dungan and Dr. Richard Readinger arrived—they resuscitated the baby before going on to their clinic visits. The success of the outreach concept pioneered by the Cardiology Department would lead to the creation of satellite clinics in other pediatric medical services.

Reverend Charles G. Johnson joined the staff in February 1983 as the hospital's first full-time chaplain. A native of Brinkley, Arkansas, Reverend Johnson came to Children's from Corpus Christi, Texas, where he had served as an associate minister of Travis Baptist Church. He had previously served as a chaplain in health care facilities in Texas and Kentucky.

"As chaplain," he explained, "I will respond to obvious traumatic experiences, but I hope also to be able to be a facilitator when the question is asked, 'Where is God in the midst of this illness?' A chaplain has few answers, but hopefully does have the ability to live out a personal existence with others in a genuine relationship of trust and love."

The first-ever national telethon for children's hospitals took place over the Memorial Day weekend of May 28-29, 1983. The "Children's Miracle Network Telethon" raised funds for pediatric hospitals across the nation. Unlike other national telethons, however, every penny raised in Arkansas would remain in the state—going directly to Arkansas Children's Hospital.

Each hour of the eighteen-and-a-half-hour telethon included forty-five minutes of all-star Hollywood entertainment originating from the Osmond

Family studios in Orem, Utah, and fifteen minutes originating from the studios of KTHV-Arkansas 11 in Little Rock. Jim Ed Brown served as host of the local segment of the telethon, and Arkansas' First Lady Hillary Clinton, state Chair of the event, also hosted a portion of the program. Numerous hospital staff members appeared on the telethon along with many former patients and their families.

Thousands of Arkansans helped "make a miracle happen" over the Memorial Day weekend by making gifts and pledges of approximately $400,000—the largest amount ever raised by a telethon in Arkansas up to that time. A pledge by Jones Toyota-Volvo and Jones Brothers Datsun-Isuzu of Little Rock was the largest single gift to the fund-raising effort. The Jones organization pledged $50 for every new car sold over a four-month period—a mimimum of $40,000. Herbert Jones, president of Jones Toyota-Volvo, appeared on the local segment of the telethon to present the first month's gift—a check for more than $12,000—to host Jim Ed Brown.

"The name *Children's Miracle Network Telethon* is especially fitting in Arkansas," reflected Larry Woodard, president of the Arkansas Children's Hospital Foundation. "It is a miracle that a state with as small a population as ours raised more money than all but two other markets participating in the telethon. Only Denver and Columbus received more...pledges than ACH. We were ahead of even the Los Angeles local telethon."

The telethon, which would become an annual event, was sponsored by the Osmond Foundation, a philanthropic organization established in 1970 by the family of entertainers Donny and Marie Osmond to support children's hospitals and other child health-related institutions worldwide. It was held in conjunction with the National Association of Children's Hospitals and Related Institutions Inc.

Leland R. McGinness, who had led Arkansas Children's Hospital for eleven eventful years, retired as its Chief Executive Officer on August 26, 1983. Dr. Randall L. O'Donnell, administrator since 1980, was appointed by the Board of Trustees as the new CEO. The change in administrative leadership was announced by Board president James Dyke. "The Board of Trustees and the entire hospital community are deeply grateful to Mr. McGinness for the leadership and dedication he has provided during his tenure," said Dyke. "It is his commitment and vision which have been the driving force in making Arkansas Children's Hospital what it is today—a pediatric medical center of excellence which is one of the finest in the country."

Dr. Randall O'Donnell

"Leland McGinness is truly a man of vision, and he had the dedication and the drive to make that vision a reality," reflected Dr. O'Donnell. "One of my favorite quotations comes to mind whenever I think of Mr. McGinness. 'To accomplish great things we must not only act, but also dream, not only plan but also believe.' Few people ever have the opportunity to realize a dream. Leland McGinness is one of those few—and what he has done will benefit the children of Arkansas for decades to come.

"Personally, I consider Mr. McGinness to have been a very fine mentor; he taught me a great deal, and I consider it a privilege to have worked with him. His patience and his faith that we could build a pediatric medical center of excellence served as a confidence-builder and an example to the entire staff.

"His philosophy was simple. 'We can, we shall, we must.' I don't know how many times I've heard him say that, no matter how large the obstacle facing us," asserted Dr. O'Donnell. "And I think it's a good philosophy for us to continue following as we strive to build upon the achievements of the past."

When McGinness had joined Arkansas Children's Hospital in June 1972, the facility had ninety-three beds and an annual budget of less than $1.3 million. Under his dynamic leadership, it had grown to include 160 beds and twenty NICU bassinets, making it one of the twenty largest pediatric hospitals in the nation, with a budget in 1983, of more than $40 million. The number of employees had grown from approximately 175 in 1972 to almost 1,000 in 1983.

"The fact that our goal—the creation of a children's medical center of excellence—was achieved, accomplished by a group of people dedicated to being advocates for children, is the thing that I'm proudest of," McGinness said in looking back on his tenure. "The opportunity to be identified with a group of people who have that spirit, that commitment—that is my most cherished remembrance."

McGinness would continue to be an advocate for the children of Arkansas. Following a three-month vacation, he would return to the hospital, working several days each week, as a special assistant to Dr. O'Donnell in conjunction with special projects for the institution, and in December 1991, would assume the responsibilities of Evening Administrator.

Building on the accomplishments of the past and the excellence of the present, Dr. O'Donnell outlined his vision of the future. "I see us branching out to meet the needs of children in surrounding states, becoming even more of a regional center for pediatric health care," he explained.

Dr. O'Donnell continued, "I see increasing patient activity in ongoing acute care, in a growing intermediate care capacity, and in other areas of medicine such as behavioral medicine. We'll be looking into the possibility of enhancing our activities in those specialized areas in the future.

"I see us staying current with the rapid advances in medical technology. We are a 'high-tech' institution now, but we must continue to have the most modern equipment, especially that which has particular application for children. We're at the cutting edge in medical technology today," asserted Dr. O'Donnell, "and we're going to stay there. I envision our reaching a point where parents with a child in need of medical attention will automatically think of Children's Hospital."

Formal dedication ceremonies for the hospital's newly-expanded emergency care facilities were held on November 11, 1984. The "ribbon" was made of gauze and the "ribbon-cutters" were a pair of surgical scissors. The new area was named in honor of Cecil and Alice Pearson of Dallas, Texas, whose $100,000 gift had made it possible. The Pearsons were on hand for the occasion, along with other dignitaries, hospital staff members and supporters.

The Pearsons' donation had been made as a "challenge gift" in conjunction with the 1984 "Children's Miracle Network Telethon," which had aired in June. The Pearsons had pledged to match every dollar phoned in up to $50,000. And if their goal was met, they pledged to double their gift for a total of $100,000. Arkansans had responded by phoning in pledges totaling more than $75,000, which coupled with corporate gifts brought the telethon's grand total to more than $555,000.

Each child admitted to the medical facility now received a copy of *My Hospital Activity Book*. Created by the Child Life Department and produced with funds provided by the Arkansas Jaycee Women, the book was designed to involve children in learning about the hospital and coping with their experiences while a patient there.

This book grew out of Dr. O'Donnell's concern for the special needs of hospitalized children. "I've always been interested in the needs and emotions of hospitalized children," he explained, "but it wasn't until my daughter Darby was hospitalized at three weeks of age in May 1992 that I gained a real sensitivity to the stress that parents are under when their child is ill."

The more than eighty nurses, nurse technicians, social workers and other professionals who worked on the hospital's "Rainbow Units"—*Three-Gold, Three-Green, Three-Orange* and *Three-Blue*—shared Dr. O'Donnell's awareness of these special needs and emotions. "Emotional support for the child and family can be as important as medical treatment in many cases," asserted Marcella Kindred, R.N., head nurse on Three-Orange and Three-Blue.

Three-Orange was a sixteen-bed orthopedic unit which served patients with fractures, dislocated hips, spina bifida, spinal surgery and other orthopedic conditions. Many of them had long stays of three or four weeks. "Patients on Orange are more confined than on other units," said Kindred. "About eighty-five percent of them cannot get out of bed because of traction. They become bored easily and need special attention."

Hematology/Oncology patients occupied Three-Gold. Patients on this thirteen-bed unit often had frequent hospitalizations and most were very ill. "Most of these children have long stays—up to three months or more," said Fiona McDermott, R.N., head nurse on Three-Gold and Three-Green. "We really get to know these kids and their families since Three-Gold becomes their second home."

Three-Blue was a sixteen-bed surgery unit. "Patients scheduled for heart surgery begin and end their hospital stay on Blue," said Marcella Kindred. "The unit also serves as a 'stepdown' for patients from the Pediatric Intensive Care Unit." Other surgical patients cared for on Three-Blue included those who underwent hernia surgery, appendectomies and tonsillectomies. Length of stay was usually shorter than for the other units.

"From the minute children are admitted to Three-Blue, one of us is there to meet their needs," Ruth Simcox, R.N., a staff nurse on the unit observed in a 1984 interview. "Ninty-nine percent of my job is that initial meeting with parents and child, getting them settled in before any procedures start. If I can gain their trust and confidence then, working with them the rest of the time is easy."

What does it take to be a pediatric nurse in daily contact with children and their families? "You have to be able to get along with people—all types of people," reflected surgery nurse Lea Goodson. "You have to be understanding and you have to really care about the families. But number one has to be love of the job—you have to love kids to nurse kids."

Patients with diabetes, asthma, head injuries and cystic fibrosis were treated on Three-Green. This seventeen-bed unit also included four isolation rooms for children with infectious diseases.

Cystic fibrosis (CF) is a genetic disease in which the body's mucous glands secrete an abnormally thick mucous and the sweat glands produce an unusually salty sweat. This mucous clogs the bronchial tubes making it difficult to breath. These abnormal secretions can also lead to a variety of other complications, including chronic pulmonary disease, pancreatic insufficiency, excessively high sweat electrolytes and in some cases cirrhosis of the liver.

"Cystic Fibrosis is a masquerader," explained Dr. Robert Warren, director of the hospital's pulmonary program, in a 1984 interview. "The disease's pulmonary symptoms are often mistakenly attributed to asthma, chronic bronchitis, whooping cough and other respiratory disturbances.

"Some CF victims have few synptoms for years," he added, "while others are born very sick. The disease is almost totally unpredictable, even when it is reaching its final stages." Often, when asked about a patient's prognosis, Dr. Warren responded, "My crystal ball isn't working today."

Many CF patients come to Arkansas Children's Hospital for a "tune-up"—two or three weeks of high-powered therapy with potent antibiotics, intensive respiratory treatments and assessments of nutritional status and respiratory capabilities. Such hospitalizations become necessary when a patient's lungs become infected by the bacteria trapped in their mucus. These "tune-ups" also provide the opportunity for CF patients to visit with one another and share the uncertainties that each experiences.

"Even fifteen years ago, it was unusual for a CF child to survive through adolescence," said Shirley Holt, a respiratory therapist on the Children's Hospital CF Team. "But today many live to enjoy adulthood, thanks to the many advances in antibiotics, nutrition and respiratory therapy.

"These kids have been told all their lives that they're going to die," said Holt, "but now they find that they've somehow accidentally grown up instead, and they don't know what to do with themselves."

It was for this reason that Holt and two other CF team members—Jennie Crawford, a nurse practitioner, and Barbara Bunten, a social worker—formed a CF support group in early 1985 as an outgrowth of the Adult Cystic Fibrosis Clinic at Arkansas Children's Hospital.

"Adult CF patients simply want to be part of the crowd," said Holt in a 1986 interview. "The support group allows them to share experiences, such as how much to tell a prospective employer, how to deal with friends' reactions or whether or not to tell a date."

"Working with the CF Team is both rewarding and frustrating," added Crawford. "It's often difficult to draw the line in becoming emotionally involved with CF patients. These people have become our friends, but while Shirley and I see ourselves as just starting our lives, looking forward to homes, babies, families, that sort of thing, we also see the CF kids winding down their lives. It's sometimes hard for us to cope with the fact that we have so much to be thankful for."

While it was sometimes difficult to work with terminally-ill patients, staff members on Three-Green spoke of their cystic fibrosis patients with great admiration. Shirley Ward, a respiratory therapist who sometimes worked with CF patients, reflected in 1984, "I don't know whether you have to be special to be a CF kid, or whether CF makes you special—but there's something incredible about these young people." Shirley Holt echoed her co-worker, "It's a privilege to work with these kids," she declared. "They have allowed us to occupy a very special part of their lives."

Ground was broken in October 1985 for a new $10 million education/research building which would house outpatient clinics, classrooms, an auditorium, laboratories and physicians' offices. The structure's educational facilities would be used by medical students, postdoctoral residents and nursing students. A major gift toward construction of the new building was made possible by the Roy and Christine Sturgis Charitable and Educational Trust of Dallas, Texas, which donated $1.5 million—the largest single gift ever made to the hospital up to that time. The multi-purpose structure, which would be named in honor of the Sturgis family, was scheduled to be completed in March 1987.

Another expansion of the NICU transport system occurred in November 1985 when the hospital added a helicoper named Angel One. "With Angel One, transport patients can be moved directly from one hospital to another, so that the transfer by ambulance to the airport or hospital is eliminated," explained Dr. O'Donnell. "Now, a critically ill child anywhere in Arkansas

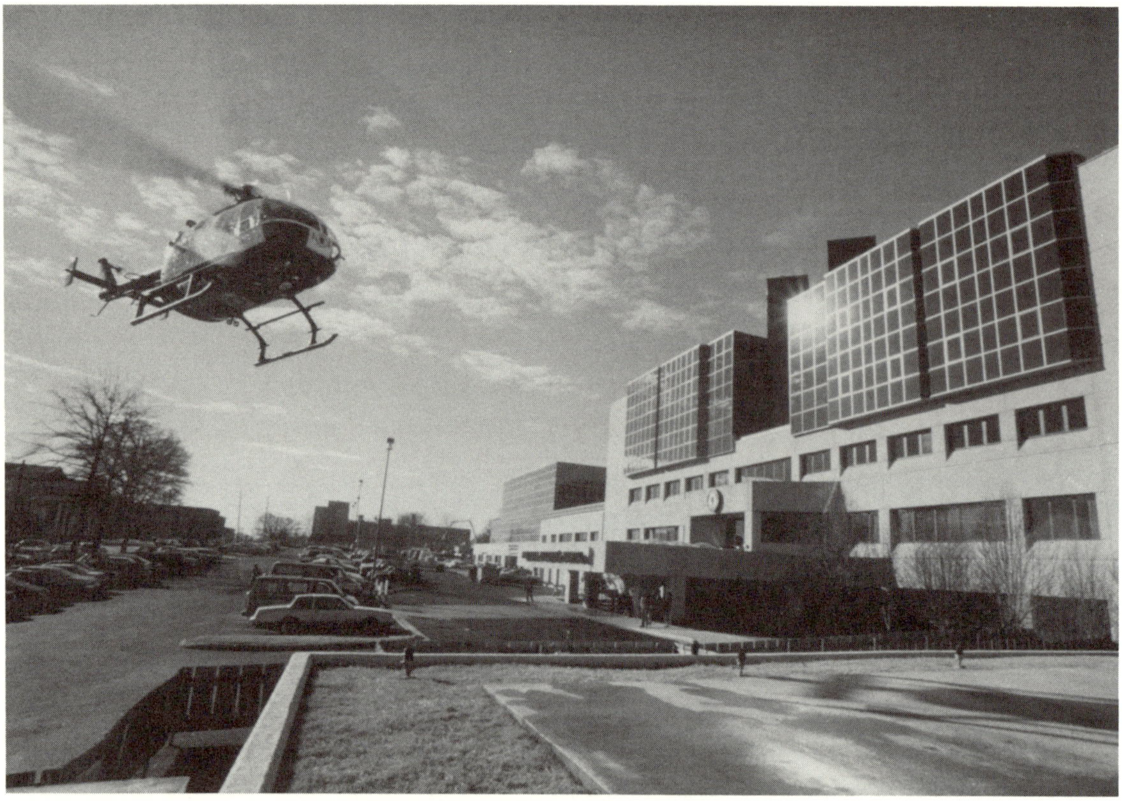

Angel One landing, ca. 1985

can be transferred within hours to one of our state-of-the-art intensive care units."

Dr. O'Donnell also noted that the NICU transport system had recently been cited by the Southern Regional Task Force on Infant Mortality as a major contributing factor in the state's dramatically improved infant mortality rate. The 1983 infant mortality rate in Arkansas was 10.7 per 1,000 births—the lowest of any southern state and below the national average of 10.9. The helicopter would be used for the majority of emergency air transports. The airplane, however, would continue to be used for longer flights and as a back-up for the helicopter in inclement weather or whenever more than one aircraft was needed.

Expansion of the system into a three-vehicle emergency NICU transport operation—van, airplane and helicopter—was welcomed by physicians across the state. "I couldn't practice the kind of medicine I do without knowing the back-up from Children's was there," reflected pediatrician Dr. Yoland Condrey of Mountain Home in a 1988 interview.

Fellow pediatrician Dr. Lester Austin of Jonesboro agreed. Referring to the transport system as "my Linus blanket," he explained that, "At Methodist Hospital in Jonesboro, we have a level-two nursery for our babies. While that's good, we also know that it's not enough for many of the high-risk babies of our area. We have to have a more intensive, more specialized level of care for those babies and the transport system makes that care available. At Children's Hospital, they're saving those newborns, and that makes things better for all of us throughout the state."

Gerald and Carolyn Hamra assisted by son Ryan (left), along with CEO Dr. Randall O'Donnell, Hillary Clinton, and her daughter Chelsea, break ground for the hospital's therapeutic pool. February 14, 1986.

Dignitaries such as United States Senator Dale Bumpers, Betty Bumpers, Governor Bill Clinton, Hillary Clinton and Little Rock Mayor Tom Prince were on hand the afternoon of August 16, 1985, for the formal dedication of the hospital's new Gerald F. Hamra Rehabilitation Center. Hamra, Chair of the Board and CEO of Wendy's restaurants of Little Rock, had challenged viewers of the third annual "Children's Miracle Network Telethon" by pledging to match every dollar phoned in up to $75,000. The Rehabilitation Center, which would provide physical and occupational therapy, was chosen to bear Hamra's name because of his special interest in that area of medicine due to his having had polio as a child.

At the ceremonies, Hamra announced that he would lead a campaign to raise $150,000 to construct a therapeutic pool for the Rehabilitation Center. The pool would add a new dimension to the therapy provided to patients with arthritis, burns, neuromuscular injuries and other conditions.

The first donation toward the new pool came from special guest R. David Thomas, Founder and Senior Chair of the Board of Wendy's International. Thomas also presented a plaque to Hamra, who was the top fund raiser among all Wendy's owners nationwide for the 1985 telethon.

In April 1985 the Association for the Care of Children's Health, an international organization dedicated to meeting the psychological, social, emotional and educational needs of hospitalized children and their families, selected Arkansas Children's Hospital from among fourteen nationwide nominees to receive its 1985 Distinguished Service Award. Programs such as Child Life and Education, Social Work and Patient Education were cited, as well as the institution's overall commitment to meeting the needs of hospitalized children.

Generous Arkansans met and surpassed the challenges made during the forth annual "Children's Miracle Network Telethon" on the weekend of May 31-June 1, 1986. Thousands of individuals, businesses and organizations helped raise more than $1,135,000 for Arkansas Children's Hospital. It was Arkansas's first-ever million dollar telethon. And when the toteboard total went over $1 million, it meant that the hospital qualified to receive another $1 million—an endowment gift earmarked for the hospital's cardiovascular program and made as a challenge gift by David Clark, president of Interstate Airlines of Little Rock, and his employees.

An endowment gift is one which keeps on giving, since the gift itself is invested and the interest generated is used for the ongoing costs of the program. Under the guidelines of the telethon, endowment funds could not be counted on the toteboard, but Clark explained that he and his employees wanted to make the gift as a challenge to telethon viewers.

This $1 million gift—the largest single endowment gift ever received by Arkansas Children's Hospital up to that time—made the cardiovascular program its first major medical service to be permanently endowed. The endowment gift was David Clark's second pledge to the annual fund drive. During the 1985 telethon, he had phoned in to match the $75,000 challenge gift made by Gerald Hamra of Wendy's of Little Rock.

Another challenge gift came from long-time hospital supporter Stella Boyle Smith. She promised to donate $35,000 if telethon viewers phoned in $100,000 in pledges. Arkansans responded by calling in nearly $130,000 in pledges—a total that when combined with other telethon-related gifts, put the toteboard over the one million dollar mark.

Charles B. Whiteside succeeded James T. Dyke as president of the Board of Trustees in November 1986. Whiteside was vice president of Merrill Lynch Pierce Fenner and Smith Investment Securities Inc. A member of the hospital's governing body for twelve years, he had served as treasurer and as chair of the executive committee.

More than 100 guests attended the formal dedication of the hospital's new $300,000 therapeutic pool on August 17, 1986. The pool was named—as was the rehabilitation center which housed it—in honor of Gerald F. Hamra. Among those attending were Hamra, Congressman Tommy Robinson, former Governor Frank White and special guest R. David Thomas.

The floor of the 20-by-25-foot pool—flush with the room's floor when not in use—could be raised or lowered hydraulically, from a six-inch depth for small children to a five-foot depth for older patients. "Besides its therapeutic value for those with burns, arthritis, cystic fibrosis or orthopedic problems," explained Isabel Finnell, Director of Rehabilitation Services, "it lets us add enjoyment to a sometimes painful process."

By July 1987 Phase Two of the hospital's long-range expansion project was well underway. The emergency room entrance had been moved to the southwest corner of the hospital, other entrances and streets had been closed and a 180-foot crane had appeared in front of the medical facility. The project included the addition of a fourth and fifth floor to the east wing of the main building and the expansion of the emergency room, ambulatory surgery and various ancillary services.

These two new floors would add seventy-five beds and approximately 70,000 square feet of floor space. Financed by the sale of bonds—the same method used to finance construction of the Sturgis Building—the project was scheduled to be completed in the Spring of 1988. The new fourth floor would house:

- ❖ A twelve-bed Adolescent Medicine Unit which would provide care for children ages twelve to twenty-one. This unit would include a recreation center and programs geared to the special psychosocial needs of teenagers, and would be the only medical unit of its type in the state.
- ❖ A thirteen-bed General Medicine Unit which would provide additional beds to relieve the pressure caused by the high census on the four Rainbow Units.
- ❖ A twenty-bed Progressive Care Unit which would provide care for children requiring long-term rehabilitation due to accident-related trauma or other disabling conditions.
- ❖ A twelve-bed Neurology/Neurosurgery Unit which would provide care for children with neurological, neuropsychiatric, neuromuscular and neuro-orthopedic disorders.

The new fifth floor would house the Child Study Center which would be relocated from the University of Arkansas for Medical Science. This inpatient program would treat children under the age of thirteen with a primary psychiatric diagnosis. Outpatient services for the Child Study Center would also be moved to Arkansas Children's Hospital.

The contract with Comprehensive Care Corporation had expired in October 1986, and the adolescent psychiatric program was now being operated solely by Arkansas Children's Hospital. Renamed Turning Point, the unit would be relocated to the new fifth floor. The area currently housing Turning Point would be used for the relocation of several ancillary services.

Under the hospital's management, the unit would treat more acute cases—those with suicidal intent or psychosis. It would also be expanded to forty beds—twenty adolescent beds and twenty beds designated for patients ages three to twelve. Length of stay would be reduced with a greater emphasis on outpatient treatment.

Phase Two would also include expansion of the cafeteria, kitchen and food storage areas on the north side of the hospital. Radiology, Pediatric Neurology and Pulmonary Function, Purchasing, Rehabilitation Services, Dental, Eye and ENT clinics, Medical Records, Respiratory Therapy, Heart Station and PICU Waiting Room were also slated for expansion.

The new fourth floor would be named the "Stella Boyle Smith Patient Pavilion" in honor of the hospital's long-time friend and supporter who had recently made a $500,000 gift to the institution. Her half-million dollar donation would become part of the already established Stella Boyle Smith Endowment Fund. The money from this gift would be used for operational support of existing medical programs, creation of new services and the purchase of medical equipment.

Smith remembered when the institution was an orphanage, and had participated in the groundbreaking ceremonies for the first hospital. She had also helped found its first auxiliary, and remembered sponsoring card parties and other fund-raising events over the years—in addition to donating generously to the hospital many times herself.

"As a volunteer in the 1920s and 30s," she recalled, "there wasn't anything I didn't do. I scrubbed the operating room floor on my hands and knees many times, I washed baby clothes, I de-liced the kids. I'd go over there and see things that needed to be done, and I'd just do them, that's all."

Over the years, Smith had donated more volunteer hours to the institution than any other single person. She had not only scrubbed the children,

Long-time ACH supporter Stella Boyle Smith (left)
looks on as Larry Woodard, president of ACH Foundation, CEO Dr. Randall O'Donnell, and his daughter Darby hang a plaque naming the hospital's new fourth floor in her honor, October 1988

she had brought them presents, had taken them to her home for special meals and had followed their progress after their return home.

In addition to caring for and helping the children in those early years, Smith had also functioned as one of the hospital's first and best fund raisers when money ran short. "Of course, I was just a volunteer and didn't get anything for my efforts—except the devil if I didn't raise enough money!" she remembered with a laugh. And from her days of collecting quarters to recent years when she had been instrumental in encouraging many other generous Arkansans to contribute to Children's, she had continued to be an important fund raiser and donor for the hospital.

Smith had been honored by the hospital in 1978 as a "Distinguished Friend of Arkansas Children," one of only two persons ever to receive the award. "The current expansion," she reflected in a 1987 interview, "will make the hospital one of the best anywhere when it's completed. But," she added, "expansion itself has never been the most important thing to me.

I've always just had the children in mind. I'd do things I thought would help to save their lives or make them happier."

In discussing the major reasons for the current expansion, Dr. O'Donnell observed, "In today's competitive health care climate, growing is the equivalent of survival. Right now, we simply do not have room to meet all of the needs of children and their families in the state.

"We're expanding the Emergency Room because we've seen such explosive growth in that area. Our ER originally was designed to accommodate 5,000 to 6,000 patient visits a year, but through June of the current fiscal year, we've already seen 28,000 patients there. Within the next two years, we anticipate well over 50,000 ER visits annually.

"In view of the high census that we continually maintain, there is also a need for additional beds as well as for expansion of ancillary services. In today's competitive enviroment," concluded Dr. O'Donnell, "with so many others seeking a share of the pediatric health care market, we simply cannot afford to stand still."

The new Roy and Christine Sturgis Educational Building was formally dedicated on July 20, 1987. Arkansas First Lady Hillary Rodham Clinton delivered the keynote address in which she praised the institution's commitment not only to excellence in patient care, but to education and research as well.

Webster Hubbell and Wilson Jones of Little Rock's Rose Law Firm attended the dedication on behalf of the Roy and Christine Sturgis Charitable and Educational Trust of Dallas, whose $1.5 million gift had made the education/research facility a reality. It would house several outpatient clinics, a 200-seat auditorium, four classrooms, a clinical laboratory and various research labs, medical library, support services and more than sixty-five physicians offices.

Phillip K. Gilmore was named Administrator and Chief Operating Officer of Arkansas Children's Hospital on August 10, 1987. The position had been vacant for four years, since Dr. O'Donnell had been named Chief Executive Officer. As administrator, Gilmore would be responsible for the day-to-day operation of the medical facility.

A native of Lena, Mississippi, Gilmore came to Little Rock from El Dorado, Arkansas, where he had served as Associate Administrator of Warner Brown Hospital from 1981 to 1986, before being named President and Administrator in November 1986. He held a Master's degree in Microbiology from the University of Southern Mississippi, and a Master's in Health Administration from the Washington University School of Medicine in St. Louis.

"We have experienced firsthand the love and caring which is shown to families who come here and as a result we have a strong love for the hospital and what it is doing for the children of our state," said Gilmore.

When his son, Jonathan was born in June 1986, the infant was jaundiced. After nearly two months of observation and tests for blood or other problems which might cause the condition, he began to get worse. "He would break out in a cold sweat when he took a bottle," remembered his father.

"Jonathan was hospitalized in El Dorado. After several days the situation became critical. He was breathing 160 breaths a minute and was on oxygen. Our pediatrician said that he couldn't go on working that hard to breathe, and that they'd done all they could for him at Warner Brown. He said we'd have to go to Children's where he could be put on a ventilator."

Angel One flew the critically ill child to Little Rock while Gilmore and his wife drove to Little Rock by car. Upon arriving at Children's, they were met by a team of medical specialists ready to take their son to surgery. "It was a tremendous relief," recalled Gilmore, "to know what the problem was—a rare congenital heart defect—and that it could be repaired immediately."

The Gilmores were further impressed with the care that Jonthan received from the nurses, child life specialists, waiting room attendants and other staff members. "We fell in love with Children's and wanted to do anything we could for it," said Gilmore.

During the following year, Gilmore was asked to speak about his family's experience at several hospital fund raisers. Although he had recently been promoted to President and Administrator of Warner Brown Hospital, when the opportunity arose in August 1987 to become Administrator and Chief Operating Officer of Arkansas Children's Hospital, he accepted.

Three patients, dozens of staff members, construction workers and supporters of the pediatric medical facility gathered on March 15, 1988, to sign their names to a steel beam before it was hoisted into place atop the fifth floor, "topping out" the new addition. "Arkansas Children's Hospital will never be finished expanding and growing," Dr. O'Donnell told the crowd. "We will continue to provide the finest medical services for all the children of Arkansas."

B. Douglas (Doug) Brandon succeeded Charles B. Whiteside as president of the Board of Trustees in November 1988. Brandon was president of Brandon Furniture Company and served in the state senate. He had been a member of the Board since 1980, and for the previous year had served as its vice-president.

Also in November 1988 Hillary Clinton was elected to a seat on the Board. In addition to her role as the state's First Lady, she was an attorney with the Rose Law Firm and was a national leader in education and community affairs. She had served as Chair and host of the local segment of the annual "Children's Miracle Network Telethon" for the past six years.

In January 1989 the Trustees approved construction of a new "Children's Care Center" to be located at the south end of the Sturgis Building, which would double the capacity of the outpatient clinic. Construction was to begin in the spring and was expected to be completed early the following year.

The delivery of a 22,000-pound magnet in January 1989 signaled that the new Magnetic Resonance Imaging (MRI) Center was nearing completion. Opened in late February, the Center was named in honor of the hospital auxiliary. The MRI magnet, with a pull 30,000 times stronger than the earth's gravity, could create sophisticated internal images of every part of the body providing the most accurate diagnosis of a wide variety of medical problems.

The Heart Catheterization Laboratory, which had first opened in 1979, was also undergoing renovation. Its high-tech diagnostic equipment was being made even more advanced with the addition of computerized digital subtraction which would greatly enhance the pictures used to locate and diagnose heart defects in even the smallest infants.

On March 6, 1989, the new "Wal-Mart Adolescent and Young Adult Unit" was officially opened. Named in recognition of the outstanding support given by Wal-Mart stores throughout Arkansas, northern Louisiana and northeast Texas during the annual telethon, the unit would provide care for teenagers with eating disorders, medical conditions such as diabetes, those injured in accidents and a host of other medical problems.

"Our unit provides an appropriate setting for the special needs of teenagers," observed Dr. Brian Hardin, Director of Adolescent Medicine. "We have a recreation area where we can have movies, pizza parties or classroom activities. And we're geared to adolescent issues—issues like independence, readjusting to their school schedule after an illness, even things like helping them apply for a Social Security card."

Eleven members of the Osmond Family—including Donny and Marie—attended the formal dedication of the new "Osmond/Children's Miracle Network Progressive Care Unit" on May 8, 1989. Named in recognition of the family's work with the annual telethon, the unit would primarily serve children in need of long-term rehabilitation due to accident-related trauma but would also be available to those with spina bifida, cerebral palsy and other disabling conditions.

"Our goal is to help them become functional, independent adults," declared Dr. Vikki Stefans, Medical Director of the Progressive Care Unit. "We will focus on learning new skills and preparing for the return to the community and independent living. From the moment children arrive, we will begin planning which skills they need to learn or re-learn to insure a successful return to home, family and school—a return to productive living."

The 1980s had been an era of extraordinary growth and development for Arkansas Children's Hospital. By 1990 it was the sixth largest pediatric medical facility in the nation. "As we enter a new decade," reflected Chief Executive Officer Dr. Randall O'Donnell in January of that year, "one of our primary objectives must be never to lose that ... sense of caring and closeness for which we've always been known."

Dr. O'Donnell with the Osmond Family, May 8, 1989

Nine

BY 1990, ONE-SIXTH OF the manufactured goods produced in Arkansas were being exported to other nations. Foreign manufacturers such as the French-owned Falcon Jet in Little Rock and the Japanese-owned electronics firm Sanyo Corporation in Forrest City now had major factories in the state. Income for the average Arkansan was seventy-seven percent of the national average per-capita income and was increasing faster than the national average.

Arkansas still ranked low in terms of spending on education, but during the 1980s state government, led by Governor Bill Clinton, had sought to improve education by mandating higher standards for students, teachers and schools. The state had made great strides in the years since World War II. Now, as they looked toward the dawn of the twenty-first century, Arkansans faced new and challenging issues, many of which reflected a growing concern for the environment.

As its economy grows and its population increases, can Arkansas always count on a plentiful supply of clean water? Should it "export" water to western and southwestern states in the future? Should its forest be clear-cut—cut over and replanted in large sections? Do the soil erosion and stream silting which can result from clear-cutting outweigh the growing worldwide demand for timber products? These and other difficult questions would require answers in the years ahead.

Nowhere were the challenges of the future more eagerly anticipated than at Arkansas Children's Hospital. By 1990, with the exception of liver transplants, any pediatric procedure offered anywhere in the world could be performed there. In March of that year, Chief Executive Officer Dr. Randall O'Donnell reflected on the medical facility's level of sophistication in an interview with the *Arkansas Times* magazine. "You either can do a heart transplant in the middle of the night or you can't. We can."

Margaret Bogle, Ph.D., resigned as director of the hospital's Nutritional Services Department in May 1990 to become director of its newly created De-

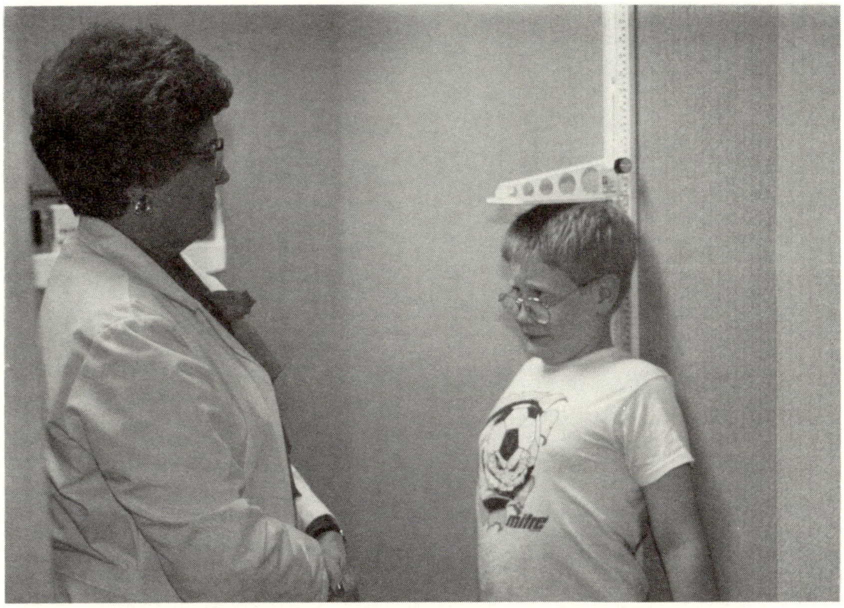

Margaret Bogle Ph.D., with eight-year-old Ben Herring, 1991

partment of Clinical Nutrition and Research. Under Dr. Bogle's direction, this department would implement new and innovative programs in clinical nutrition. "We're dedicated to establishing a Nutrition Center committed to the three-pronged mission of Children's Hospital—clinical care, education and research," said Dr. Bogle.

Clinical care—consulting with physicians regarding disease processes and how to provide specific nutrients through food, counseling families on nutritional concepts and developing formulas to meet the needs of infants who had metabolic needs which could not be met with commercially available products—was already an integral part of clinical nutrition's role at the hospital.

Education would also receive strong emphasis in this new department, which would participate in a dietetic intern program with the University of Arkansas Medical Center and the Veterans' Administration Hospital. In addition to providing lectures to junior medical students and residents, clinical nutritionists would teach in informal settings, participating along with doctors, nurses and others in direct patient care.

"Research is the area with the most potential for growth, and that growth is already well underway," asserted Dr. Bogle. "In our planned Nutritional Assessment Program we will be able to establish nutritional standards for both healthy and sick children in the areas of energy expenditure and body composition. We will use sophisticated equipment to correlate nutritional status with the impact of disease, which in turn will allow us to implement nutritional therapies based on the data collected.

"We'll have 'metabolic beds' where we can do nutrient-balance studies. For instance, we'll be able to record the amounts of foods eaten and specific nutrients absorbed by children's bodies and perform lab and other tests to see how they are being used. The effects of drugs on nutrients will also be monitored directly. These examples," declared Dr. Bogle, "are just a hint of what can and will be accomplished once our Department of Clinical Nutrition and Research is in full operation."

"Give and it shall be given unto you." Elmer Ferguson, president of the DeWitt Bank and Trust Company of DeWitt, Arkansas quoted this Bible verse at the dedication of the "Elmer and Gladys Ferguson Neuroscience Unit" in August 1990. "I'm thrilled about this new unit and I'm glad we were able to make the gift," said Gladys Ferguson.

The couple had made their donation in the form of a $250,000 challenge gift during the 1990 Children's Miracle Network Telethon. "We felt it would encourage others to give," explained Elmer Furguson. "And we've received letters from people letting us know that because of our challenge, they called in a pledge. We've had people tell us stories...about how they have been helped by the hospital—services they couldn't get elsewhere. We also like the fact that children whose parents can't pay for their treatment are accepted by the hospital."

"The Fergusons have been friends of Arkansas Children's Hospital for many years, providing support both individually and in the form of corporate donations from DeWitt Bank and Trust Company. While they have never had a child, grandchild or great-grandchild at the hospital, their gift to support the Neuroscience Unit has helped us create one of this country's finest such programs for children," said Dr. O'Donnell at the dedication. "And it will allow us to become a national leader in this medical specialty."

Children with brain tumors, seizures or other neurological problems were treated on this new unit. Among the innovative procedures performed was "brain mapping"—a complex process which determines the exact spot in a child's brain responsible for sending the signals which cause seizures. The seizures could then be eliminated by removing the affected portion of the brain without causing damage to functions such as speech and motor skills.

Sophisticated video electroencephalograms (EEGs) were also available. These video EEGs allowed a comparison between a child's seizure activity with a video tape of physical activity, enabling physicians to develop a more accurate assessment.

Rhizotomy was another new surgical procedure performed on the unit. This surgery decreases spasticity in cerebral palsy patients while increasing strength and mobility. "We make an incision in the lower part of the back to expose the nerve rootlets. During the surgery we record responses of the muscles to nerve rootlet stimulation," explained neurosurgeon Dr. Frederick Boop. "The nerves which respond normally are left alone and the ones that respond in a spastic manner are cut."

Kathy McElduff, Speech Language Pathologist, works with Sidney Wolfe of Mena, ca. 1991.

"Fully half of all inpatients at Arkansas Children's Hospital have some type of neurological problem, from patients with seizures to those with infectious diseases like meningitis," asserted Dr. Stephen Bates, Director of Pediatric Neurology. "We accept patients with more complicated neurological problems for this special unit. Our neurologists and neurosurgeons then work together with specially trained nurses, occupational, physical and speech therapists, social workers, pharmacists and others to provide the best possible care."

Also in August 1990 the tenth anniversary of the Neonatal Intensive Care Unit (NICU) was celebrated with a reunion attended by more than 500 former patients, their families and friends. In his welcoming remarks, Dr. Robert Arrington, Director of Neonatology, estimated that the NICU had treated over 3,500 infants during its first decade. "There are babies who weighed only one or two pounds when they came to us who today are walking around enjoying the festivities," stated Dr. Arrington.

The reunion's program honored Governor Bill Clinton and the Arkansas Legislature as "Arkansas Children's Hospital Heroes" for having appropriated the funds eleven years earlier to construct the state's first designated level-three NICU. The unit had grown from its original twelve beds in 1980 to thirty beds in 1990. Six neonatalogists, several general pediatric surgeons, numerous pediatric specialists and more than ninety specialized nurses now maintained top quality care around the clock. In addition, respiratory therapists, social workers and chaplains provided continuous care to the newborn and premature infants and their families.

Speaking for the parents whose children had been premature, suffered birth defects or other serious medical problems, Governor Clinton credited the NICU staff along with the transport team for the drop in the state's infant mortality rate. "It's thanks largely to this unit and the dedicated people here," he affirmed.

In May 1991 "Race to the Future" was the theme of the annual "ACH Employee Campaign." In past years, employees had helped raise funds for expansion of the hospital, purchase of the Angel One transport helicopter, and renovation of the cafeteria. The 1991 Campaign would help raise part of the $1.5 million needed by October to qualify for a $500,000 matching grant from the Mabee Foundation of Tulsa. This grant would go toward construction of the proposed Arkansas Children's Hospital Research Institute.

The two-week Employee Campaign raised almost $29,000. "By raising more than ever before, our employees have proven that we will win the 'race to the future,'" declared Larry Woodard, President of the Arkansas Children's Hospital Foundation. "Thanks to their generosity and loyalty...our research institue is that much closer to being a reality."

More than 250 friends of Doug Brandon and Children's Hospital gathered on September 10, 1991, to dedicate the B. Douglas Brandon Conference Center, which occupied the first floor of the South Campus Building. This seven-story structure located at 1120 Marshall Street had been purchased by the

Doug Brandon, September 10, 1991

hospital in 1989. Dr. O'Donnell thanked Brandon—the outgoing president of the Board of Trustees—for his years of service. "Doug Brandon has given his time, talents and influence to help Arkansas Children's Hospital attain its stature as one of the leading pediatric medical centers in the nation."

Brandon thanked his wife, Sissi, and family for allowing him to devote time to the hospital. "I hope each of my children try to do it the way I've done it and give back to their community," he added.

The new Brandon Conference Center featured a 124-seat auditorium equipped with state-of-the-art video, slide projection and sound systems and four smaller classrooms which could be converted into two larger ones with a combined seating capacity of 240. Continuing education activities for medical professionals, hospital conferences and hospital-sponsored community education activities would be held at the facility.

Diane Mackey succeeded Brandon as president of the Board of Trustees in September 1991. A former assistant U.S. attorney, Mackey was a partner with the Friday, Eldredge and Clark Law Firm where she specialized in environmental law. A member of the Board for eleven years, she was also a past president of the hospital auxiliary.

On October 7, 1991, Dr. O'Donnell and Dr. Harry Ward, Chancellor of the University of Arkansas for Medical Sciences (UAMS), signed an agreement to build a pediatric research institute at Arkansas Children's Hospital. "This is a very big moment in the life of Arkansas Children's Hospital, particularly in its affiliation with UAMS," said Dr. O'Donnell. The research facility, he added, would aid the hospital in fulfilling its three-fold mission—excellence in clinical care, education and research.

Also on hand to sign this agreement were Mackey, Charles Whiteside, President of the Board of Directors of the Arkansas Children's Hospital Research Institute Inc. and B. Alan Sugg, Ph.D., President of the University of Arkansas system. The research institute, the first phase of which was completed in January 1992, is housed in a four-story, 115,000 square-foot building located on the institution's South Campus next to the Brandon Conference Center.

With an estimated cost of $25 million, the research institute will be completed as contributions from donors allow. More than $5 million has already been raised for Phase One—a $7.5 million renovation of the first floor. This area is now the site of a state-of-the-art animal facility, where physicians and researchers will use animals to study diseases and conditions in infants and children. The second, third and fourth floors will house research laboratories and office space for researchers.

"Our plans are for the research institute to broaden our scope to encompass all the physical, mental and emotional factors that determine the well-being of children and their families. Research here 'from the family to the gene' can result in discoveries that today we can only dream about," said Dr. Robert Fiser, Chair of the UAMS Department of Pediatrics and Vice President of the Arkansas Children's Hospital Research Institute.

Researchers will study every aspect of pediatric health care with an emphasis on the development of the brain and the central nervous system. The main focus will be the effects of nutrition and toxicology on the nervous system. Other programs are planned in alcohol and drug abuse, child and family relationships and the effect of environment on school readiness.

"Right now," reflected Dr. Fiser in an interview with the *Arkansas Times* magazine, "Vanderbilt University does more research than any pediatric department in the U.S. I told my Board that in ten years—no, we'll up that—in five years—we're going to do better than Vanderbilt.

"Building on research which is already underway, we're going to become the best place in the U.S. to study the developing nervous system. We're going to have a research institute better than Sloan-Kettering [in New York]. I honestly think we can do this. I told our faculty, 'You don't have to win, but in ten years somebody's got to be nominated for a Nobel Prize.'"

Dr. O'Donnell agreed. "Just look at what we've already accomplished," he said. "We've added 1,400 jobs in the last ten years. We're one of the largest employers in the state. And five years from now our research institute has the potential of being similar in size to the hospital. We're already twelve times the size we were eight to ten years ago, so just doubling doesn't sound so implausible."

Why is it important to establish a research institute at Arkansas Children's Hospital? "Conducting research in the area of pediatric medicine which requires new diagnostic and treatment techniques," explained Thomas Badger, Ph.D., Scientific Director of the ACH Research Institute. "It will enable our physicians to be as knowledgeable as any in the world and will increase their ability to provide the best possible medical care to young Arkansans. Enhancing recruitment and retention of faculty will also be important pluses. Our research institute will concentrate on areas of research in which we are already strong such as nutrition.... And because of the type of research we will be conducting, we will be able to take clinical problems out of the lab and back to the patient."

During fiscal year 1991-1992 the pediatric medical facility which now had 268 beds, admitted 9,088 children and young adults. Another 221,014 visited its 47 outpatient clinics which were staffed by 322 physicians, many of whom were the only subspecialists of their kind in the state. Treatments ranged from delicate heart surgeries to setting broken bones. More than 1,200 of those receiving treatment were transported to the hospital by its state-of-the-art "Angel One Transport Network," which now included two medically equipped helicopters, two twin-engine, turbo-propeller airplanes and three transport vans.

Before being admitted to the hospital every inpatient had to visit the same department—Admissions. "If they are admitted to the hospital, we see them here," said Carol Hudgens, Director of Admissions. "and to many people's surprise, we do more than just type their names into a computer.

"If a family is going to have a large financial responsibility, we help them look at what options are available. Often they are eligible for Medicaid, Children's Medical Services or charity and they don't even know it. The easy part about our job is that we never have to turn anyone away. We're going to see a child no matter what, if they can or cannot pay. But it's our job to do everything we can to help them financially."

"It's never boring here," added Hudgens. "We have plenty to keep us busy. We admit patients through the emergency room from midnight to 7 A.M. We see families when they are at their worst. No one wants their child to be in the hospital, but once the family realizes that we will go out of our way to help them, they are thankful."

Financial Counselors sometimes travel throughout Arkansas and even out of state to help families complete Medicaid and insurance claims. "Some of our patients' families are never here at Children's," explained Admissions Manager Cathy Fox. "For instance, if a newborn is transported here by helicopter, its mother may still be in the hospital elsewhere and not be able to come in. In that case, we will go to her to complete the Medicaid application.

"Sometimes we have to track down families once we get to their home town because they don't have a home phone. No one is required to go on a home visit. It's something we volunteer to do. Many times going into a home really opens our eyes to what some of these families are going through. It makes all of us want to try harder to help them."

Medical Director Dr. Betty Lowe was named vice president-elect of the American Academy of Pediatrics in July 1992. She would take office as vice president in October and would serve as 1993-94 American Academy of Pediatrics President. The Academy, a 30,000-member professional medical society headquartered in Elk Grove, Illinois, was active in child advocacy and support for all pediatricians. Dr. Lowe had been a member of both the national Academy and its Arkansas chapter since 1971. She had served as a district Chair for the national Academy and as a member of its executive board since 1986. She was the first woman to serve as a district Chair, and the first person from Arkansas Children's Hospital to serve as president of the Academy.

"The selection of Dr. Lowe is most fitting because of the contributions she has made as doctor, teacher, administrator and author in more than thirty years of practicing pediatric medicine," said Dr. O'Donnell. "We are as

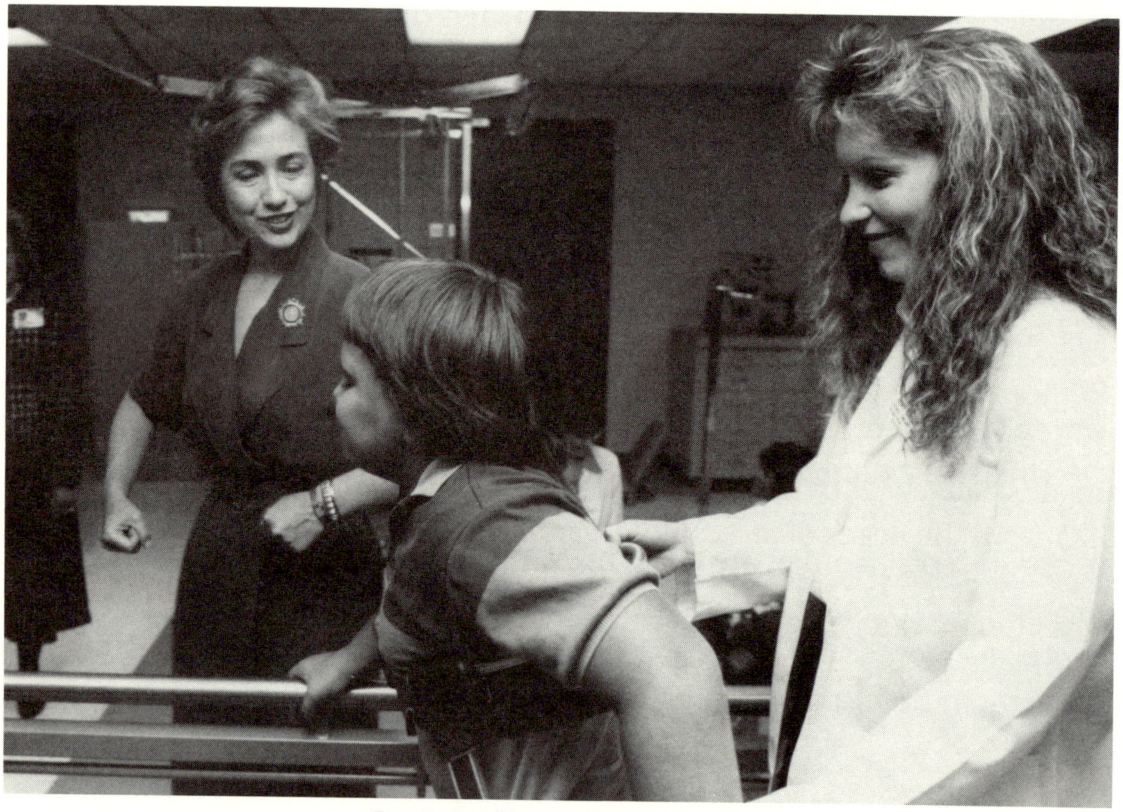

First Lady Hillary Rodham Clinton
encourages Charles Garnett and his physical therapist Renee Bennett during a visit to the Gerald F. Hamra Rehabilitation Center. July 22, 1993

proud of her national achievements as we are to have her expertise and experience at Children's Hospital."

Governor Bill Clinton—a long-time advocate of pediatric health care—was elected president of the United States on November 2, 1992. The nation's new First Lady Hillary Clinton had served as Chair and co-host of the annual "Children's Miracle Network Telethon" from the first telethon in 1988 through 1992. She had joined the Board of Trustees in 1988 and served until January 1993 when she was voted Board Member Emeritus.

"I learned many lessons at Arkansas Children's Hospital over the years," she reflected in July 1993, "and they are lessons that I am trying to bring to bear...as we look at trying to improve our entire health care system. I want every child in America to have access to a facility like this and to know that a hospital is not just a place where you go when you're sick, but also a place that tries to reach out to the community to prevent you from being sick."

Phillip K. Gilmore was appointed Interim Chief Executive Officer of Arkansas Children's Hospital on November 17, 1992, following the resignation of Dr. Randall O'Donnell, who resigned to become CEO of Children's Mercy Hospital in Kansas City, Missouri. Gilmore had served as Administrator and Chief Operating Officer of ACH since August 1987.

"I'm grateful for the confidence the Board of Trustees has in me to take on this task during the interim because I want us to continue to work to provide...the highest quality of care," said Gilmore the day after his appointment was announced. "I will continue overseeing the day-to-day operations, but I will also be looking at the hospital in a broader view. I think my experience the last five years in dealing with the hospital's day-to-day operations will help me to maintain the momentum we have."

Looking back on his twelve years at Children's, Dr. O'Donnell reflected in an interview with the *ACH News*. "The thing I'm proudest of is that we can serve the needs of any child, regardless of their family's resources, and that we give just one class of care—first class. And I think our special emotional support for children and families is second to none.

"The employees of Arkansas Children's Hospital have an important part to play," he added. "Every person is an expert at his or her job. Each one helps make the hospital better. Think back to what you are proudest of in your own area. Who made it happen? You did. You made it happen, working together with others in your department and throughout the hospital."

As Interim CEO, Phillip Gilmore worked closely with the Arkansas Legislature in an effort to resolve problems related to a shortfall in revenue for the state Medicaid program. During this period, he also made several interim appointments to key administrative positions left vacant by staff members who resigned to accept similar positions in Kansas City with Dr. O'Donnell at Children's Mercy Hospital.

Among those resigning to go to Kansas City was former Chief Executive Officer Leland McGinness, who had served as Evening Administrator since December 1991. He had accepted a position as Chief of Staff/Special Assistant to Dr. O'Donnell.

"I depart with deep feelings of love and affection for Arkansas Children's Hospital. Spiritually and emotionally I will never leave," wrote McGinness in a letter dated April 1, 1993. "During the last twenty plus years I have had the honor of ... helping translate into reality the concept that the children of Arkansas should have available continuous, easily accessible, high quality, comprehensive health care. I remain awed by the success of this endeavor."

Dr. Jonathan R. Bates

Following an extensive nationwide search for the best qualified individual, Jonathan Richard Bates, M.D. was named the new Chief Executive Officer of Arkansas Children's Hospital on May 24, 1993. A native of Ann Arbor, Michigan, Dr. Bates was a graduate of the University of Missouri School of Medicine and had served his internship and residency in pediatrics at the Children's Hospital in Boston. He came to Little Rock from Long Beach, California, where he had served as administrator of the 193-bed Memorial Miller Children's Hospital and as Senior Vice President of the 729-bed Long Beach Memorial Medical Center.

"His extensive education and vast experience make Dr. Bates the most qualified person to lead ACH through this era of continued growth and health care reform," affirmed Board president Diane Mackey. "He has a thorough knowledge of the workings of health care and is interested in providing access to cost-efficient, high quality health care for every child in Arkansas."

Reflecting on the future, the pediatrician-turned-administrator observed, "Children's health care in the next five to ten years will be heavily influenced by two factors: the development of health care reform and the impact of managed care. ACH has excellent opportunities in both regards. We have a number of statewide clinics, consulting programs and other outreach activities. And we have the critical mass of expertise needed by managed care plans. In the years ahead ACH will be even more active in developing a system of care for children throughout the state. We've made a promise to the children of Arkansas to be there when they need us, and as the health care picture changes and competition and risk increase, we will keep that promise."

Whatever changes the future may bring, Arkansas Children's Hospital will continue to be a place of care, love, and hope for the children of the state.

Bibliography

Berry, Fred and John Novak. *The History of Arkansas,* Little Rock: Rose Publishing Company, 1987

Donovan, Timothy P. and Willard Gatewood, eds. *The Governors of Arkansas—Essays in Political Biography*. Fayetteville: University of Arkansas Press, 1981.

DuVall, Leland, ed. *Arkansas Colony and State*. Little Rock: Rose Publishing Company, 1973.

Ferguson, John L. and J. H. Atkinson. *Historic Arkansas*. Little Rock: Arkansas History Commission, Arkansas State Board of Education, 1966.

Herndon, Dallas T., ed. *Centennial History of Arkansas*. 3 vols. S.J. Clark Publishing Company, 1922.

Leveritt, Mara. Miracle On Wolfe Street. *Arkansas Times* Magazine. Little Rock, March 1990.

Mitchell, Ruth. *Arkansas Heritage*. Little Rock: Rose Publishing Company, 1986.

Rogers J.S. *History of Arkansas Baptists*. Little Rock: The Executive Board of the Arkansas Baptist State Convention, 1948.

Thomas, D.Y., ed. *Arkansas and Its People—A History, 1541-1930*. 4 vols. American Historical Society, 1930.

The Book of Arkansas, Little Rock: The Arkansas Gazette, 1913.

Who's Who In Little Rock 1921. Little Rock, 1921.

Index